LET MY PEOPLE GO

Valarie Owen

WORD OF FAITH
LEADERSHIP AND BIBLE INSTITUTE

All Scripture quotations
from the King James Version
of the Bible unless otherwise stated

Other Books:

Healing in His Wings

Forgiveness: A Covenant of Love

In The Beginning God . . .

All illustrations by Tom Elliott

ISBN 0-914307-10-X
Printed in the United States of America
Copyright © 1983 WORD OF FAITH PUBLISHING
PO Box 819000, Dallas, Texas 75381

*Shalom to my special friends
in the Eagle's nest, Jerusalem.*

"Yet the number of the Children of Israel
shall be as the sand of the sea,
which cannot be measured nor numbered;
and it shall come to pass,
that in the place where it was said unto them,
Ye are not my people,
there it shall be said unto them,
Ye are the sons of the living God."
                                    Hosea 1:10

TABLE OF CONTENTS

Introduction

PART I: **EXODUS**   **The Second Book of Moses**

Chapter 1   The Egyptian Bondage 1
Chapter 2   Holy Ground 5
Chapter 3   Let My People Go 33
Chapter 4   Crossing the Red Sea 77
Chapter 5   The Song of Moses.......................... 91
Chapter 6   Bread and Meat From Heaven...........101
Chapter 7   The Smitten Rock...........................109
Chapter 8   The Mosaic Covenant 117
Chapter 9   The Tabernacle of Moses 137
Chapter 10   The Priesthood 229
Chapter 11   The Golden Calf 249

PART II: **LEVITICUS**   **The Third Book of Moses**

Chapter 12   Holiness 269

PART III: **NUMBERS**   **The Fourth Book of Moses**

Chapter 13   From Sinai to Kadesh-Barnea.............291
Chapter 14   Departure from Sinai.....................301

PART IV: **DEUTERONOMY**   **The Fifth Book of Moses**

Chapter 15   The Law Restated..........................349
Chapter 16   The Death of Moses 373

Summary

INTRODUCTION

In the Greek language the first five books of the Bible are called the PENTATEUCH, and in the Hebrew language they are referred to as the TORAH. Genesis, the first book of Moses, was covered in a separate volume.

Although the first parents rebelled against the authority of God, He continued to communicate with man through chosen vessels in order to get His redemptive plan on the earth. This plan was developed by progressive revelation; God gave a sequence of revelations, each of which added to some previous revelations not only of Himself, but of His salvation plan which was culminated in Christ Jesus our Lord and Saviour.

With each new revelation came the demand for total trust and obedience to God's purposes and will in the earth. In the second book of Moses, called Exodus, God shows us how He called a man to deliver His people out of Egyptian bondage where they had been enslaved for 430 years, and equipped him with a rod for his task. In Genesis, we have the beginning of all things. In this book we study how God formed His nation, His chosen, and brought them to a place where they would have to turn to Him for their freedom, and this would require a total dependence upon the Lord God of Abraham, Isaac, and Jacob.

Among Christendom there is an apathy that is especially pronounced in regard to the study of the Old Testament. In some denominational circles, it is totally disregarded as history, having no relevance to the church of today. By man it is thought to be dull reading and hard to understand. But for those who know the Old Testament, it is a great source of delight for therein lies our Jewish heritage (roots).

The concept of the kingdom of God involves the entire message of the Bible. From His temptation to His crucifixion, Jesus punctuated His ministry by citing the Old Testament. He offered Himself as a fulfillment of the law of Moses.

This book contains nothing original; I have not attempted to put forth any new revelations from God. All has been written, rewritten, and preached down through the many centuries of earth's history; but effort has been made to relate the central themes of the books of the law in a simple and unencumbered way so as not to confuse the earnest heart or laden it with too many side issues, though all is important to our learning.

The book of Exodus gives us the story of the departure of the children of Israel from Egypt, the journey into the wilderness of Sinai, the giving of the law, and the building of the tabernacle. There are many types of Christ in this book; perhaps too numerous to cover all of them. In the third book of Moses called Leviticus, the study is devoted to the worship and holiness of the redeemed people of God. The words that dominate the pages of this book are (1) priest, (2) sacrifices, (3) blood, and (4) offerings. The approximate date is believed to be about 1450–1410 B.C. It is called Leviticus because it contains the laws and order of the Levitical priesthood. The fourth book of Moses is called Numbers, and its title comes from the numbering of the children of Israel. History and law are intermixed in this story. The fifth book of Moses is called Deuteronomy, and contains both history and law with much repetition. It is often referred to as the second law.

Each of these five books deals in depth with the sovereignty of God in His mighty acts. These acts are as those found in the creation story—His call of Abram, the birth of Isaac, the protection He gave to Joseph down in Egypt, the call of Moses, and the parting of the Red Sea, which covers only a small portion of the revelation of God as to His Holiness and Character.

How incomplete would be our knowledge of creation and the sovereign plan of God to redeem this earth if we did not pursue the wilderness journey as Godleads His chosen from Egypt to the land He promised to Abraham. It is through the study of the Old Testament characters that we come face to face with the faithful Almighty God and His inability to change. He has declared that where there is no blood there is no salvation. It is redemption by blood that occupies a prominent place in the story now unfolding, and may it prove to be an oasis in the desert of life for those who have yet to experience His matchless Grace in the new birth. The Blood of the Lamb is the answer to the great question of Israel's tie and relationship to Yahweh, the God of Abraham, Isaac, and Jacob. Perhaps the greatest chapter in the entire Bible is Exodus 12, describing the blood-sprinkled door posts down in Egypt, for it represented the answer to all the needs of the children of Israel and the generations yet to come. *"For all have sinned and come short of the glory of God," (Romans 3:23)* and the Blood of the Lamb is God's promise of deliverance. *". . . when I see the blood, I will pass over you, and the plague shall not be upon you to destroy you, when I smite the land of Egypt" (Exodus 12:13).* We are shielded by the Blood of the Lord Jesus Christ.

When Israel was a child, then I loved him, and called my son out of Egypt.   *(Hosea 11:1)*

THE SECOND BOOK OF MOSES

EXODUS

(Map)

Chapter 1

THE EGYPTIAN BONDAGE

The word Exodus means "exit or departure." The second book of Moses is the story of redemption. It graphically describes the going out of the chosen people from the land where they had suffered helplessly as slaves for generations. This mass exodus of the children of God from the land of Egypt was by divine, miraculous intervention. They were delivered by God through His chosen prophet, Moses. This typifies the new birth by the Spirit of God as He leads one from the Kingdom of darkness into the kingdom of light. From the Patriarchs to the Exodus is believed to have been about 1606–1462 B.C.

"Now there arose up a new king over Egypt, which knew not Joseph." *(Exodus 1:8)*

At this point in time, Egypt was the world power (1600–1200 B.C.). The children of Israel, now called Israelites, had suffered over 400 years under the cruel hand of one Pharaoh after another. They had helplessly served the Egyptians as their slaves from one generation to another.

Jacob and his twelve sons went into Egypt (Joseph was already there) during a severe famine; in time each of the brothers died, ending that generation. But, God had promised that Abraham's seed would be as the sands of the sea. In Egypt his descendants increased rapidly in numbers, and the Hebrew people multiplied developing into a great nation filling the land of Ghosen which was a fulfillment of Divine Promise. In Genesis 12:1-3, the call and promise to Abram is given: *"Now the Lord had said unto Abram, get thee out of thy country, and from thy kindred, and from thy father's house, unto a land that I will show thee: And I will make of thee a great nation, and I will bless thee, and make thy name great; and thou shalt be a blessing: And I will bless them that bless thee, and curse him that curseth thee: and in thee shall all families of the earth be blessed."* Abram moved in faith, but he never saw the promised land nor set his foot upon it. God told him his descendants would sojourn in a strange land, become slaves to its inhabitants, and be entreated with evil for four hundred years; but God said He would judge the nation who cursed His people; He would then bring them forth so they could worship Him.

Through envy Joseph's brothers sold him into slavery, and he was carried down into Egypt where he found favor with the Pharaoh. In time there arose a king who had made no promises to Joseph in behalf of his family, and he feared the Hebrews would increase to the point of revolt for they were spreading over the land causing a population explosion. He decreed that all male children should be killed at birth, and the children of God must go into slavery and bondage to the king. Yet the God of Abraham, Isaac and Jacob was masterminding the entire plan. He would lead His people into Egypt and initiate the steps that would lead them out.

"Therefore they did set over them taskmasters to afflict them with their burdens. And they built for Pharaoh treasure cities, Pithom and Raamses."

(Exodus 1:11)

The more they afflicted the Hebrews, the more God multiplied them until they became an ever-increasing threat to Pharaoh, and great fear fell upon the land. The Egyptians made life hard for the children of Israel and caused them to serve them with rigor and long, hard hours of slave labor. They worked long hours in the fields, built the cities, made the bricks, and some worked in the Egyptian homes as servants where they were beaten and mistreated. The Hebrew[1] midwives were instructed to kill all male children at birth, but they feared God and braved the king's wrath. God richly blessed them because they feared Him, and He gave them families and houses. *"Them that honor Me I will honor, and they that despise Me shall be lightly esteemed"* (1 Samuel 2:30).

The children of Israel going down into Egypt, increasing there under hard conditions, and coming out under the capable leadership of Moses, serves to show how God uses natural means for supernatural ends, and makes all things work together to His glory as well as for the good of His people.

---

[1]Josephus, the Jewish historian recorded these midwives to be Egyptian.

3

God In Control

In the land of Goshen, God began to prepare His people to inherit the Promised Land. The land of Goshen is to this day considered the richest province of Egypt. But to the Israelites, this had become the land of bondage.

The enemy may oppose God's chosen ones, but God will ever prove Himself to be the greater power. From the outset, this story is presented as a struggle between Yahweh and Pharaoh, who had made the lot of Israel exceedingly hard. But under this pressure, these determined people of God prospered and multiplied. The Egyptians eyed these Semites[2] with mixed emotions of anger, hatred, and envy. Certainly nothing good could come from the land of Ghosen. These strange people were somewhat ''unnerving,'' and their God most unpredictable.

---

[2]Semites—a member of any of various ancient and modern peoples including the Hebrews and Arabs. Descendants of Seth.

Chapter 2

HOLY GROUND

The Birth of Moses

And there went a man of the house of Levi, and took to wife a daughter of Levi. And the woman conceived, and bare a son: and when she saw him that he was a goodly child, she hid him three months. And when she could no longer hide him, she took for him an ark of bulrushes, and daubed it with slime and with pitch, and put the child therein; and she laid it in the flags by the river's brink. And his sister stood afar off, to wit what would be done to him. And the daughter of Pharaoh came down to wash herself at the river; and her maidens walked along by the river's side; and when she saw the ark among the flags, she sent her maid to fetch it. And when she had opened it, she saw the child: and, behold, the babe wept. And she had compassion on him, and said, This is one of the Hebrews' children. Then said his sister to Pharaoh's daughter, Shall I go and call to thee a nurse of the Hebrew women, that she may nurse the child for thee? And Pharaoh's daughter said to her, go. And the maid went and called the child's mother. And Pharaoh's daughter said unto her, Take this child away, and nurse it for me, and I will give thee thy wages. And the woman took the child, and nursed it. And the child grew, and she brought him unto Pharaoh's daughter, and he became her son. And she called his name Moses: and she said, Because I drew him out of the water. (Exodus 2:1-10)

Jannes and Jambres

Josephus, the Jewish historian, recorded that during the heighth of Israel's afflictions in Egypt, one of the sacred scribes, who was very successful in foretelling, told the king of Egypt there would be a child born to the Israelites, and if he were reared, would bring the Egyptians' dominion low, and raise the status of the Hebrew people. He reported to the Pharaoh that this man would excel all men in virtue, and great glory would be ascribed to him throughout the ages. Dr. Bernard wrote that there were two of these prophets instead of one, and the Targum of Jonathan named the two famous antagonists of Moses as Jannes and Jambres. Paul made mention of these two men in 2 Timothy 3:8, *"Now as Jannes and Jambres withstood Moses, so do these also resist the truth: men of corrupt minds, reprobate concerning the faith."*

This was so feared by the king that he demanded all male babies born to the Hebrews be thrown into the river. He further decreed that any parent who failed to drown their male babies would be destroyed. But not even a king can outwit the purposes of God, not even with ten thousand subtle devices can he match the wisdom of the Lord. Centuries later, another king tried to kill the Christ child. *"Now when Jesus was born in Bethlehem of Judaea in the days of Herod the king, behold there came wise men from the east to Jerusalem. Saying, Where is he that is born King of the Jews? for we have seen his star in the east, and are come to worship him. When Herod the king had heard these things, he was troubled, and all Jerusalem with him . . . Go and search for the young child; and when ye have found him, bring me word again, that I may come and worship him also . . . Then Herod, when he saw that he was mocked of the wise men, was exceeding wroth, and sent forth, and slew all the children that were in Bethlehem, and in all the coasts thereof, from two years old and under, according to the time which he had diligently inquired of the wise men"* (Matthew 2:1-16).

In the Exodus account of the birth of Moses, it is not revealed that Amram, the father, had anything to do with saving the child's life. Only three people are mentioned: Jochebed (mother); Miriam (sister); and Pharaoh's daughter. But in Hebrews 11:23 we read, *"By faith Moses, when he was born, was hid three months of his parents, because they saw he was a proper child; and they were not afraid of the king's commandment."* It was not the faith of Moses referred to here, but the faith of his parents who were from the tribe of Levi.

With the birth of Moses to this somewhat obscure couple, we are reminded that God does not need mighty men, nor men who are prominent and well-known, to fulfill His cause and purpose: *"But God hath chosen the foolish things of the world to confound the wise; and God hath chosen the weak things of the world to confound the things which are mighty; and base things of the world, and things which are despised, hath God chosen, yea, and things which are not, to bring to nought things that are: that no flesh should glory in His presence." (2 Corinthians 1:27-29).*

This was definitely the couple God chose to bring His people out of Egypt. He did it because of their faith; they did not fear the edict of the king. They hid the baby for three months in their home, but when he could no longer be hid, they got a papyrus basket and coated it with tar and pitch. Moses was taken to the Nile river and placed among the reeds along the bank while his sister, Miriam, watched the ark from a distance to see what would happen.

When Pharaoh's daughter went to the Nile to bathe, she saw the ark and sent her slave girl to get it. When she opened the basket, the baby was crying and she took pity upon him. She recognized that Moses was a Hebrew baby, but he had won her heart. Miriam inquired if she wanted one of the Hebrew women to nurse the child for her. Miriam got the mother and brought her to Pharaoh's daughter who instructed her to take the child and nurse him for ample wages. So Moses was nursed and weaned by his own mother; then she took him back to Pharaoh's daughter, and he became her son. She named him Moses, ". . . Because I drew him out of the water."

The Ark

The exact form or size of the little ark[1] is not known. It may have been a basket, boat or box; it was made of the leaf of the papyrus, a reedy plant which grew along the banks of the Nile used by the Egyptians for baskets, boats, wails, and sometimes even for food. Slime or bitumen mentioned here is the same substance used by the slaves for the making of bricks in Egypt. When cold it is very brittle; but when mixed with tar it becomes firm and fixed. Amram and Jochebed did a most unusual thing. They placed Moses in the very river where other babies were being drowned. The mother laid him in the flags by the river's bank. These parents moved by faith and not by sight. Human reasoning would have carried the child as far away from the river as possible. Though the child was brought to the brink of death, he was preserved in an "ark." So it is in our salvation; we are brought to the shores of death, and our only salvation is found in His invitation to enter into the "Ark of Safety," through the shed blood of Jesus Christ. This further typifies the tender care with which the Father in Heaven extends to the babes in Christ. He guards their steps and directs their path in life. God is in control of the lives dedicated to Him.

It was God who put it into the heart of this Egyptian princess to go to the particular spot where the ark was found. He caused her to be moved with compassion when she saw the baby, and beheld its weeping. It was God alone who caused this daughter of the haughty monarch to allow Miriam to seek out the child's mother for a nurse. In Romans 11:36, we read, *"For of him, and through*

---

[1]Same Hebrew word used in connection with Noah's Ark which clearly typified Christ.

*him, and to him, are all things: to whom be glory for-
ever. Amen."* This was Pharaoh's wisdom turned to fool-
ishness, and Satan's devices defeated. *"He taketh the wise
in their own craftiness: and the counsel of the froward
is carried headlong" (Job 5:13).*

Early Days of Moses

It would be preposterous to suppose that Pharaoh's
daughter did not know of the king's decree proclaiming
all male Hebrew children be thrown into the river or put
to death. She knew she was supposed to kill the child;
instead she had compassion on him, and gave him back
to his mother to nurse and wean him until he could be
taken into the Egyptian courts.

Moses grew to manhood amidst the luxuries of the
royal Egyptian households. God had caused him to become the grandson of the very man who demanded his
death. In Proverbs 21:30, we read, *"There is no wisdom
nor understanding nor counsel against the Lord."* The
program of Pharaoh was confounded and the program of
Jehovah God was sustained and advanced. Moses received
his education and training under the careful supervision
of Pharaoh's daughter; he learned reading, writing, arch-
ery, various other physical activities, and training in the
administrative field to teach him responsibility for the position he was to gain in the courts. God took years to mold
and form the character of Moses for the work he had
called him to do. He was a channel through which God's
Divine purpose could flow.

Moses in Midian

*"And it came to pass in those days, when Moses was
grown, that he went out unto his brethren, and looked
on their burdens: and he spied an Egyptian smiting an*

Hebrew, one of his brethren. And he looked this way and that way, and when he saw that there was no man, he slew the Egyptian, and hid him in the sand. And when he went out the second day, behold two men of the Hebrews strove together: and he said to him that did the wrong, Wherefore smitest thou thy fellow? And he said, Who made thee a prince and a judge over us? Intendest thou to kill me, as thou killedst the Egyptians? And Moses feared, and said, Surely this thing is known. Now when Pharaoh heard this thing, he sought to slay Moses. But Moses fled from the face of Pharaoh, and dwelt in the land of Midian: and he sat down by a well. Now the priest of Midian had seven daughters: and they came and drew water, and filled the troughs to water their father's flock. And the shepherds came and drove them away: but Moses stood up and helped them, and watered their flock. And when they came to Reuel their father, he said, How is it that ye are come so soon today? And they said, An Egyptian delivered us out of the hand of the shepherds, and also drew water enough for us, and watered the flock. And he said unto his daughters, And where is he? why is it that ye have left the man? Call him, that he may eat bread. And Moses was content to dwell with the man: and he gave Moses Zipporah, his daughter. And she bare him a son, and he called his name Gershom: for he said, I have been a stranger in a strange land. And it came to pass in process of time, that the king of Egypt died: and the children of Israel sighed by reason of the bondage, and they cried, and their cry came up unto God by reason of the bondage. And God heard their groaning, and God remembered his covenant with Abraham, with Isaac, and with Jacob. And

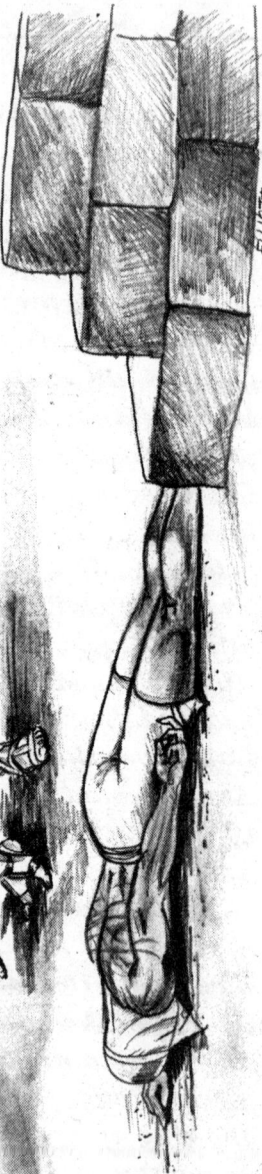

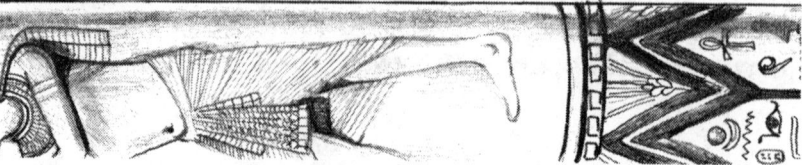

God looked upon the children of Israel, and God had respect unto them.''   *Exodus 1:11-25*

As Moses grew to manhood perhaps it was not always easy for him to understand where his loyalties lay. No doubt he loved his adopted mother, and members of the royal family; but he could not help being disturbed by the mistreatment of his true kinsmen, the Hebrews. They were being treated like animals by the taskmasters under whom they worked. His own mother had taught him that he was not a true Egyptian. She taught him the Hebrew language, and told him stories of his people. He knew about the early fathers of his nation—Abraham, Isaac, and Jacob, and Jacob's twelve sons—and the one true God Whom they had worshipped.

When Moses was forty years old, he walked among the Hebrews and was grieved over their plight in Egypt. He saw an Egyptian beating one of his brethren; he killed him, and hid his body in the sand. In Hebrews 11:24-28, it is recorded that Moses refused to live any longer in the pleasures of Pharaoh's court: *"By faith Moses, when he was come to years, refused to be called the son of Pharaoh's daughter; Choosing rather to suffer affliction with the people of God, than to enjoy the pleasures of sin for a season; Esteeming the reproach of Christ greater riches than the treasures in Egypt: for he had respect unto the recompense of the reward. By faith he forsook Egypt, not fearing the wrath of the king: for he endured, as seeing him who is invisible. Through faith he kept the passover, and the sprinkling of blood, lest he that destroyed the firstborn should touch them."*

The record of Moses begins with Exodus 2, and ends in Deuteronomy 34. Thus, we see that four of the five books of Moses were written to make known the acts of this great man of God, and all of those acts were performed "by faith."

The life of Moses was divided into three definite periods:

  (1) Forty years in the court of Pharaoh
  (2) Forty years in the desert
  (3) Forty years with Israel in the wilderness

According to Stephen's statement in Acts 7:25, God had at some time spoken to Moses and made known to him that he was to be Israel's deliverer: *"For he (Moses) supposed his brethren would have understood how that God by his hand would deliver them: but they understood not."* Moses believed God and refused to be called the son of Pharaoh any longer. He made the choice by faith. If he had looked at the treasures of Egypt in the same way Lot looked at Sodom, we would not have the record of Moses as it is today. He believed God with the faith of his forefather Abraham. Though Moses did not see Christ clearly with the natural eye, he anticipated His coming long before He came. Christ was made manifest to the Old Testament prophets. We have this truth recorded in 1 Corinthians 10:4, *". . . did all drink the same spiritual drink: for they drank of that spiritual Rock that followed them: and that Rock was Christ."* Jesus told the Pharisees, *"Had ye believed Moses, ye would have believed me: for he wrote of me"* (John 5:46). Though Moses lived centuries before Christ, he counted the reproach of Christ as more gain to him than anything Egypt held. He looked forward to that glorious day when all who have suffered for Christ's sake will be rewarded abundantly. If we confess Jesus, He will confess us. If we suffer with Him, we will reign with Him.

Returning to the text, when we are told that Moses looked "this way and that way . . ." He attempted to carry out spiritual ends by carnal means, which had so often led his ancestors into sin and suffering. He would become a deliverer before he was called to it by God. He would accomplish it by other means than those which God would appoint. When God is fully trusted, we need not look "this way and that way." This is proof that when the Holy Spirit writes a man's history, He presents him to us as he is, and faithfully sets forth all his failures and imperfections. While, in the New Testament, when He comments upon such history, He merely gives the real principle and main result of a man's life.

Moses Rejected

God had to teach Moses first by failure. He thought that his brethren would have understood that their deliverance was to come through him; but they rejected him, and questioned his loyalty since he was a prince in the court of the Egyptians. His move was premature. He was forty years ahead of God in his timing for their deliverance. He had to be drained of all his self-will and self-reliance. His education was incomplete. Besides, the Hebrew people had not yet come to the pitch of anguish referred to in verse 23, when the king of Egypt died, and the children of Israel forsook the false gods to which they had given their allegiance in order to return to the God of their fathers.

Thus, Moses got a rude awakening when he assumed his own people would have understood the slaying of the

Egyptian; he found they did not want him for a leader, and they suspected that he would kill them as he had killed the Egyptian. This was Moses' first sample of their ingratitude not only towards him as their deliverer, but towards Yahweh, the God of their fathers, who had promised to bring them out of Egypt when the time was right. The hammer fell, and fearing for his life Moses fled to the land of Midian, a pilgrim and a stranger.

Midian was the peninsula of Sinai, a desolate, barren area between two gulfs. Likely he crossed this triangular peninsula to the eastern side around the Gulf of Akabah (northwestern Arabia), where the Midianites, the descendants of Abraham and Keturah lived. One writer stated that Moses could not have made that journey without the help of the Bedouin along the way. These Midianites were Sand-Crossers, Bedouin of the desert, with a vague claim to pasturelands in the peninsula of Sinai. It was so like God to prepare a shelter and home for the fugitive.

Moses rested on a well as the seven daughters of Reuel, the priest of Midian, came to water their father's flock. Moses protected the women against the violence of the shepherds, who drove away their flocks. When they reported the incident to their father, they called Moses an Egyptian, suggesting that he was still wearing Egyptian dress. He was invited into the home of the priest, and in time Reuel gave Moses his daughter, Zipporah, for his wife, and two sons were born to this union there in Midian. Reuel, the father-in-law of Moses, seemed to have worshipped the God of Abraham, even as his name implies: Reuel, the "friend of El," the latter being the designation which the patriarchs gave to God, as El Shaddai, "God Almighty." Reuel is also called Jethro and Jether, which means "excellency," and may have been his official title as chief priest of the tribe.

Moses named his first son Gershom (expulsion, banishment), and the second son he called Eliezer, *"my God is help" Exodus (18:4).* In the process of time the king of Egypt died, and God had prepared Moses for the task which lay ahead of him. He was now eighty years old, and for the past forty years had lived in the solitude of the Midian desert; but his steps were ordered by the Lord. Now the time was right to bring the children of Israel out of   bondage down in Egypt. Many, many times he must have thought about the Hebrews who were enslaved by the Egyptians, as he tended his father-in-law's sheep year after year. We are given no record of his thoughts during that time, but God waited until every hope of being sent back had faded before He met Him at the burning bush and renewed His Word to him. Moses was no longer impulsive and self-motivated. He had learned to be still and know the voice of God. Moses had had to learn that God's clocks are never one minute behind.

The Flame of Fire (1463 B.C.)

"Now Moses kept the flock of Jethro his father in law, the priest of Midian: and he led the flock to the backside of the desert, and came to the mountain of God, even to Horeb. And the angel of the Lord appeared unto him in a flame of fire out of the midst of a bush: and he looked, and, behold, the bush burned with fire, and the bush was not consumed. And Moses said, I will now turn aside, and see this great sight, why the bush is not burnt. And when the Lord saw that he turned

aside to see, God called unto him out of the midst of the bush, and said, Moses, Moses, And he said, Here am I. And he said, Draw not nigh hither: put off thy shoes from off thy feet, for the place whereon thou standest is holy ground. Moreover he said, I am the god of thy father, the God of Abraham, the God of Isaac, and the God of Jacob. And Moses hid his face; for he was afraid to look upon God. And the Lord said, I have surely seen the affliction of my people which are in Egypt, and have heard their cry by reason of their taskmasters; for I know their sorrows; And I am come down to deliver them out of the hand of the Egyptians, and to bring them up out of that land unto a good land and a large, unto a land flowing with milk and honey; unto the place of the Canaanites, and the Hittites, and the Amorites, and the Perizzites, and the Hivites, and the Jebusites. Now therefore, behold, the cry of the children of Israel is come unto me: and I have also seen the oppression wherewith the Egyptians oppress them. Come now therefore, and I will send thee unto Pharaoh, that thou mayest bring forth my people the children of Israel out of Egypt. And Moses said unto God, Who am I, that I should go unto Pharaoh, and that I should bring forth the children of Israel out of Egypt? And he said, Certainly I will be with thee; and this shall be a token unto thee, that I have sent thee: when thou hast brought forth the people out of Egypt, ye shall serve God upon this mountain." (Exodus 3:1-12)

In the first part of his life, Moses was schooled in the finest of Egyptian culture. He was well-trained in the ways and wisdom of this world; in the second part of his life he was trained in that perfect wisdom that comes from above. God has His own special ways of preparing his servants for their earthly task; man's efforts are totally unacceptable in His sight. One writer stated that when God is about to do any of His great works, He first silently prepares all for it. Not only the good seed to be scattered, but the breaking up of the soil for its reception is His.

Shepherd Moses

Years had passed since the prince fled from Egypt. He was now a bedouin dressed in the dusty desert garb of the Sand-Crossers. He had for four decades been far-removed from the grandeur of the Egyptian courts with its vast temples, the many gods, and the golden palace of the Pharaoh, Seti I, who had decreed the death of all the male Hebrew children. Forty years had passed since young Moses had served his military duties at the quarries, or perhaps, as army overseer of "his kinfolk" working in the Delta. Josephus recorded that Moses was a captain in the Egyptian armies.

The king of Egypt had died, and the children of Israel cried by reason of their heavy burdens. Where was the God of their forefathers? Had He not promised to deliver them? While the children of God moaned and cried out, He had already prepared the way for their deliverance. He had not only chosen Moses to be the saviour of His people, but had trained him for the enormous task he would undertake. (Seti was probably the Pharaoh of the oppression; Ramses, the Pharaoh of the Exodus.)

On that specific day, ordained by God, the nomadic shepherd Moses wandered far and wide seeking pasture and water for his flock. On the back side of the desert he came to Mount Horeb, the mountain of God. It was there that Moses had his encounter with Deity.

The southern end of the peninsula of Sinai consists of a confused mass of peaks (the highest above 9,000 feet). The great central group among these mountains is that of Horeb, and one special height in it is Sinai, the "mount of God." It is here amidst this awful desolation that the most fertile places in the "wilderness" are to be found. Even today part of this plateau is quite green. Thus, to this place the Bedouin drive their flocks when summer has parched all the lower districts.

It was here, in the early summer, that Moses probably drove Jethro's flock for pasture and water. Behind him, to the east, lay the desert; before him rose the "mountain of God," in magnificent grandeur. The stillness of that place was unbroken; the faintest of sounds would fall distinctly on the ear; all at once truly a "sight" to behold. Here, at Horeb, God appeared to Moses as the Angel of the Lord, in a FLAME OF FIRE, out of the midst of a burning bush. The bush continued to burn as was not consumed. It was not the bush burning that got the attention of Moses, but the fact that it was not consumed by the flames that caused him to investigate. The burning bush was symbolic of the children of Israel yet in Egypt, and the voice of God was calling for their deliverance from its fiery furnaces. Nothing in Egypt had ever afforded such a sight; God in a burning bush tells us even now that if we are in a fiery furnace, so is He. Just as the bush was not consumed, neither are we. *"The Lord of hosts is with us, the God of Jacob is our refuge" (Psalm 46).* This is ample provision for every existence. Though our God is a consuming fire, it is not to consume us, but to consume all in us and about us which is contrary to His Holiness.

Moses declared that he would inspect the bush and see why it had not burned. Yahweh called to him out of the midst of the burning bush. The bush, in contrast with the more noble and lofty trees (cedars of Lebanon), represented the people of Israel in their humiliation, despised by the world yet loved and chosen of God. *"Moses, Moses . . ."* came the voice of Almighty God from the flames, *"Do not come near; take off your shoes for the place where you are standing is Holy Ground."* Just a moment before, the place where he stood was common ground, now it was Holy, and the Glory of God shone all around Moses as he said, *"Here am I."*

At that moment the temple of God was a burning bush. The fire was representative of the Glory and Presence of God. Moses received his commission to deliver Israel from a burning bush. Barefooted and submissive, he listened to God.

The God of Abraham, Isaac and Jacob had come down to deliver His people out of the hands of the Egyptians just as He had promised to Abraham centuries before. *". . . I am the God of thy father, the God of Abraham, the God of Isaac, and the God of Jacob. And Moses hid his face; for he was afraid to look upon God" (Exodus 3:6)*. Thus, the Lord stood revealed before Moses as the covenant-keeping God, the God of all grace.

Seven things the Lord said:

(1) I have seen the affliction of my people

(2) I have heard their cry

(3) I know their sorrows

(4)   I am come down to deliver them

(5)   Out of the hand of the Egyptians

(6)   To bring them up out of that land unto a good land

(7)   I will send thee unto Pharaoh to bring them out

In verse 11, Moses revealed in a few words the mighty lessons he had learned in the desert's silence when he asked of Jehovah, *"Who am I?"* The servant of God needed to be encouraged. His mind must have quickly flashed back to the time when he had tried to gain the favor of his people only to be rejected and humiliated by his own kin. Moses was earnestly seeking an answer from God. God said, *"Certainly I will be with thee . . ."* God told Moses that He was giving him a token (promise) that He was sending him back to Egypt to deliver His people. That token being that when Moses led the children of Israel out of Egypt, they would worship Him on that very mountain.

I Am That I Am

"And Moses said unto God, Behold, when I come unto the children of Israel, and shall say unto them, The God of your fathers hath sent me unto you; and they shall say to me, What is his name? what shall I say unto them? And God said unto Moses, I AM THAT I AM: and he said, Thus shalt thou say unto the children of Israel, I AM hath sent me unto you. And God said moreover unto Moses, Thus shalt thou say unto the children of Israel, The Lord God of your fathers, the God of Abraham, the God of Isaac, and the God of Jacob, hath sent me unto you: this is my name forever, and this is my

*memorial unto all generations. Go, and gather the eld-
ers of Israel together, and say unto them, The Lord God
of your fathers, the God of Abraham, of Isaac, and of
Jacob, appeared unto me, saying, I have surely visited
you, and seen that which is done to you in Egypt. And
I have said, I will bring you up out of the affliction of
Egypt unto the land of the Canaanites, and the Hittites,
and the Amorites, and the Perizites, and the Hivites, and
the Jebusites, unto a land flowing with milk and honey.
And they shall hearken to thy voice: and thou shalt
come, thou and the elders of Israel, unto the king of
Egypt, and ye shall say unto him, The Lord God of the
Hebrews hath met with us: and now let us go, we beseech thee, three days' journey into the wilderness, that
we may sacrifice to the Lord our God. And I am sure
that the king of Egypt will not let you go, no, not by a
mighty hand. And I will stretch out my hand, and smite
Egypt with all my wonders which I will do in the midst
thereof: and after that he will let you go. And I will give
this people favour in the sight of the Egyptians: and it
shall come to pass, that, when ye go, ye shall not go
empty: But every woman shall borrow of her neighbour, and of her that sojourneth in her house, jewels of
silver, and jewels of gold, and raiment: and ye shall put
them upon your sons, and upon your daughters; and
ye shall spoil the Egyptians.'' (Exodus 3:13-22)*

Certainly Moses knew of some of the obstacles and
difficulties he would meet in this new commission from
God. He was well aware of the fact that there were many
gods in Egypt, and that the children of Israel were also
familiar with them. He had very good reason to question
the Lord about who He was. In other words, what was

Moses to tell them to still their doubts and fears about God's purpose towards them. He had already asked of the Lord, *". . . who am I?"* Now it was, *"Who are You?"* Had God so chosen, He could have sent an angel to deliver His people; or He could have appeared in person to set them free. Moses was His emptied vessel, made ready for the Master's use. And God replied, *"I AM THAT I AM . . . you tell them I AM has sent you to deliver them . . ."* Moses knew that his own name would make no noticeable impression upon God's people; most of them had swayed towards the idolatries of the Egyptians. They would want to know which god he was representing; what is his character; prove to us who he is. I AM is the great Jehovistic name of God. Dr. Pentecost says, "It contains each tense of the verb 'to be,' and might be translated, 'I was, I am, and I shall always continue to be.'" The I Am of the burning bush now stands fully declared in the blessed Person of our Saviour who said, "I am the bread of life," "I am the good Shepherd," "I am the door," "I am the light of the world," "I am the way, the truth and the life," "I am the true vine." He is the eternal I AM; the same yesterday, today, and forever.

Deliverance Announced

Step by step God outlined His plan for their deliverance to Moses, and commanded him to go to Egypt, gather the elders before him, and say to them that the God of their fathers had seen their afflictions, and was ready to deliver them. The elders would have a listening ear. God directed that Moses and the elders would go unto the Pharaoh and ask to be set free. He said at first they will not be released; but eventually by the power of His mighty stretched out arm, they would come out of Egypt carrying the spoils of Egypt.

EXCUSES OF MOSES:	PROMISES FROM GOD:
(1) Who am I	(1) I will be with you
(2) Who are you	(2) The I AM
(3) No message	(3) Covenant-Keeping God
(4) No authority	(4) Rod of God
(5) No gift of speech	(5) His enabling
(6) I stutter	(6) Send Aaron as spokesman
(7) Send someone else	

"And Moses answered and said, But, behold, they will not believe me, nor hearken unto my voice: for they will say, The Lord hath not appeared unto thee."

(Exodus 4:1)

Here Moses lays bare before God the unbelief of the children of Israel. The conjunction "and" connects the last verse of chapter three with the first verse of chapter four as a continued story. In spite of all God has outlined to Moses, he claimed they would not listen to him. God said to Moses, *"What is that in your hand?"*

Moses replied, "It is a rod."

"Cast it on the ground, Moses."

When he cast the rod on the ground, it became a serpent and Moses fled from it in fear.

This scene has reference to the calling of Moses. Hitherto Moses had wielded the shepherd's crook. At God's command he was to cast it away; his calling had now changed. He would have to meet not only the old enemy, "the serpent," but the might of Pharaoh, of which the serpent was the well-known Egyptian emblem. The serpent was the symbol of royal and divine power on the diadem of every Pharaoh as the emblem of the land, its religion, and government.

God had asked the impossible of Moses when He commanded him to stretch forth his hand and take the serpent by the tail. He obeyed, and the snake turned back into a rod in his hand. This symbolized the overthrow of the power of Egypt at the command of God.

"That they may believe that the Lord God of their fathers, the God of Abraham, the God of Isaac, and the God of Jacob, hath appeared unto thee. And the Lord said furthermore unto him, Put now thine hand into thy bosom. And he put his hand into his bosom: and when he took it out, behold, his hand was leprous as snow. And he said, Put thine hand into thy bosom again. And he put his hand into his bosom again; and plucked it out of his bosom, and, behold, it was turned again as his other flesh. And it shall come to pass, if they will not believe thee, neither hearken to the voice of the first sign, that they will believe the voice of the latter sign." *(Exodus 4:5-8)*

Leprosy is a well-known type of sin. Many symbolisms are involved in this second sign to Moses. Suffice it to say, the nation of Israel had become leprous; defiled in every way.

In Numbers 11:11-12, we read, ". . . Have I conceived all this people, that Thou shouldest say to me, Carry them in thy bosom?" But God was showing forth

His power to cleanse the leprous nation, and bring them forth by the hand of His servant Moses. He placed his hand once more in his bosom, and the hand came out white as the other — the flesh restored. God proved to Moses that he was equipped with the necessary power to execute deliverance to Israel.

"And it shall come to pass, if they will not believe also these two signs, neither hearken unto thy voice, that thou shalt take of the water of the river, and pour it upon the dry land: and the water which thou takest out of the river shall become blood upon the dry land."
(Exodus 4:9)

This sign was first to be a sign to Israel, and afterwards a plague upon Egypt. All this failed to satisfy Moses. He had yet another reason why he could not go to Egypt to deliver God's people from slavery. He was not eloquent; he was slow of speech. In other words, he stuttered. Maybe he was not really the instrument God needed for so great a task. He could just as easily send someone else.

"And the anger of the Lord was kindled against Moses, and he said, Is not Aaron the Levite thy brother? I know that he can speak well. And also, behold, he cometh forth to meet thee: and when he seeth thee, he will be glad in his heart. And thou shalt speak unto him, and put words in his outh: and I will be with thy mouth, and with his mouth, and will teach you what ye shall do. And he shall be thy spokesman unto the people: and he shall be, even he shall be to thee instead of a mouth, and thou shalt be to him instead of God. And thou shalt take this rod in thine hand, wherewith thou shalt do signs."
(Exodus 4:14-17)

Moses forfeited the dignity of being Jehovah's sole instrument in that glorious work which He was about to accomplish. The anger of the Lord was kindled against him for his unbelief and lack of trust. Aaron would now stand in the same relation to Moses, now King as a prophet to God.

Moses returned home and talked this over with Jethro, his father-in-law, and requested leave to go to his people in Egypt. Jethro sent him forth with his blessings.

"And the Lord said unto Moses in Midian, Go, return into Egypt: for all the men are dead which sought thy life. Moses set out for Egypt with his wife, two sons, and the rod in his hand." (Exodus 4:19)

God talked with Moses as they traveled. He told him to do all the miracles He had shown him before Pharaoh; but He warned him that the king would be stubborn and would not let them go.

"And thou shalt say unto Pharaoh, Thus saith the Lord, Israel is my son, even my firstborn: And I say unto thee, Let my son go, that he may serve me: and if thou refuse to let him go, behold, I will slay thy son, even thy firstborn. And it came to pass by the way in the inn, that the Lord met him, and sought to kill him. Then Zipporah took a sharp stone, and cut off the foreskin of her son, and cast it at his feet, and said, Surely a bloody husband art thou to me. So he let him go: then she said, A bloody husband thou art, because of the circumcision." (Exodus 4:22-26)

God repeated His command to Moses for him to return to Egypt. He was to tell the Pharaoh that he was holding God's people in bondage, and he must let them go.

God acknowledged Israel as His firstborn son; He told Moses to tell the king, *"Let my son go that he may worship me, or I will slay your youngest son."*

The scene suddenly changed. God met Moses and his family at the inn where they were spending the night, and threatened to kill him. Zipporah took a flint knife, cut off the foreskin of her young son, and threw it at the feet of her husband and cried, *"You are a bloody husband to me because of the circumcision!"* But the Lord let him alone. Apparently, this important matter had long been neglected, and had to be tended to before he could be an ambassador for God. Jehovah was about to fulfill His covenant engagement to Abraham; the sign of that covenant was circumcision, which the son of Moses had not received because of the objections of its mother. If Moses persisted in ignoring such Divine requirements, it would have cost him his life. By this act he is forcibly reminded of the Holiness of the God with whom he was dealing.

We are not told how God sought to kill him, but it would seem that he was stricken down and rendered helpless because his wife had to perform the act of circumcision on their son. This last act had to be done before Moses totally qualified for his mission down in Egypt.

In verse 27, we see that God works from both ends of the line. While He was dealing with Moses, He was also speaking to his brother Aaron, telling him to go into the wilderness and meet Moses on the mount of God. It was there that Moses related all that had happened to Aaron. The mount speaks of elevation; elevation of spirit through communion with the Most High. After the servant of God has been on the mount with Him, then he is ready to go forth and represent Him on the plains.

Aaron and Moses returned to Egypt and summoned the elders of the people of Israel to a meeting. (The elders are to be viewed as representatives of the people.) Aaron told them what Jehovah had said to Moses. Moses performed the miracles as they watched, and they believed the time had really come for their deliverance. They bowed their heads and worshipped God.

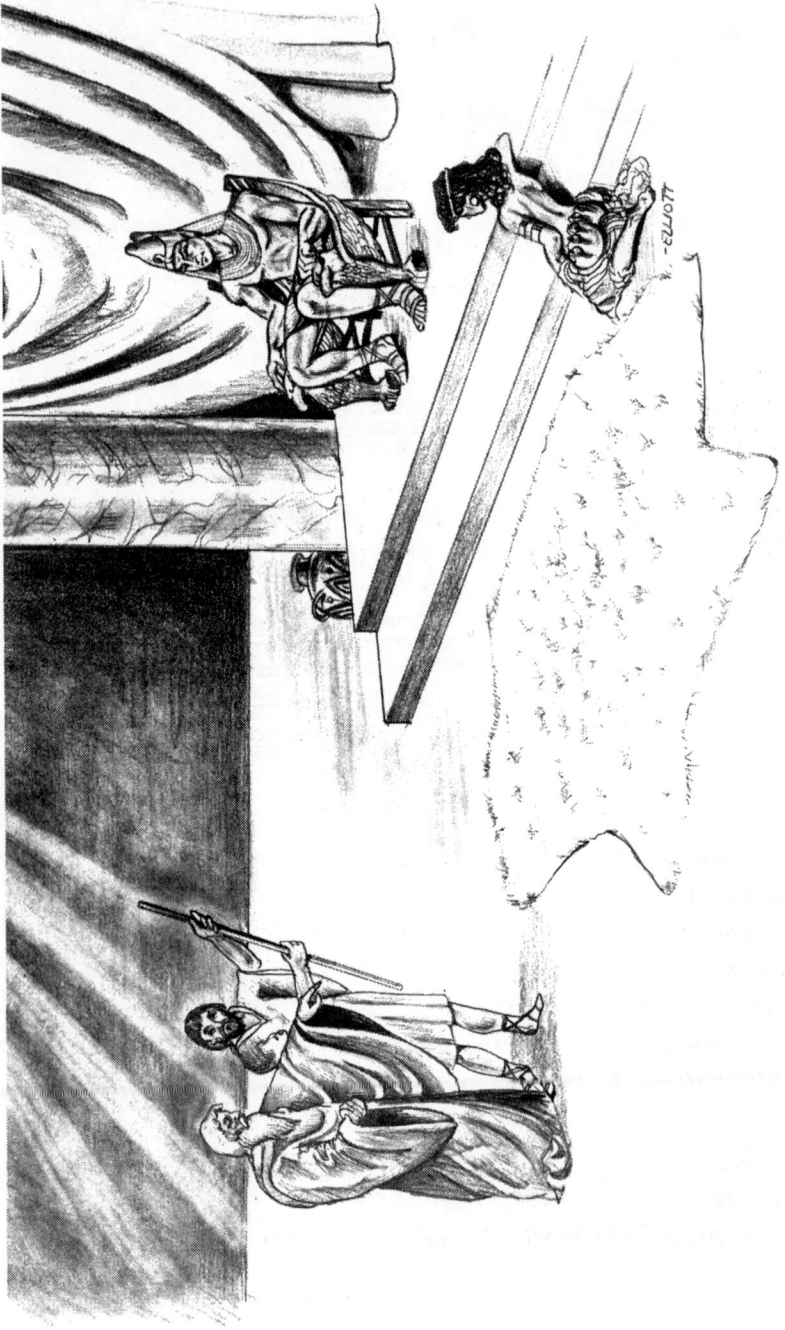

Moses and Aaron Before Pharaoh

Chapter 3

LET MY PEOPLE GO

Bricks Without Straw

"And afterward Moses and Aaron went in, and told Pharaoh, Thus saith the Lord God of Israel, Let my people go, that they may hold a feast unto me in the wilderness. And Pharaoh said, Who is the Lord, that I should obey his voice to let Israel go? I know not the Lord, neither will I let Israel go. And they said, The God of the Hebrews hath met with us: let us go, we pray thee, three days' journey into the desert, and sacrifice unto the Lord our God; lest he fall upon us with pestilence, or with the sword. And the king of Egypt said unto them, Wherefore do ye, Moses and Aaron, let the people from their works? get you unto your burdens. And Pharaoh said, Behold, the people of the land now are many, and ye make them rest from their burdens. And Pharaoh commanded the same day the taskmasters of the people,

*and their officers, saying, Ye shall no more give the peo-
ple straw to make brick, as heretofore: let them go and
gather straw for themselves. And the tale of the bricks,
which they did make heretofore, ye shall lay upon them;
ye shall not diminish aught thereof: for they be idle;
therefore they cry, saying, Let us go and sacrifice to our
God. Let there more work be laid upon the men, that
they may labour therein; and let them not regard vain
words.''*   *(Exodus 5:1-9)*

The very thought of losing Israel caused the Pharaoh
to clutch them with greater eagerness and watch them
with greater vigilance. The demand by this unknown god
to let the people go was absolutely absurd and ridiculous;
he would not let them go, and just for asking, he would
see that their work was made next to impossible.

*"Why do you two men take the people away from
their work?"* shouted the king. He immediately sent orders to the taskmasters and officers he had set over the
people that they were to receive no more straw, and their
production quotas must increase instead of decrease.
*"Make them sweat; teach them not to listen to Moses
and Aaron,"* demanded the king.

The taskmasters of the people told them Pharaoh had
ordered them to find straw wherever they could, so the
people scattered throughout all the land to gather stubble
instead of straw. The Egyptian taskmasters laid the whip
to their backs with greater force; they made impossible
demands and whipped them without mercy when they
did not produce. Quotas fell short and backs bled from
the beatings. The Israeli foremen went to Pharaoh and
pleaded with him, but to no avail. As they left the palace,

Moses and Aaron were waiting for them. The foremen swore at them, contending all this was their fault for they had caused the king to put a sword in the hands of their taskmasters to kill them.

"And Moses returned unto the Lord, and said, Lord, wherefore has thou so evil entered this people? Why is it that thou has sent me? For since I came to Pharaoh to speak in thy name, he hath done evil to this people; neither hast thou delivered thy people at all."

(Exodus 5:22-23)

Moses had been sorely tried. He had gone to Pharaoh to ask for the release of the people, and not only was he mocked by the king, but he lost favor again with the children of God. He did what he should have done; he turned to the Lord for an answer. He questioned, as many do, why the Lord had bothered to send him: had he not failed in his mission? Had he not asked God to send a more qualified person to do this job? In his moments of distress, he accused God of doing evil to them. While the Pharaoh sat smug in his palace, the God of Israel was directing Moses in another attack.

This first meeting with Pharaoh had served to determine the relationship of all concerned in reference to the Commands of God: (1) it brought out the hatred of Pharaoh, ripening for judgment; (2) it brought out the unbelief of Israel; and (3) it brought out the weakness of Moses.

The Established Covenant

"Then the Lord said unto Moses, Now shalt thou see what I will do to Pharaoh: for with a strong hand shall he let them go, and with a strong hand shall he drive

them out of his land. And God spake unto Moses, and said unto him, I am the Lord: And I appeared unto Abraham, unto Isaac, and unto Jacob, by the name of God Almighty, but by my name JEHOVAH was I not known to them. And I have also established my covenant with them, to give them the land of Canaan, the land of their pilgrimage, wherein they were strangers. And I have also heard the groaning of the children of Israel, whom the Egyptians keep in bondage; and I have remembered my covenant. Wherefore say unto the children of Israel, I am the Lord, and I will bring you out from under the burdens of the Egyptians, and I will rid you out of their bondage, and I will redeem you with a stretched out arm, and with great judgments. And I will take you to me for a people, and I will be to you a God: and ye shall know that I am the Lord your God, which bringeth you out from under the burdens of the Egyptians. And I will bring you in unto the land, concerning the which I did swear to give it to Abraham, to Isaac, and to Jacob; and I will give it you for an heritage: I am the Lord. And Moses spake so unto the children of Israel: but they hearkened not unto Moses for anguish of spirit, and for cruel bondage. And the Lord spake unto Moses, saying, Go in, speak unto Pharaoh king of Egypt, that he let the children of Israel go out of his land. And Moses spake before the Lord, saying, Behold, the children of Israel have not hearkened unto me; how then shall Pharaoh hear me, who am of uncircumcised lips?'' (Exodus 6:1-12)

In chapter six, God again revealed Himself as the GREAT I AM. He spoke to Moses giving him the plan for what lay ahead. This entire prophecy was revealed in detail to Abraham centuries before in Genesis 15, when God cut the blood covenant with him while he relaxed in a deep sleep: *"And when the sun was going down, a deep sleep fell upon Abram; and lo, an horror of great darkness fell upon him. And he said unto Abram, Know of a surety that thy seed shall be a stranger in a land that is not theirs, and shall serve them; and they shall afflict them four hundred years; And also that nation, whom they shall serve, will I judge: and afterward shall they come out with great substance"* (verses 12-14).

The time was right for Moses to deliver the children of Israel from their bondage. God prolonged the deliverance by the hand of Moses so that He might show forth His power to the wicked Egyptian dynasty. God told Moses that in the end the Pharaoh would be glad to see the Hebrew people leave his land. Over and over He reminded Moses that He is the I AM—I AM THE LORD! Pharaoh is a type of Satan in this world, and he does not give up his prey so easily. The key word in the Pentateuch is COVENANT.

In this chapter, after some failures at his task, Moses sought the face of Jehovah, and He assured him He had heard their groanings and was prepared to bring them forth into a land flowing with milk and honey. In verse 3, the Lord told Moses that the fathers of old knew Him only by His title JEHOVAH, but they had not lived to experience all that was included in His covenant name. In Hebrews 11:13, we are told, *"These all died in faith, not having received the promises, but having seen them afar off, and were persuaded of them, and embraced them, and confessed that they were strangers and pilgrims on the earth."* They did not know Him as the God of miracles; under Moses the children of Israel would know. Divine Titles are a most important subject of study for they are inseparably connected with a sound interpretation of Scripture. Elohim and Jehovah are not employed loosely on the pages of the Bible. Each has a definite significance, and the distinction is carefully preserved. Elohim (God) is the name which speaks of the Creator and Lord of His creatures. Jehovah (the Lord) is His title as connected with His people by covenant relationship.

Thus, to dispel all of Moses' fears, the Lord continually reminded him that He was the I AM; a covenant-keeping God. He had heard their cries, and would redeem them, and claim them for His own people.

It would be of special interest to note the seven "I WILL's" just in this section alone: (1) I will bring you out from under the burdens of the Egyptian; (2) I will rid you from their bondage; (3) I will redeem you with a stretched out arm and with great judgments; (4) I will take you to me for a people; (5) I will be to you a God; (6) I will bring you into the land I promised to Abraham, Isaac, and Jacob; and (7) I will give this land to you for an heritage.

Moses was encouraged by the Lord, but when he spoke to the children of Israel, they would not listen to him. Once again the Lord commanded Moses to appear before Pharaoh and insist he let the children go. Moses responded saying if the Hebrew brethren would not listen when he spoke, he knew Pharaoh would not hearken to him. Moses soon forgot it was the Lord who was ordering his steps. The task seemed too great for him in his own strength; however, the Lord had already said He would bring them out with the strength of His stretched-out arm, and He would bring judgment upon the land.

We note seven reasons for the plagues brought upon the Egyptians: (1) judgment for treatment of Israel; (2) judgment against Pharaoh and the Egyptians—first born; (3) judgment upon the Egyptian gods—witchcraft; (4) public manifestation of the mighty power and strength of Almighty God; (5) to show man's responsibility; (6) for signs to His own people; and (7) to manifest God's plan for Israel's redemption from the grip of Satan;

With persistence and patient endurance, the Lord dealt with Moses in the midst of all his complaints. While Moses talked with the Lord and dealt with Pharaoh, the children of Israel were scattered all over the land looking for straw to make bricks. Pharaoh responded to God's demand with an unqualified "no," declaring he knew not their God. The story of Moses' encounter with the Pharaoh is exciting, charged with suspense as step by step the episode unfolds, and we are in the midst of the battle between Pharaoh (Satan) and the Yahweh of Israel.

Moses' Commission Renewed

Exodus 7 begins with a continuation of the conversation between God and Moses. Moses had been pouring out his weaknesses before the Lord, and God in turn, encouraged him by telling him he was His ambassador to Pharaoh, and Aaron his spokesman. Moses told Aaron everything God said to him, and Aaron related God's messages to Pharaoh for Moses. However, from this chapter on, we find a marked change in Moses. No longer does he appear before God timid, hesitant, and discouraged. The anointing of God fell upon him for the job which lay ahead. The conflict from this point on would not be one of words, but of deeds. It is now open war! Here before us is the great conflict between good and evil. Pharaoh has taken fiendish delight in persecuting the Lord's people and openly defying their God. Through the work of His mediator, God continues in the midst of battle, to deliver His chosen ones—His elect.

These five chapters form one distinct section. We have (1) the ten judgments from the hand of the Lord; (2) the resistance of Jannes and Jambres; (3) the four objections of Pharaoh; and (4) the final act of God for deliverance.

The entire land of Egypt was made to tremble and fear beneath the successive blows from the rod of God. That same rod is spoken of as our comfort and guide.

In Psalm 105:26-45, the inspired Psalmist has given a condensed view of the appalling inflictions which the hardness of Pharaoh's heart brought upon his land and his people. He had set himself to resist God, and the consequences were judicial blindness and hardness of heart. The following verses give witness to the fact that none can resist the sovereign will of God and survive:

"He gave them hail for rain, and flaming fire in their land. He smote their vines also and their fig trees; and brake the trees of their coasts. He spake, and the locusts came, and caterpillars, and that without number, And did eat up all the herbs in their land, and devoured the fruit of their ground. He smote also all the firstborn in their land, the chief of all their strength. He brought them forth also with silver and gold: and there was not one feeble person among their tribes. Egypt was

glad when they departed: for the fear of them fell upon them. He spread a cloud for a covering; and fire to give light in the night. The people asked, and he brought quails, and satisfied them with the bread of heaven. He opened the rock, and the waters gushed out; they ran in the dry places like a river. For he remembered his holy promise, and Abraham his servant. And he brought forth his people with joy, and his chosen with gladness. And gave them the lands of the heathen: and they inherited the labour of the people; That they might observe his statutes, and keep his laws. Praise ye the Lord."

(Psalms 105:26-45)

It was God who hardened the heart of Pharaoh; the method used was rejection to light. God had revealed Himself to the king, and he had wantonly refused His commands.

"But Pharaoh shall not hearken unto you, that I may lay my hand upon Egypt, and bring forth mine armies, and my people the children of Israel, out of the land of Egypt by great judgments. And the Egyptians shall know that I am the Lord, when I stretch forth mine hand upon Egypt, and bring out the children of Israel from among them."   *(Exodus 7:4-5)*

God would take full opportunity to display His mighty power. A dark background was required to bring forth Divine Light. In Matthew 18:7, we read, *"It must needs be that offences come, but woe to that man by whom the offence cometh."*

Moses was eighty years old, and Aaron was eighty-three years old when they approached Pharaoh in behalf of the Yahweh of Israel for His people. The scriptures record that they did as the Lord instructed; they went in to Pharaoh again, Aaron took the rod and cast it down before Pharaoh and his servants, and it became a snake. Pharaoh's wise men came forth, his sorcerers, the magicians of Egypt, Jannes and Jambres, and they conjured up snakes by enchantment. Their rods became snakes, but Aaron's rod swallowed up their rods. Again, He hardened Pharaoh's heart, and he did not hearken to the Lord God of Israel. In Proverbs 21:1, we read, *"The king's heart is in the hand of the Lord, as the rivers of water: He turneth it whithersoever He will."* It says in Revelation 17:17, *"For God hath put in their hearts to fulfill His will, and to agree, and give their kingdom unto the Beast."*

There were only three miracles the magicians of Egypt were able to imitate: (1) the rods being turned into serpents (7:12); (2) turning the water into blood (7:22); and (3) bringing up of frogs (8:7). Keep in mind all they do is by the energy and direction of Satan.

The Ten Plagues of Egypt

(1) WATERS TURNED TO BLOOD

"Get thee unto Pharaoh in the morning; lo, he goeth out unto the water; and thou shalt stand by the river's brink against he come; and the rod which was turned to a serpent shalt thou take in thine hand. And thou shalt say unto him, The Lord God of the Hebrews hath sent me unto thee, saying, Let my people go, that they may serve me in the wilderness: and behold, hitherto thou wouldest not hear. Thus saith the Lord, In this thou shalt know that I am the Lord: behold, I will smite with the rod that is in mine hand upon the waters which

*are in the river, and they shall be turned to blood. And
the fish that is in the river shall die, and the river shall
stink; and the Egyptians shall loathe to drink of the
water of the river.''*   *(Exodus 7:15-18)*

As mentioned, in the ten plagues we have the perfection of God's judgments against the gods of Egypt. In chapter 12:12, we read, *"For I will pass through the land
of Egypt this night, and will smite all the firstborn in
the land of Egypt, both man and beast; and against all
the gods of Egypt I will execute judgment: I am the
Lord."*

The Egyptians worshipped the River Nile as a god. They called it "the Father of the gods." To fully appreciate the depth of this act by God against the Egyptian priests, we need to realize there was nothing they held in greater abhorrence than blood, seldom admitting any bloody sacrifices. Surely their horror was quite extreme when they found the river they worshipped turned into blood, which they regarded with such utter disgust. So, the extent of this calamity will be seen when we remember that the waters of the Nile were to the Egyptians then, as now, a great source of dependence for drinking and culinary purposes. Since it seldom rains, well water cannot be collected, the spring water is hard and unwholesome, and wells are seldom ever found there. The Egyptians say the Nile water is sweet as honey and sugar.

*"And the Lord spake unto Moses, Say unto Aaron,
Take thy rod, and stretch out thine hand upon the
waters of Egypt, upon their streams, upon their rivers,
and upon their ponds, and upon all their pools of water,
that they may become blood; throughout all the land of*

Egypt, both in vessels of wood, and in vessels of stone." *(Exodus 7:19)*

This he did in the sight of Pharaoh, and in the sight of his servants; and all the waters in the river, and in storage vessels were turned to blood. Fish died, the river stank, and the people had no water, except for the children of Israel protected over in the land of Goshen.

But the magicians of Egypt used their magic and turned water into blood; Pharaoh returned to his palace unimpressed. This plague lasted for seven days.

(2) THE FROGS

The "frogs" were consecrated to the deity of "Osiris," the greatest of the Egyptian gods.

"And the Lord spake unto Moses, Go unto Pharaoh, and say unto him, Thus saith the Lord, Let my people go, that they may serve me. And if thou refuse to let them go, behold, I will smite all thy borders with frogs. And the river shall bring forth frogs abundantly, which shall go up and come into thine house, and into thy bedchamber, and upon thy bed, and into the house of thy servants, and upon thy people, and into thine ovens, and into thy kneadingtroughs. And the frogs shall come up both on thee, and upon thy people, and upon all thy servants. And the Lord spake unto Moses, Say unto Aaron, Stretch forth thine hand with thy rod over the streams, over the rivers, and over the ponds, and cause frogs to come up upon the land of Egypt. And Aaron stretched out his hand over the waters of Egypt; and the frogs came up, and covered the land of Egypt. And the magicians did so with their enchantments, and brought up frogs upon the land of Egypt. Then Pharaoh called

*for Moses and Aaron, and said, Entreat the Lord, that
he may take away the frogs from me, and from my people; and I will let the people go, that they may do sacrifice unto the Lord. And Moses said unto Pharaoh,
Glory over me: when shall I entreat for thee, and for thy
servants, and for thy people, to destroy the frogs from
thee and thy houses, that they may remain in the river
only? And he said, Tomorrow. And he said, Be it according to thy word: that thou mayest know that there
is none like unto the Lord our God. And the frogs shall
depart from thee, and from thy houses, and from thy
servants, and from thy people; they shall remain in the
river only. And Moses and Aaron went out from Pharaoh: and Moses cried unto the Lord because of the frogs
which he had brought against Pharaoh. And the Lord
did according to the word of Moses; and the frogs died
out of the houses, out of the villages, and out of the
fields. And they gathered them together upon heaps:
and the land stank. But when Pharaoh saw that there
was respite, he hardened his heart, and hearkened not
unto them; as the Lord had said."*

(Exodus 8:1-15)

With each plague God sent another request and warning to the king. The second plague was also connected
with the Nile river, and it must be remembered that the
frog was also connected with the most ancient forms of
idolatry in Egypt. Again, the object of their worship had
become a curse to them. God warned that the frogs would
cover the land, enter their bedrooms, fill their cooking
vessels, and jump out of the kneadingtroughs. The Egyptians were quite accustomed to hoards of small croaking
frogs coming out of the mud after the annual flooding of

the Nile; they were quickly consumed by the ibis (a large wading bird).

The supernaturalness of their appearance lay in the extraordinary number, and in the fact that as soon as Aaron stretched forth his hand, at the command of God, the frogs appeared. The magicians succeeded in imitating Moses by bringing an untold number of frogs upon the land, but it is apparent they were unable to remove the curse for in verse 8 Pharaoh called for Moses and Aaron to entreat the Lord to remove the plague from his house and his people, and he would let the people go to worship their God.

Moses gave the king further proof that the plagues were from God when he gave the king the option of determining a time he pleased for their removal. Verse 9 from the Hebrew reads, *"Nullum occurrit tempus regi— no time fixed on by the king shall be objected to; have thou this honor over me, tell me against when I shall entreat for thee."* This was designed for Pharaoh's conviction. Moses left the king and interceded in behalf of the Pharaoh who had promised to let the people go. The frogs died, and Pharaoh hardened his heart when he saw there was a respite. He refused to let the people go.

(3) THE LICE

With no apparent warning, God commanded Moses and Aaron to stretch out the rod and smite the land with lice.[1] A scrupulous, external cleanliness was observed by the priests. This plague shocked and disgraced them.

"And the Lord said unto Moses, Say unto Aaron, Stretch out thy rod, and smite the dust of the land, that

---

[1]Hebrew word "sciniphes," actually means "gnats" so small they are hardly visible to the eye, but carry a powerful sting which is painful, and very irritating to the eyes.

it may become lice throughout all the land of Egypt. And they did so; for Aaron stretched out his hand with his rod, and smote the dust of the earth, and it became lice in man, and in beast; all the dust of the land became lice throughout all the land of Egypt. And the magicians did so with their enchantments to bring forth lice, but they could not: so there were lice upon man, and upon beast. Then the magicians said unto Pharaoh, This is the finger of God: and Pharaoh's heart was hardened, and he hearkened not unto them; as the Lord had said.''
(Exodus 8:16-19)

The plague of frogs were produced out of the water, but these lice out of the dust of the ground. God proved to the Pharaoh, and to the world, that He has many arrows in His quiver. We note a steady advance in the severity of the plagues. The magicians were helpless; they gave witness to Pharaoh that this had to be the hand of God.

(4) THE FLIES

Egyptians worshipped several deities whose province was to drive out flies. The god of Ekron (2 Kings 1:2) was a fly deity, known as Zebub or Beel-zebub, prince of flies. In Matthew 12:24-27, Jesus is called Beel-zebub, the prince of the devils: *"But when the Pharisees heard it, they said, This fellow doth not cast out devils, but by Beelzebub the prince of the devils. And Jesus knew their thoughts, and said unto them, Every kingdom divided against itself is brought to desolation; and every city or house divided against itself shall not stand: And if Satan cast out Satan, he is divided against himself; how shall then his kingdom stand? And if I by Beelzebub cast out devils, by whom do your children cast them out? therefore they shall be your judges.''*

"And the Lord said unto Moses, Rise up early in the morning, and stand before Pharaoh; lo, he cometh forth to the water; and say unto him, Thus saith the Lord, Let my people go, that they may serve me. Else, if thou wilt not let my people go, behold, I will send swarms of flies upon thee, and upon thy people, and into thy houses: and the houses of the Egyptians shall be full of swarms of flies, and also the ground whereon they are. And I will sever in that day the land of Goshen, in which my people dwell, that no swarms of flies shall be there; to the end thou mayest know that I am the Lord in the midst of the earth. And I will put a division between my people and thy people: tomorrow shall this sign be. And the Lord did so; and there came a grievous swarm of flies into the house of Pharaoh, and into his servants' houses, and into all the land of Egypt: the land was corrupted by reason of the swarm of flies. And Pharaoh called for Moses and for Aaron, and said, Go ye, sacrifice to your God in the land. And Moses said, It is not meet so to do; for we shall sacrifice the abomination of the Egyptians to the Lord our God: lo, shall we sacrifice the abomination of the Egyptians before their eyes, and will they not stone us? We will go three days' journey into the wilderness, and sacrifice to the Lord our God, as he shall command us. And Pharaoh said, I will let you go, that ye may sacrifice to the Lord your God in the wilderness; only ye shall not go very far away: entreat for me. And Moses said, Behold, I go out from thee, and I will entreat the Lord that the swarms of flies may depart from Pharaoh, from his servants, and from his people, tomorrow: but let not Pharaoh deal deceitfully any more in not letting the

*people go to sacrifice to the Lord. And Moses went out
from Pharaoh, and entreated the Lord. And the Lord did
according to the word of Moses; and he removed the
swarms of flies from Pharaoh, from his servants, and
from his people; there remained not one. And Pharaoh
hardened his heart at this time also, neither would he
let the people go."*   *(Exodus 8:20-32)*

These were so-called dog-flies, which not only infested the palace and houses, but wasted the land by de-
positing their eggs everywhere. This was a most painful
plague, for the flies fastened upon every uncovered sur-
face such as the eyelids and corners of the eyes, and their
bites caused sores and inflammation. It was announced to
Pharaoh as he went to the river early in the morning, probably with a procession in order to open the solemn fes-
tival which was held one hundred and twenty days after
the first rise of the Nile about the end of October or the
early part of November. God sent word that the land
would literally be covered with these flies if he did not
let the Hebrew people go so they could sacrifice to their
true God. All would be covered but the land of Goshen,
which he would protect, *". . . to the end thou mayest
know that I am the Lord in the midst of the earth"* *(verse
22)*.

The Curse

First compromise: Pharaoh said, *"All right! All
right! Go sacrifice to your God, but do it in this land.
Do not go into the wilderness,* to which Moses replied,
*"No! The Egyptians hate our God, and they will kill us.
God has commanded us to go a three-day journey into*

the wilderness and sacrifice to Jehovah our God. That is His command."

Second compromise: *"All right! All right! But do not go too far. Now, plead with God for me."*

Moses warned Pharaoh not to lie to him; but just as soon as the curse of flies was lifted, the king hardened his heart again and refused to let the people go.

(5) PESTILENCE

The Egyptians worshipped several animals as sacred deities. Apis, the sacred bull, was an outstanding god. When Pharaoh's heart was hardened after he had promised to let God's people go, he was warned of another plague that was on the way. This would strike their animals, even their most sacred gods. This was surely God's wrath revealed from heaven against the ungodly. But, once again, the Lord promised that the people over in Goshen would be severed from the plague.

But Pharaoh's heart was hardened and he did not let the children of Israel go.

"Behold, the hand of the Lord is upon thy cattle which is in the field, upon the horses, upon the asses, upon the camels, upon the oxen, and upon the sheep: there shall be a grievous murrain . . . And the Lord did that thing on the morrow, and all the cattle of Egypt died: but of the cattle of the children of Israel died not one."   *(Exodus 9:3, 6)*

(6) THE BOILS

"And the Lord said unto Moses and unto Aaron, Take to you handfuls of ashes of the furnace, and let Moses sprinkle it toward the heaven in the sight of Pha-

raoh. And it shall become small dust in all the land of Egypt, and shall be a boil breaking forth with blains upon man, and upon beast, throughout all the and of Egypt.''   *(Exodus 9:8-9)*

The magicians could not stand before Moses and Aaron because the blisters had covered their bodies. Still, Pharaoh refused to listen to these men of God. Medical deities were helpless; Molock was a medical deity (Acts 7:43).

(7)   RAIN, HAIL, AND FIRE

Isis and Osiris were the gods of weather and fire and were worshipped for their protection. These gods of weather were helpless in the midst of the plague of hail, rain, and fire.

God sent yet another warning to Pharaoh to prove to him there was no other god like the God of the Hebrews in all the earth.

"For I will at this time send all my plagues upon thine heart, and upon thy servants, and upon thy people; that thou mayest know that there is none like me in all the earth. For now I will stretch out my hand, that I may smite thee and thy people with pestilence; and thou shalt be cut off from the earth. And in very deed for this cause have I raised thee up, for to shew in thee my power; and that my name may be declared throughout all the earth. As yet exaltest thou thyself against my people, that thou wilt not let them go?''

(Exodus 9:14-17)

Moses stood before the Pharaoh of Egypt and declared to him that these plagues would be worse than all the others. He expounded the Word of God to that heathen king and demanded the release of the Hebrew children: *"Do you think you can stand before the face of the God of all creation? He could have killed you by now! Tomorrow you will be plagued by a hailstorm across this nation this land has never known. It will lay the place in total ruin."*

Moses stretched forth his hand and the Lord sent thunder, hail and lightning so terrible the people coruched in fear. Men and animals alike were killed. The land of Goshen lay undisturbed by the plagues.

"And the Lord said unto Moses, Stretch forth thine hand toward heaven, that there may be hail in all the land of Egypt, upon man, and upon beast, and upon every herb of the field, throughout the land of Egypt. And Moses stretched forth his rod toward heaven: and the Lord sent thunder and hail, and the fire ran along upon the ground; and the Lord rained hail upon the land of Egypt. So there was hail, and fire mingled with the hail, very grievous, such as there was none like it in all the land of Egypt since it became a nation. And the hail smote throughout all the land of Egypt all that was in the field, both man and beast; and the hail smote every herb of the field, and brake every tree of the field. Only in the land of Goshen, where the children of Israel were, was there no hail. And Pharaoh sent, and called for Moses and Aaron, and said unto them, I have sinned this time: the Lord is righteous, and I and my people are wicked. Entreat the Lord (for it is enough) that there be no more mighty thunderings and hail; and I will let you go, and ye shall stay no longer. And Moses said unto him, As soon as I am gone out of the city, I will spread abroad my hands unto the Lord; and the thunder shall

cease, neither shall there be any more hail; that thou mayest know how that the earth is the Lord's. But as for thee and thy servants, I know that ye will not yet fear the Lord God. And the flax and the barley was smitten: for the barley was in the ear, and the flax was bolled. But the wheat and the rie were not smitten: for they were not grown up. And Moses went out of the city from Pharaoh, and spread abroad his hands unto the Lord: and the thunders and hail ceased, and the rain was not poured upon the earth. And when Pharaoh saw that the rain and the hail and the thunders were ceased, he sinned yet more, and hardened his heart, he and his servants." (Exodus 9:22-34)

And Pharaoh refused to let the children of Israel go so they could worship God in the wilderness.

(8) LOCUSTS

Since Pharaoh's pride still refused to bend to the will of God, Moses was instructed to announce another, and yet more fearful, plague to cover the land of Egypt. However, the Lord strengthened Moses' faith by telling him that the hardening of Pharaoh and his servants was decreed by Him. He used these signs in order that Israel might perceive that He was Jehovah. We note the progressive severity of these plagues, and how Moses' attitude changed each time. Hitherto, he had been content with repeating each demand as he was instructed by the Lord; but now the failure of the king to keep his royal word had changed and altered the relations between them. The king had forfeited all claim to his respect. He had proven over and over that he was not a man of his word, but an outright liar. The confessions of his sins were followed by no efforts of change. He was no longer ignorant of Jehovah, but willfully obstinate and defiant. He hated the Israelites with a passion. Moses altered his tone. He would not long treat him as a king, but as an outright sinner.

"And the Lord said unto Moses, Go in unto Pharaoh: for I have hardened his heart, and the heart of his servants, that I might shew these my signs before him: And that thou mayest tell in the ears of thy son, and of thy son's son, what things I have wrought in Egypt, and my signs which I have done among them; that ye may know how that I am the Lord." (*Exodus 10:1-2*)

God assured Moses that the ten plagues must be inflicted upon Egypt not only for the release of His people, but also for the magnifying of His Name, and that all generations to come must rehearse it in the ears of their children's children. They must be aware of His overruling power, authority, and dominion on the earth. All of these plagues would stand out in history as undeniable proof that He was the I AM, and to be worshipped by all His creation.

The gods "Iris," and "Serapis" were worshipped by the Egyptians to protect their land from locusts. The east wind was never feared because of protection from the Red Sea, and locusts came from the east.

"And Moses and Aaron came in unto Pharaoh, and said unto him, Thus saith the Lord God of the Hebrews, How long wilt thou refuse to humble thyself before me? Let my people go, that they may serve me. Else, if thou refuse to let my people go, behold, tomorrow will I bring the locust into thy coast: And they shall cover the

face of the earth, that one cannot be able to see the earth: and they shall eat the residue of that which is escaped, which remaineth unto you from the hail, and shall eat every tree which groweth for you out of the field: And they shall fill thy houses, and the houses of all thy servants, and the houses of all the Egyptians; which neither thy fathers, nor thy fathers' fathers have seen, since the day that they were upon the earth unto this day. And he turned himself, and went out from Pharaoh.''   *(Exodus 10:3-6)*

Moses spoke with authority the words which the Lord God had instructed him to speak, then he turned and hastily left the court. He had no more to add. We are to speak what the Lord tells us to speak in any situation and to cease from adding our thoughts to the matter. He knew in his heart that God was almost finished with Pharaoh.

The court officials came before Pharaoh and interceded in behalf of the people. It seemed their king would destroy them completely by his hardness. Next they spoke in behalf of the people of Israel, begging their king to let the Hebrews go and worship their God before Egypt lay in complete ruins. So Moses and Aaron were brought back before Pharaoh.

"And Moses and Aaron were brought again unto Pharaoh: and he said unto them, Go, serve the Lord your God: but who are they that shall go? And Moses said, We will go with our young and with our old, with our sons and with out daughters, with our flocks and with our herds will we go; for we must hold a feast unto the Lord. And he said unto them, Let the Lord be so with you, as I will let you go, and your little ones: look to it;

for evil is before you. Not so: go now ye that are men, and serve the Lord; for that ye did desire. And they were driven out from Pharaoh's presence." (Exodus 10:8-11)

Compromise Three: In other words, the Pharaoh said, "All right, go serve your God, you men, but not the children; leave them behind. Never will you take the little ones with you! Get out!"

But the locust came with the east wind, blowing straight from the desert, and lasting all day and all night. The locust covered the entire land for God had commanded that what the hail and fire had not destroyed, the locust would finish off. This plague of locust was so severe that it blotted out the sun, and the land lay in total darkness during that time. Nothing was left—not a tree or green plant remained. But all was well over in the land of Goshen which was protected by the mighty hand and power of God that they might know the God of Abraham, Isaac, and Jacob was calling for His people to come out from among the unclean thing, and be reunited to Him.

"Then Pharaoh called for Moses and Aaron in haste; and he said, I have sinned against the Lord your God, and against you. Now therefore forgive, I pray thee, my sin only this once, and entreat the lord your God, that he may take away from me this death only. And he went out from Pharaoh, and entreated the Lord. And the Lord turned a mighty strong west wind, which took away the locust, and cast them into the Red Sea; there remained not one locust in all the coasts of Egypt. But the Lord hardened Pharaoh's heart, so that he would not let the children of Israel go." (Exodus 10:17-20)

How gracious and long-suffering is our God! But God alone knew the evil thoughts of the Pharaoh, and He worked in line with them to release His Own people. In answer to the intercession of His servant, Moses, the Lord sent a strong west wind, and drove the locust into the Red Sea.

(9) THE DARKNESS

The Egyptians worshipped Ra, the sun god. Pharaoh was called the child of the sun. Unannounced, the darkness fell like a heavy blanket across the land of Egypt; but there was light over in the land of the Hebrews.

"And the Lord said unto Moses, Stretch out thine hand toward heaven, that there may be darkness over the land of Egypt, even darkness which may be felt. And Moses stretched forth his hand toward heaven; and there was a thick darkness in all the land of Egypt for three days: They saw not one another, neither rose any from his place for three days: but all the children of Israel had light in their dwellings. And Pharaoh called unto Moses, and said, Go ye, serve the Lord; only let your flocks and your herds be stayed: let your little ones also go with you. And Moses said, Thou must give us also sacrifices and burnt offerings, that we may sacrifice unto the Lord our God. Our cattle also shall go with us; there shall not an hoof be left behind; for thereof must we take to serve the Lord our God; and we know not with what we must serve the Lord, until we come thither. But the Lord hardened Pharaoh's heart, and he would not let them go. And Pharaoh said unto him, Get thee from me, take heed to thyself, see my face no more; for in that day thou seest my face thou shalt die. And

*Moses said, Thou hast spoken well, I will see thy face
again no more.''*   *(Exodus 10:21-29*

Compromise Four: Pharaoh called again for
Moses, for the land of Egypt had been rendered totally
helpless by this ninth plague. No one dared venture from
his dwelling; no one could cook, fetch water, or visit a
neighbor.

Then Pharaoh called for Moses and offered him his
fourth compromise with the attitude that this was his last
offer, and evil would befall Moses if this suggestion was
refused.

He said, *"Go on, worship your God, but you are to
let your flocks and herds stay here; I will let you take
the children though."* Satan disputed with great perseverance every inch of Israel's way out of Egypt. In this
offer from Pharaoh, the devil sought to get the children
of Israel out in the wilderness with no way to sacrifice
unto their God. He will whisper in the ear, "Go a little
ways, but do not get carried away with this thing about a
deeper walk. Above all, spare your children. They do not
need to hear about healing and prosperity; keep them
where they are. All right, go on to church, but leave your
pocketbook at home. God does not need your money!"
On and on he spews out his lies of compromise.

Pharaoh had made a miserable attempt to make the
best of two worlds. God has said we cannot serve Him and
the world at the same time. We must be totally separated
from Egypt, which is a type of the world. If Satan could
not induce them to sacrifice in the land, he would send
them out of the land without sacrifice. In 2 Timothy 4:10,
we read where Demas was caught in such a snare, *"For*

Demas hath forsaken me, having loved this present world . . .'' Ananias and Sapphira fell dead because they withheld from God, and lied to the Holy Ghost (Acts 5).

This danger was very real, and Moses did not fall into the trap. He knew if their possessions remained in Egypt, so would their affections. God had called for total separation.

Moses replied that not as much as a hoof would be left behind. The king became furious and ordered him out of the court again, screaming that Moses and Aaron were never to show their face in the court again upon sentence of death.

"Very well," Moses answered, *"you will never see my face again."* He knew they would have to go a full three days into the wilderness, taking all they owned, before they would hear a hint from the Lord as to sacrifice and worship. We, too, must take that three-day journey with the Lord in order to enter in unto His fullness in this life, and be transformed into His likeness. Depart from the way of evil, and leave not a trace behind.

Matthew Henry wrote, *"Impotent Malice! To threaten him with death who was armed with such a power, and at whose mercy he had so often laid himself. What will not hardness of heart and contempt of God's word and commandments bring men to?"*

When men refuse the Word of God, rebel against His commandments, and turn their feet into the path of evil, God will permit strong delusions to come upon them. The same Word that softens hearts can cause another to turn cold and hard as stone.

—ELLIOTT

(10)   THE DEATH OF THE FIRSTBORN

The contest between Jehovah and Pharaoh was just about to end. He had been given ample opportunity to repent and turn from his wickedness. Warning after warning, plague after plague had been sent, but still Pharaoh refused to acknowledge God, and feared Him not. He offered to compromise with God and his people, but he refused to "let them go." This story clearly sets forth the folly of fighting against the Lord, and resisting His commandments. In Proverbs 16:1-3, 33, we read, *"The preparations of the heart in man, and the answer of the tongue, is from the Lord. All the ways of a man are clean in his own eyes; but the Lord weigheth the spirits. Commit thy works unto the Lord, and thy thought shall be established . . . The lot is cast into the lap; but the whole disposing thereof is of the Lord."* Also, in Proverbs 19:21, we read, *"There are many devices in a man's heart; nevertheless the counsel of the Lord, that shall stand."*

When the Lord God has purposed a thing, no man can change it. *"For the Lord of hosts hath purposed, and who shall disannul it? and His hand is stretched out, and who shall turn it back?"* (Isaiah 14:27) Those who walk in pride, God will bring low. Even today we hear people say, "Who is the Lord that I should serve him?"

The first three verses of chapter 11, must have been spoken to Moses before his last interview with Pharaoh. Verse one should be rendered: *"And Jehovah had said unto Moses . . ."* To fully understand Moses' confident reply to the king's last challenge, we should insert them at the last of chapter 10. Probably Exodus 11:4, and what follows form part of Moses' reply to Pharaoh which began in 10:29.

"And the Lord said unto Moses, Yet will I bring one plague more upon Pharaoh, and upon Egypt; afterwards he will let you go hence: when he shall let you go, he shall surely thrust you out hence altogether. Speak now in the ears of the people, and let every man borrow of his neighbour, and every woman of her neighbour, jewels of silver, and jewels of gold. And the Lord gave the people favour in the sight of the Egyptians. Moreover the man Moses was very great in the land of Egypt, in the sight of Pharaoh's servants, and in the sight of the people. And Moses said, Thus saith the Lord, About midnight will I go out into the midst of Egypt. And all the firstborn in the land of Egypt shall die, from the firstborn of Pharaoh that sitteth upon his throne, even unto the firstborn of the maidservant that is behind the mill; and all the firstborn of beasts. And there shall be a great cry throughout all the land of Egypt, such as there was none like it, nor shall be like it any more. But against any of the children of Israel shall not a dog move his tongue, against man or beast: that ye may know how that the Lord doth put a difference between the Egyptians and Israel. And all these thy servants shall come down unto me, and bow down themselves unto me, saying, Get thee out, and all the people that follow thee: and after that I will go out. And he went out from Pharaoh in a great anger. And the Lord said unto Moses, Pharaoh shall not hearken unto you; that my wonders may be multiplied in the land of Egypt. And Moses and Aaron did all these wonders before Pharaoh: and the Lord hardened Pharaoh's heart, so that he would not let the children of Israel go out of his land."

(Exodus 11:1-10)

The tenth and last plague was directed against all the heathen deities at one time. One stroke more would Jehovah bring upon all of Egypt. Not only would the Pharaoh gladly let His people go, but they would go carrying the spoils of their victory by asking the Egyptians for their gold and silver jewels. God caused his people to find favor in the sight of the enemy.

This last plague would touch not only the royalty who lived in the palace, but it would strike down the occupants of the whole of Egypt; except it would not touch Israel, His firstborn. At this point Moses received his instructions which carry over into chapter 12 for their fulfillment.

The Lord told Moses He would send another plague which would cause the Egyptians to beg the Hebrews to leave their land; they would offer them their silver and gold, and anxiously shove them out. So, Moses announced to the Pharaoh what was about to take place at midnight; when the Lord passed over the land, all the oldest sons would be slain—from the firstborn of Pharaoh to the maidservant behind the mill, to the firstborn of the beasts.

If the death of the cattle had humbled the king, the death of his child would not have been necessary. God is a God of love and He is longsuffering and not willing that anyone should perish. Careful note must be made of the total protection God gave to His own people. Also, Moses and Aaron were not ordered to summon this plague. No, God said He would handle this Himself. It would take place in the dead of night; when they were all asleep. All their firstborn should sleep the sleep of death, but not silently so as not to be found until the next morning. The wail of death would resound throughout the entire land. Families would stand by helplessly and see their firstborn suffer the agonies of death. Yet, while angels drew their swords against the Egyptians, there should not be so much as a dog's bark at any of the children of Israel.

Moses announced to Pharaoh that this last plague would cause him to take notice that Jehovah *". . . makes a difference between the Egyptians and the Israelis. All your officials will come running to me, bowing low and begging us to leave the country. Only then will we go!"* With that, Moses left the palace in a fit of anger, for the Lord had told him that Pharaoh would not listen and would not let the people go.

The fourteenth day of Nisan had arrived, and after Moses had delivered the Divine ultimatum, he left forever the Palace of the Pharaohs.

The Passover Lamb

"And the Lord spake unto Moses and Aaron in the land of Egypt, saying, This month shall be unto you the beginning of months: it shall be the first month of the year to you. Speak ye unto all the congregation of Israel, saying, In the tenth day of this month they shall take to them every man a lamb, according to the house of their fathers, a lamb for an house: And if the household be too little for the lamb, let him and his neighbour next unto his house take it according to the number of the souls; every man according to his eating shall make your count for the lamb. Your lamb shall be without

blemish, a male of the first year: ye shall take it out from the sheep, or from the goats: And ye shall keep it up until the fourteenth day of the same month: and the whole assembly of the congregation of Israel shall kill it in the evening. And they shall take of the blood, and strike it on the two side posts and on the upper door post of the houses, wherein they shall eat it. And they shall eat the flesh in that night, roast with fire, and unleavened bread; and with bitter herbs they shall eat it. Eat not of it raw, nor sodden at all with water, but roast with fire; his head with his legs, and with the purtenance thereof. And ye shall let nothing of it remain until the morning; and that which remaineth of it until the morning ye shall burn with fire. And thus shall ye eat it; with your loins girded, your shoes on your feet, and your staff in your hand; and ye shall eat it in haste; it is the Lord's passover. (Exodus 12:1-11)

Redemption By Blood

"For I will pass through the land of Egypt this night, and will smite all the firstborn in the land of Egypt, both man and beast; and against all the gods of Egypt I will execute judgment: I am the Lord. And the blood shall be to you for a token upon the houses where ye are: and when I see the blood, I will pass over you, and the plague shall not be upon you to destroy you, when I smite the land of Egypt." (Exodus 12:12-13)

A Memorial of Redemption

"And this day shall be unto you for a memorial; and ye shall keep it a feast to the Lord throughout your generations; ye shall keep it a feast by an ordinance for-

ever. *Seven days shall ye eat unleavened bread; even the first day ye shall put away leaven out of your houses: for whosoever eateth leavened bread from the first day until the seventh day, that soul shall be cut off from Israel. And in the first day there shall be an holy convocation, and in the seventh day there shall be an holy convocation to you; no manner of work shall be done in them, save that which every man must eat, that only may be done of you. And ye shall observe the feast of unleavened bread; for in this selfsame day have I brought your armies out of the land of Egypt: therefore shall ye observe this day in your generations by an ordinance forever. In the first month, on the fourteenth day of the month at even, ye shall eat unleavened bread, until the one and twentieth day of the month at even. Seven days shall there be no leaven found in your houses: for whosoever eateth that which is leavened, even that soul shall be cut off from the congregation of Israel, whether he be a stranger, or born in the land. Ye shall eat nothing leavened; in all your habitations shall ye eat unleavened bread. Then Moses called for all the elders of Israel, and said unto them, Draw out and take you a lamb according to your families, and kill the pass-over. And ye shall take a bunch of hyssop, and dip it in the blood that is in the basin, and strike the lintel and the two side posts with the blood that is in the basin; and none of you shall go out at the door of his house until the morning. For the Lord will pass through to smite the Egyptians; and when he seeth the blood upon the lintel, and on the two side posts, the Lord will pass over the door, and will not suffer the destroyer to come in unto your houses to smite you. And ye shall observe*

*this thing for an ordinance to thee and to thy sons for-
ever. And it shall come to pass, when ye be come to the
land which the Lord will give you, according as he hath
promised, that ye shall keep this service. And it shall
come to pass, when your children shall say unto you,
What mean ye by this service? That ye shall say, It is the
sacrifice of the Lord's passover, who passed over the
houses of the children of Israel in Egypt, when he smote
the Egyptians, and delivered our houses. And the people
bowed the head and worshipped. And the children of
Israel went away, and did as the Lord had commanded
Moses and Aaron, so did they."*   *(Exodus 12:12-28)*

Death of Firstborn

*"And it came to pass, that at midnight the Lord
smote all the firstborn in the land of Egypt, from the
firstborn of Pharaoh that sat on his throne unto the
firstborn of the captive that was in the dungeon; and all
the firstborn of cattle. And Pharaoh rose up in the night,
he, and all his servants, and all the Egyptians; and there
was a great cry in Egypt; for there was not a house
where there was not one dead."*   *(Exodus 12:31-36)*

The Exodus

*"And he called for Moses and Aaron by night, and
said, Rise up, and get you forth from among my people,
both ye and the children of Israel; and go, serve the
Lord, as ye have said. Also take your flocks and your
herds, as ye have said, and be gone; and bless me also.
And the Egyptians were urgent upon the people, that
they might send them out of the land in haste; for they
said, We be all dead men. And the people took their*

*dough before it was leavened, their kneadingtroughs
being bound up in their clothes upon their shoulders.
And the children of Israel did according to the word of
Moses; and they borrowed of the Egyptians jewels of silver, and jewels of gold, and raiment: And the Lord gave
the people favour in the sight of the Egyptians, so that
they lent unto them such things as they required. And
they spoiled the Egyptians.''*   *(Exodus 12:31-36)*

First Stage of Their Journey

*"And the children of Israel journeyed from
Rameses to Succoth, about six hundred thousand on
foot that were men, beside children. And a mixed multitude went up also with them; and flocks, and herds,
even very much cattle. And they baked unleavened
cakes of the dough which they brought forth out of
Egypt, for it was not leavened; because they were thrust
out of Egypt, and could not tarry, neither had they prepared for themselves any victual. Now the sojourning
of the children of Israel, who dwelt in Egypt, was four
hundred and thirty years. And it came to pass at the end
of the four hundred and thirty years, even the selfsame
day it came to pass, that all the hosts of the Lord went
out from the land of Egypt. It is a night to be much observed unto the Lord for bringing them out from the
land of Egypt: this is that night of the Lord to be observed of all the children of Israel in their generations.
And the Lord said unto Moses and Aaron, This is the
ordinance of the passover: There shall no stranger eat
thereof: But every man's servant that is bought for
money, when thou hast circumcised him, then shall he
eat thereof. A foreigner and an hired servant shall not*

eat thereof. In one house shall it be eaten; thou shalt not carry forth aught of the flesh abroad out of the house; neither shall ye break a bone thereof. All the congregation of Israel shall keep it. And when a stranger shall sojourn with thee, and will keep the passover to the Lord, let all his males be circumcised, and then let him come near and keep it; and he shall be as one that is born in the land: for no uncircumcised person shall eat thereof. One law shall be to him that is homeborn, and unto the stranger that sojourneth among you. Thus did all the children of Israel; as the Lord commanded Moses and Aaron, so did they. And it came to pass the selfsame day, that the Lord did bring the children of Israel out of the land of Egypt by their armies.''

(Exodus 12:37-51)

"And the Lord spake unto Moses and Aaron in the land of Egypt saying, 'This month shall be unto you the beginning of months: it shall be the first month of the year to you" (April 1, 1462)[1] Recorded here is a very interesting change in the order of time. The common civil year was rolling on its ordinary course when Jehovah interrupted it in reference to His people; thus, in principle He taught them that they were to begin a new era in company with Him. Redemption was to constitute the first step in a new life; henceforth, all former things had passed away, and all had become new. "This teaches a plain truth. A man's life is really of no account until he begins to walk with God, in the knowledge of full salvation and settled peace, through the precious blood of the Lamb. Previous to this, he is, in the judgment of God, and

---

[1]Dates taken from the Chronological Bible.

69

in the language of Scripture, 'dead in trespasses and sins;' and he is, 'alienated from the life of God.' His whole history is a complete blank, even though, in man's account, it may have been one uninterrupted scene of bustling activity. All that which engages the attention of the man of this world—the honors, the riches, the pleasures, and the attractions of life, when examined in the light of the judgment of God, when weighed in the balances of the sanctuary, must be accounted as a dismal blank, a worthless void, utterly unworthy of a place in the records of the Holy Ghost" (Arthur Pink).

The Bible teaches us that the "wages of sin is death." Therefore, we have no difficulty in perceiving that it is the question of SIN which is raised here and dealt with by God.

Since the Israelites were as much sinners in the eyes of God as the Egyptians, we must understand that although God purposed to deliver His children out of Egypt, He would do it only on a righteous basis. Holiness can never ignore sin. When the angels sinned, God did not spare them (2 Peter 2:4). The elect are *"children of wrath even as others"* (Ephesians 2:3). God made no exception with Jesus, His Own Son, *"For he hath made him, who knew no sin, to be sin for us, that we might be made the righteousness of God in him"* (2 Corinthians 5:21). Another thought along this line comes from Psalm 32:1: *"Happy is he whose transgression is forgiven, whose sin is covered." We can receive life and happiness only through the Lord Jesus Christ, and the shed blood of the Lamb of God. Outside of Him all is vanity and vexation of soul and spirit. "In Him alone true and eternal joys are to be found; and we only begin to live when*

we begin to live in, live on, live with, and live for Him"
(C.H.M.).[2]

All of the claims of justice would have to be met. But how? By a substitute. Sentence of death – –but it fell upon the innocent victim. That which was without blemish died for all who were ever born of Adam and Eve. *"From the sole of the foot even unto the head there is no soundness in it, but wounds, and bruises, and putrifying sores. They have not been closed, neither bound up, neither mollified with ointment"* (Isaiah 1:6).

The entire value of the blood of the pascal lamb lay in its being a type of the Lord Jesus Christ, Who was the Lamb slain from the foundation of the world. Before us we have one of the most significant chapters in the entire Bible.

From now on the month of April would be the first and most important month of the Jewish calendar. Annually, on the tenth day of this month, each family must get a male lamb, one year old, either a sheep or goat, without any defects. (Moses was to announce this to all of Israel before their departure.)

In the evening, on the fourteenth day of this month, all these lambs were to be killed, and their blood placed on the two side posts and on the upper part of the door posts of their houses. God instructed Moses to tell the people to use the blood of the Lamb eaten in that home. Everyone was to eat roast lamb that night. If there were two very small families, they were allowed to share a lamb that night.

---

[2]C. H. MacKintosh

It must not be eaten raw or boiled, but roasted. It must be accompanied with unleavened bread and bitter herbs. (This included the head, legs, heart, and liver.) None was to be eaten the next day. If a family had anything left, they were to burn it.

In the study of Exodus 12, we are dealing with ONE ASSEMBLY, and ONE SACRIFICE. *"The whole assembly of the congregation of Israel shall kill it in the evening"* (verse 6). The antitype we have of this is the whole church of God, gathered by the Holy Ghost, in the Name of Jesus, around the Passover table, sharing the Blood of the Lamb.

Four Rules for Preparation of the Lamb

(1)   Roasted with fire—not only was the lamb to be killed but its flesh was to be eaten. The act of eating in the scriptures signified two things: appropriation and fellowship. The Lamb was God's provision for His people. Jesus is the BREAD of life. Here, the laying down of life becomes the very sustenance of life. This we are to eat was a Lamb which had undergone the action or test of fire. The fire tried Him, and He could say, *"Thou hast proved mine heart; thou hast visited me in the night; thou hast tried me and shalt find nothing: I am purposed that my mouth shall not transgress"* (Psalm 17:3). Fire is symbolic of the Holy Ghost, and the Divine Presence of God. Jesus said in John 6:35, *"I am the bread of life; he that cometh to me shall never hunger; and he that believeth on me shall never thirst."* This caused the Jews to murmur against Him; He had claimed to be Bread from heaven; He had further claimed that His flesh was that Bread. From that time on many of His own disciples walked with Him no more.

(2) Eaten with unleavened bread—leaven is invariably used throughout Scripture as emblematical of evil. Nothing but unleavened bread could complement this feast of roasted Lamb. "A single particle of that which was the marked type of evil, would have destroyed the moral character of the entire ordinance" (C.H.M.). *"For even Christ our passover is sacrificed for us: therefore let us keep the feast, not with old leaven, neither with the leaven of malice and wickedness; but with the unleavened bread of sincerity and truth"*(I Corinthians 5:7-8).

(3) Eaten with bitter herbs—in remembrance of their bitter bondage down in Egypt; Christ will be sweet to us if sin is bitter. We cannot enjoy communion with the sufferings of Christ without remembering what it was that rendered those sufferings needful. This remembrance is like the bitter herbs that accompanied the passover feast. "The herbs which to an Egyptian's taste would no doubt have seemed so bitter, formed an integral part of Israel's redemption feast" (C.H.M.). Those who are redeemed by the Blood of the Lamb, who have entered into the joy of His fellowship, consider it a "feast" to put away all evil, and to keep the flesh (nature) in its place of death.

(4) Eaten in haste—IT IS THE LORD'S PASSOVER. Eat in haste and be prepared to leave the land of death and enter into the land of promise. The Blood which had preserved them from the fate of Egypt's firstborn, was also the foundation of their deliverance that night; their deliverance from the land of slavery, where Pharaoh's yoke had caused their cries of anguish to reach the heart of Jehovah.

Since we read in the Word that the Lamb was slain from the foundation of the world, then assuredly, redemption was in the mind of God before the foundation of the world. It was now time to bring forth the Lamb in type. The Lamb taken on the tenth day, (ten stands for redemption), and kept until the fourteenth day, shows us Christ foreordained of God from eternity, but manifest for us in time. This is the foundation of the believer's peace. He is our rest.

While the children of God were observing their passover feast, sheltered by the Blood upon the door posts, the Lord God, (the death angel), passed over the land of Egypt and killed all the firstborn, both man and beast, as judgment against all the gods of Egypt. *"And the blood shall be to you for a token upon the houses where ye are: and when I see the blood, I WILL PASS OVER YOU, and the plague shall not be upon you to destroy you, when I smite the land of Egypt"* (verse 13).

They were told to celebrate this event every year to remind them of their deliverance. The celebration was to last for seven days. For that entire period of time they were to eat no leaven in their bread (bread made without yeast).[3] It became a law that the children of Israel were to forever celebrate this feast.

God gave these commandments unto Moses, and Moses called all the elders of Israel together, and instructed them in what was about to take place and the

---

[3]The Exodus brought Israel into a new life. Old things were passed away. To have eaten of leaven would have been to deny, as it were, this great fact. The feast of unleavened bread, which followed the Passover night, lasted seven days, both as commemorative of the creation of Israel, and because the number seven is symbolic of "covenant" and "perfection." Verse 45 typifies that strangers cannot participate in communion with the redeemed. Verse 47 speaks in type that "not one of His bones were broken."

importance of following the precepts of the Lord. In verse 27, we read that the people bowed and worshipped the Lord.

That night at midnight, the God of Israel killed all the firstborn sons in the land of Egypt; but when He saw the blood upon the door post, He spread His protective shield over that house, and would not allow the destroyer to kill the firstborn of that family.

Pharaoh summoned Moses and Aaron during the night and begged them to leave, taking all they owned with them. That night the people of Israel left Rameses and started for Succoth or "booths."[4] There were 600,000 of them, plus the women and children. It is believed that either two or three million Jews left Egypt that night with all their cattle, jewels, and a mixed multitude (perhaps Egyptian neighbors). And so the people of God marched forth from the house of bondage, and headed for the land flowing with milk and honey promised to their forefathers so long ago. They moved out, no longer as fugitives, but as an army in triumph. We are reminded that not one single Israelite was delivered until the blood of the Lamb had been shed in obedience to the command of God.

---

[4]The locality of this and the place called Etham, has not been determined. Etham, "the edge of the wilderness," divides Egypt form Palestine.

Chapter 4

CROSSING THE RED SEA

Firstborn Set Apart

"And the Lord spake unto Moses, saying, Sanctify unto me all the firstborn, whatsoever openeth the womb among the children of Israel, both of man and of beast, it is mine. And Moses said unto the people, Remember this day, in which ye came out from Egypt, out of the house of bondage; for by strength of hand the Lord brought you out from this place: there shall no leavened bread be eaten. This day came ye out in the month Abib." *(Exodus 13:1-4)*

Moses told the people during the first stage of their exodus that they were to remember "this day" forever. They are reminded that during their annual celebrations they are to use no yeast; they are told to not even have it in the house. (Abstain from every appearance of evil).

When they reached the land God promised to their fathers, they were to mark as the day of their departure the end of March each year. On the seventh day of the celebration, they were to hold a great feast unto the Lord; at such a time they were to go over the story of their bondage and redemption with their children year after year.

"And it shall be when the Lord shall bring thee into the land of the Canaanites, and the Hittites, and the Amorites, and the Hivites, and the Jebusites, which he sware unto thy fathers to give thee, a land flowing with milk and honey, that thou shalt keep this service in this month. Seven days thou shalt eat unleavened bread, and in the seventh day shall be a feast to the Lord. Unleavened bread shall be eaten seven days; and there shall no leavened bread be seen with thee, neither shall there be leaven seen with thee in all thy quarters. And thou shalt shew thy son in that day, saying, This is done because of that which the Lord did unto me when I came forth out of Egypt. And it shall be for a sign unto thee upon thine hand, and for a memorial between thine eyes, that the Lord's law may be in thy mouth: for with a strong hand hath the Lord brought thee out of Egypt. Thou shalt therefore keep this Tordinance in his season from year to year. And it shall be when the Lord shall bring thee into the land of the Canaanites, as he sware unto thee and to thy fathers, and shall give it thee, That thou shalt set apart unto the Lord all that openeth the matrix, and every firstling that cometh of a beast which thou hast; the males shall be the Lord's. And every firstling of an ass thou shalt redeem with a lamb; and if thou wilt not redeem it, then thou shalt break his neck: and all the firstborn of man among thy children shalt

thou redeem. And it shall be when thy son asketh thee in time to come, saying, What is this? That thou shalt say unto him, By strength of hand the Lord brought us out from Egypt, from the house of bondage: And it came to pass, when Pharaoh would hardly let us go, that the Lord slew all the firstborn in the land of Egypt, both the firstborn of man, and the firstborn of beast: therefore I sacrifice to the Lord all at openeth the matrix, being males; but all the firstborn of my children I redeem. And it shall be for a token up on thine hand, and for frontlets between thine eyes: for by strength of hand the Lord brought us forth out of Egypt."(Exodus 13:5-16)

The sanctication of the firstborn was closely connected with the Passover. Because Jehovah had delivered the firstborn of Israel, they were to be sanctified to Him. A redeemed people become the property of the Redeemer. We are bought with a price, and we are reminded by Paul in 1 Corinthians 6:19, *"Ye are not your own; for ye are bought with a price."* In Romans 12:1, we are told, *"I beseech you therefore, brethren, by the mercies of God, that ye present your bodies a living sacrifice, holy, acceptable unto God, which is your reasonable service."*

Journey Is Resumed

"And it came to pass, when Pharaoh had let the people go, that God led them not through the way of the land of the Philistines, although that was near; for God said, Lest peradventure the people repent when they see war, and they return to Egypt; But God led the people about, through the way of the wilderness of the Red Sea: and the children of Israel went up harnessed out of the land of Egypt." (Exodus 13:17-18)

The route through the land of the Philistines would have been closer and more direct on their way to the promised land, but God (Elohim), like a loving Father, felt they might become discouraged and want to return to Egypt when they clashed with the Philistines, so He led them along a route through the Red Sea wilderness. Does this not prove that God orders the steps of His children who are totally committed to Him? God has made full provision for us.

"And Moses took the bones of Joseph with him: for he had straitly sworn the children of Israel, saying, God will surely visit you; and ye shall carry up my bones away hence with you."   *(Exodus 13:19)*

Guidance By Cloud And Fire

"And they took their journey from Succoth, and encamped in Etham, in the edge of the wilderness. And the Lord went before them by day in a pillar of a cloud, to lead them the way; and by night in a pillar of fire, to give them light; to go by day and night: He took not away the pillar of the cloud by day, nor the pillar of fire by night, from before the people." *(Exodus 13:20-22)*

"Just as Jehovah—the covenant God, the promising God, the One who heard the groanings of Israel, the One who raised up a deliverer for them—reminds us of God the Father, just as the Lamb—without spot and blemish, slain and its blood sprinkled, securing protection and deliverance from the avenging angel typifies God the Son; so this Pillar of Cloud—given to Israel for their guidance across the wilderness—speaks to us of God the Holy Spirit. Amazingly full, Divinely perfect, are these Old Testament foreshadowings. At every point the teaching of the New Testament is anticipated" (C.H.M.).

Jehovah[1] gave Israel a visible sign of His Presence. It was called a "pillar of cloud" and "a pillar of fire." Possibly, its upper portion rose up to heaven in the form of a column, and its lower part was spread out all over Israel's camp. Later on we read more about it.

The cloud was given to Israel as a gift; it was for guidance; it was for light; it was for a covering; God spoke from the cloud; it was darkness to the Egyptians; it rested upon the tabernacle as soon as it was erected.

Pharaoh Pursues Israel

Perhaps our imagination literally snaps when we try to visualize three million Jews being led through a wilderness by the Lord God Himself in a pillar of a cloud! God talked to Moses all along the way, instructing him, and he in turn directed the Jews. Besides that, they were carrying a dead man's bones—bringing one of their forefathers out of Egypt to bury him in the promised land because the request to do so had been preserved by the people for hundreds of years.

It was probably here at Etham, at the edge of the wilderness, during the second stage of their journey, that Moses received word that Pharaoh was in hot pursuit. God spoke to Moses saying they must get between Migdol and the sea, and camp along the shore lest Pharaoh should think he had them trapped in the wilderness.

"And the Lord spoke unto Moses, saying, Speak unto the children of Israel, that they turn and encamp

---

[1]Here the Lord takes command as Jehovah (Exodus 13:21) (Yahweh)

before Pihahiroth, between Migdol and the sea, over against Baalzephon: before it shall ye encamp by the sea. For Pharaoh will say of the children of Israel, They are entangled in the land, the wilderness hath shut them in. And I will harden Pharaoh's heart, that he shall follow after them; and I will be honoured upon Pharaoh, and upon all his host; that the Egyptians may know that I am the Lord. And they did so."   *(Exodus 14:1-4)*

We note in these scriptures that Pharaoh had a design to ruin Israel; therefore, God had a design to ruin Pharaoh. This takes us back to Genesis 12:2-3 *"I will make of thee a great nation, and I will bless thee, and make thy name great; and thou shalt be a blessing: And I will bless them that bless thee, and curse him that curseth thee: and in thee shall all families of the earth be blessed."* In that same chapter, we are told of a severe famine in Canaan which drove Abram on into Egypt. He lied about his wife, telling the Pharaoh she was his sister. God plagued Pharaoh and his house with great plagues because of this situation. At the Red Sea, He will finish them off. It will forever remain a fact that those who bless Israel will be blessed; and those who curse and misuse her, will be cursed and destroyed by God.

God not only told Moses how to lead the people nearer to the sea, but He gave him His reasons. Moses would have moved on without further details, for he moved by faith; but it is God's best to tell His children what He is doing, and why He is doing it. We can know perfect directions from God. In Amos 3:7 we read, *"Surely the Lord God will do nothing but He revealeth His secret unto His servants the prophets."* In Psalm 103:7, it says, *"He made known his ways unto Moses, his* acts unto the children of Israel." In John 15:15 we read, "Henceforth I call you not servants; for the servant knoweth not what his lord doeth: but I have called you friends; for all things that I have heard of my Father I have made known unto you."

Sagacious Pharaoh thought he would pursue the children of Israel, entrap them in the land, and then he could overrun them with ease. He still had not learned that He was dealing directly with the God of Israel! God stated that He would harden Pharaoh's heart so that he would chase the escaping slaves; then He would destroy Pharaoh and all his warriors.

"And it was told the king of Egypt that the people fled: and the heart of Pharaoh and and his servants was turned against the people, and they said, Why have we done this, that we have let Israel go from serving us? And he made ready his chariot, and took his people with him: And he took six hundred chosen chariots, and all the chariots of Egypt, and captains over every one of them. And the Lord hardened the heart of Pharaoh king of Egypt, and he pursued after the children of Israel: and the children of Israel went out with an high hand. But the Egyptians pursued after them, all the horses and chariots of Pharaoh, and his horsemen, and his army and overtook them encamping by the sea, beside Pihahiroth, before Baalzephon. And when Pharaoh drew nigh, the children of Israel lifted up their eyes, and, behold, the Egyptians marched after them; and they were sore afraid: and the children of Israel cried out unto the Lord. And they said unto Moses, Because there were no graves in Egypt, hast thou taken us away to die in the wilderness? wherefore hast thou dealt thus with us, to

carry us forth out of Egypt? Is not this the word that we did tell thee in Egypt, saying, Let us alone, that we may serve the Egyptians? For it had been better for us to serve the Egyptians, than that we should die in the wilderness." *(Exodus 14:5-12)*

Pharaoh and his servants led a chase after the children of Israel; he chose the very best of Egypt's chariot corps (600 in all), along with other chariots driven by his officers. He gave hard chase after them, for they had the wealth of Egypt with them. It was as if their minds had suddenly frozen, and they had given all they had away; suddenly, they became alert, realized what they had done, and in a dust cloud of anger, pursued the Hebrew people. All the fighting men of Egypt were with Pharaoh as they approached the Israelites camped beside the sea. The children of Israel were horrified when they looked up and saw them in the distance. They turned against Moses, their leader, for by nightfall, they were aware that the whole Egyptian host was encamped in their near vicinity. It was inevitable that by morning they would be consumed.

They knew the strength and rage of the enemy; they were hemmed in, and though they were large in number, they were weak in their own defense. Besides, they were all on foot, except for the women and children. Here is what was facing them: (1) Pihahiroth, a range of craggy rocks — impassable; (2) Migdol and Baalzephon, believed to be forts and garrisons upon the frontiers of Egypt; (3) the Red Sea before them; and (4) the Egyptians behind them bent on their destruction.

Somewhat troubled on every side, they cried out their words of defeat and discouragement to Moses. They had no way to look but up! Their fears set them to murmuring. The first time they murmured against Moses was when he killed the Egyptian in defense of one of his brethren, and they cried out, "Who called you to be our leader?"

These children of God looked upon their adversity with the natural eye, and their hearts began to fail them. Had they so soon forgotten the miracles back in Egypt? Had they so soon forgotten their escape by the Mighty Hand of God? Could they not see the Glory Cloud, (Shechinah), which represented the very presence of Yahweh? They looked not at the promises of God; they were distracted by the noise in the enemy's camp in the distance.

God had already told Moses what He was doing; Moses always shared his knowledge with the people. Moses now had three million Jews shouting at him, and firing questions all at one time. We see that they did not cry unto the Lord for deliverance; they cried out in despair and complaint.

The children of Israel at this time expressed the following: (1) a sordid contempt of liberty, preferring servitude before it, simply because they had met with a test or trial; (2) base ingratitude to Moses, who had been with them through all their deliverance, and who stood as a Prophet before God; and (3) by flaunting their anger in the face of Moses, they were also showing a haughty spirit against Yahweh, who had redeemed them from the house of bondage, suggesting that both Moses and Yahweh should have left them alone to serve in Egypt.

Redemption By Power

And Moses said unto the people, Fear ye not, stand still, and see the salvation of the Lord, which he will shew to you to-day: for the Egyptians whom ye have seen to-day, ye shall see them again no more forever. The Lord shall fight for you, and ye shall hold your peace. And the Lord said unto Moses, Wherefore criest thou unto me? speak unto the children of Israel, that they go forward: But lift thou up thy rod, and stretch out thine hand over the sea, and divide it: and the children of Israel shall go on dry ground through the midst of the sea. And I, behold, I will get me honour upon Pharaoh, and upon all his host, upon his chariots, and upon his horsemen. And the Egyptians shall know that I am the Lord, when I have gotten me honour upon Pharaoh, upon his chariots, and upon his horsemen. And the angel of God, which went before the camp of Israel, removed and went behind them; and the pillar of the cloud went from before their face, and stood behind them: And it came between the camp of the Egyptians and the camp of Israel; and it was a cloud and darkness to them, but it gave light by night to these: so that the one came not near the other all the night. And Moses stretched out his hand over the sea; and the Lord caused the sea to go back by a strong east wind all that night, and made the sea dry land, and the waters were divided. And the children of Israel went into the midst of the sea upon the dry ground: and the waters were a wall unto them on their right hand, and on their left. And the Egyptians pursued, and went in after them to the midst of the sea, even all Pharaoh's horses, his chariots, and his horsemen. And it came to pass, that in the morning watch the Lord looked unto the host of the

Egyptians through the pillar of fire and of the cloud, and troubled the host of the Egyptians. And took off their chariot wheels, that they drave them heavily: so that the Egyptians said, Let us flee from the face of Israel; for the Lord fighteth for them against the Egyptians. And the Lord said unto Moses, Stretch out thine hand over the sea, that the waters may come again upon the Egyptians, upon their chariots, and upon their horsemen. And Moses stretched forth his hand over the sea, And the sea returned to his strength when the morning appeared; and the Egyptians fled against it; and the Lord overthrew the Egyptians in the midst of the sea. And the waters returned, and covered the chariots, and the horsemen, and all the host of Pharaoh that came into the sea after them; there remained not so much as one of them. But the children of Israel walked upon dry land in the midst of the sea; and the waters were a wall unto them on their right hand, and on their left. Thus the Lord saved Israel that day out of the hand of the Egyptians; and Israel saw the Egyptians dead upon the sea shore. And Israel saw that great work which the Lord did upon the Egyptians: and the people feared the Lord, and believed the LORD, and his servant Moses."

(Exodus 14:13-31)

Chapter 14 opened with, *"And the Lord spoke,.."* and in verse 13, we read, *"And Moses said unto the people..."* showing us that all that God said to Moses, he in turn reported to the people.

Salvation

"And Moses said unto the people, Fear ye not, stand still, and see the salvation of the Lord, which he will shew to you to–day: for the Egyptians whom ye have

*seen to–day, ye shall see them again no more for ever.
For the Lord shall fight for you, and ye shall hold your
peace"*(verses 13-14). In the next verse (15), God spoke
to Moses and the question was not why was Moses crying
unto Him, but it was directed at the children of Israel in
the midst of their unbelief; He spoke to Moses as spokesman for the people. *"You people stop praying and
crying to Me. Let's get moving! Get going! The Egyptians are close on your heels! Use your rod, Moses!"*

God told Moses to hold the rod out over the waters,
and they would part, and the children of Israel would go
over on dry land to the other side. God hardened the
hearts of the Egyptians, and they tried to follow. It was
after the Lord had instructed Moses in what to do next that
He (the Angel of the Lord), who was leading them, moved
the cloud around behind them. It stood between the people of Israel and the Egyptians. It was darkness to the enemy and light to the children of God.

The Red Sea Divided

The parting of the Red Sea is without doubt the most
remarkable miracle recorded in the Bible[1]. From this time
on, whenever the servants of God would remind the people of the Lord's power and greatness, reference is almost
always made to the miracle at the Red Sea. Eight hundred
years afterwards, the Lord says through Isaiah, *"I am the
Lord thy God, that divided the sea, whose waves roared;
the Lord of hosts is His name"*(Isaiah 51:15). Nahum announced, *"The Lord hath His way in the whirlwind and*

---

[1]With the exception of the resuurection of Jesus.

in the storm, and the clouds are the dust of His feet. He rebuketh the sea, and maketh it dry"(Nahum 1:3,4). When the Lord renewed His promise to Israel, He took them back to this time and said, *"According to the days of thy coming out of the land of Egypt will I show unto him marvelous things"*(Micah 7:15). It was this notable event which made a lasting impression upon the enemies of the Lord. In Joshua 2:10-11, we read, *"For we have heard how the Lord dried up the water of the Red Sea for you, when ye came out of Egypt; and what ye did unto the two kings of the Amorites, that was on the other side of Jordan, Sihon and Og, whom ye utterly destroyed, and as soon as we have heard there things, our hearts did melt, neither did there remain any more courage in any man because of you; for the Lord your God, He is God in heaven above, and in earth beneath."*

We note that typically speaking, the crossing of the Red Sea speaks of Christ making a way through death for His people. The Red Sea is the boundary line of Satan's power. He has been cast into the sea, rendered powerless in the Name of Jesus. Lift up thy rod; stretch it forth over the sea; God has separated us from our enemies! We have been delivered from the watery grave of death, and translated by His power to the other side. There comes a time when we must stop praying and lift up the rod of power and authority against the devil and demand—even forbid that he operate in our presence. Moses is plainly a type of Christ; the rod, a symbol of His power and authority. In Hebrews 2:14, we have the antitype: *"That through death He might destroy him that had the power of death, that is, the Devil.'"*"Moses lifted up the rod, the Lord parted the Red Sea and the children of Israel went over on dry ground.[2] On their right hand and on their left hand, the waters were like a frozen wall of ice. God had brought forth a strong east wind during the night, and He had parted the sea for them.

The passage through the Red Sea sets forth the believer's union with Christ in His death and resurrection. In Galatians 2:20, we read, *"I am cricufied with Christ..."* In Roman 6:5, we read, *"If we have been planted together in the likeness of His death, we shall be also in the likeness of His resurrection."*

Also, the passage through the Red Sea illustrates the absolute sufficiency of the Lord God to care for His own. The entire picture of His loving care is portrayed in Psalm 91, the song of Moses.

God Himself shook off the Egyptians in the midst of the sea. He took the wheel off the chariots, and left them whirling in every direction. Moses used the rod twice at the Red Sea; the first time the waters parted; the second time, they went back together, drowning all the Egyptians.

---

[2]The place where they crossed was about twelve miles wide, 75-100 feet deep

Chapter 5

THE SONG OF MOSES

The Song Of The Redeemed

Up to this time we have not heard one single note of praise to God. This chapter is the magnificent song of triumph which the redeemed of the Lord sang on the shores of the Red Sea. This is the first song recorded in the Bible. It has been said that it is presumably the oldest poem in the world, unsurpassed by anything ever written. It is called the song of the redeemed for it originated from the hearts of a redeemed people. Praise and worship are impossible for the heart that has not been converted.

On the night of the Passover, Israel was secured from the doom of the Egyptians; at the Red Sea, they were delivered from the power of the Pharaoh and all his host. We look back upon Egypt with a song of praise upon our lips issuing forth from our very being. We have read how the complete victory of Israel was gained over the Egyptians, and now we read how it was celebrated. Moses, no doubt by Divine inspiration, indited this song, and delivered it to the children of Israel to be sung as their token of thanksgiving and praise for their freedom. "Singing is as much the languange of holy joy as praying is of holy desire" (Matthew Henry).

Their deliverance was not by works of thier righteousness, but according to the Mercy of God. In fact, they were told to stand still and see their salvation wrought by the mighty hand of God (Yahweh). He will do all things in such as way as to receive all the glory for it. "When we have received special mercy from God, we ought to be quick and speedy in out returns of praise to Him, before time and the deceitfulness of our hearts efface the good impressions that have been made. David sang his triumphant song in the day that the Lord delivered him" (Henry).

"Then sang Moses and the children of Israel this song unto the Lord, and spake, saying, I will sing unto the Lord, for he hath triumphed gloriously: the horse and his rider hath he thrown into the sea. The Lord is my strength and song, and he is become my salvation: he is my God, and I will prepare him an habitation; my father's God, and I will exalt him. The Lord is a man of war: the Lord is his name. Pharaoh's chariots and his host hath he cast into the sea. His chosen captains also are drowned in the Red Sea. The depths have covered them. They sank into the bottom as a stone. Thy right

hand, O Lord, is become glorious in power: thy right hand, O Lord, hath dashed in pieces the enemy. And in the greatness of thine excellency thou hast overthrown them that rose up against thee; thou sentest forth thy wrath, which consumed them as stubble. And with the blast of thy nostrils the waters were gathered together, the floods stood upright as an heap, and the depths were congealed in the heart of the sea. The enemy said, I will pursue, I will overtake, I will divide the spoil; my lust shall be satisfied upon them; I will draw my sword, my hand shall destroy them. Thou didst blow with thy wind, the sea covered them: they sank as lead in the mighty waters. Who is like unto thee, O Lord, among the gods? who is like thee, glorious in holiness, fearful in praises, doing wonders? Thou stretchedst out thy right hand, the earth swallowed them. Thou in thy mercy hast led forth the people which thou hast redeemed; thou hast guided them in thy strength unto thy holy habitation. The people shall hear, and be afraid: sorrow shall take hold on the inhabitants of Palestina. Then the dukes of Edom shall be amazed; the mighty men of Moab, trembling shall take hold upon them; all the inhabitants of Canaan shall melt away. Fear and dread shall fall upon them; by the greatness of thine arm they shall be as still as a stone; till thy people pass over, O Lord, till the people pass over, which thou hast purchased. Thou shalt bring them in, and plant them in the mountain of thine inheritance, in the place, O Lord, which thou hast made for thee to dwell in, in the Sanctuary, O Lord, which thy hands have established. The Lord shall reign for ever and ever. For the horse of Pha-

*raoh went in with his chariots and with his horsemen
into the sea, and the Lord brought again the waters of
the sea upon them; but the children of Israel went on
dry land in the midst of the sea. And Miriam the pro-
phetess, the sister of Aaron, took a timbrel in her hand
and all the women went out after her with timbrels and
with dances. And Miriam answered them, Sing ye to the
Lord, for he hath triumphed gloriously; the horse and
his rider hath he thrown into the sea."*

(Exodus 15:1-21)

In 2 Samuel 22, we have the song of David right after
the Lord had delivered him from the hand of his enemies,
and out of the hand of Saul, the king, who was trying to
kill him. He spoke the words of his song to the Lord: *"And
David spake unto the Lord the words of this song in the
day that the Lord had delivered him out of the hand of
all his enemies, and out of the hand of Saul: And he said,
the Lord is my rock, and my fortress, and my deliverer;
The God of my rock, in him will I trust; he is my shield,
and the horn of my salvation, my high tower, and my
refuge, my saviour; thou savest me from violence. I will
call on the Lord, who is worthy to be praised: so shall I
be saved from mine enemies."* The entire chapter is the
song David sang in thanksgiving for his deliverance.
Psalm 18 is identical to this song of praise.

In Revelation 15:3, we read another song of the redeemed, *"And they sing the song of Moses, the servant
of God, and the song of the Lamb, saying, Great and
marvelous are thy works, Lord God Almighty; just and
true are thy ways, thou King of saints."*

Seven Things God Is To Man:
  (1) My Strength
  (2) My Song
  (3) My salvation
  (4) My El (Strong One)
  (5) My Father's Elohim (Creator)
  (6) A Man of war
  (7) Jehovah (Yahweh)

The enemy of the Lord and His people had said they would pursue, overtake, divide the spoil, draw out the sword, and destroy them. This gives man a perfect example of how futile it is to fight against God and His chosen. This song is all about their Yahweh. There is no hint of self to be found in these lines. It is a tribute to the mighty miracles of God in the day that He delivered His people. It begins with redemption, and ends with His glory. It begins for us with the cross, and ends with the kingdom of God. This is the gushing forth of a soul that has been snatched from the jaws of death, and now stands on the shores of redemption, with a song in his heart — a song of praise to the Rock of our salvation.

They not only sang to the Lord, but they sang about Him. The word "Lord" occurs at least twelve times in eighteen verses. At least thirty-three times the pronouns referring to the Lord are used. How glorious are His ways; how marvelous His acts towards His Own.

In Philippians 4:4, we are told to rejoice in the Lord always. Joy is the spontaneous overflowing of a heart which is totally dedicated to the love and work of the Lord. The joy of the Lord will bring health and peace to

Let My People Go

the spirit and soul of a man. We must sit back and note the perfect ease with which God can master the designs of the devil; as in the words of Moses to the people: *"Be still. He is the God of our salvation. He will fight our battles for us. Fear not."*

Redemption By Experience

"So Moses brought Israel from the Red Sea, and they went out into the wilderness of Shur[1]; and they went three days in the wilderness, and found no water. And when they came to Marah, they could not drink of the waters of Marah, for they were bitter: therefore the name of it was called Marah. And the people murmured against Moses, saying, What shall we drink? And he cried unto the Lord; and the Lord shewed him a tree, which when he had cast into the waters, the waters were made sweet: there he made for them a statute and an ordinance, and there he proved them."

(Exodus 15:22-25)

Healing Covenant

"And said, If thou wilt diligently hearken to the voice of the Lord thy God, and wilt do that which is right in his sight, and wilt give ear to his commandments, and keep all his statutes, I will put none of these diseases upon thee, which I have brought upon the Egyptians: for I am the Lord that healeth thee. And they came to Elim where were the twelve wells of water, and three-score and ten palm trees: and they encamped there by the water."

(Exodus 15:26-27)

---

[1]Shur was the name given to a great wall built to protect Egypt from Asia, with its mighty Migdol, or fortresses.

After the songs of praise, Moses led the people of Israel onward from the Red Sea into the wilderness of Shur[1] where they stayed for three days without water. Then we read the third of twelve complaints recorded as Israel traveled towards the promised land. When they arrived at Marah, the water was so bitter they could not drink it, and they turned against Moses and complained bitterly against him.

Moses pleaded with the Lord, and the Lord showed him a tree to throw into the water to make the waters sweet. Three days and three nights they had been without water in the hot, sandy desert, and when water was found, behold, it was bitter. We always murmur when we take our eyes off the Lord, and put hope in our own strength to deliver. They seemed to have completely overlooked the fact that they had been led to Marah by the Pillar of Cloud! They were really murmuing against the Lord, instead of moses.

The type is quite apparent. The tree typifies the Cross of Christ and the Christ of the Cross. It was our blessed Lord Who, by going down into the place of death, sweetened the bitter waters for us. One is reminded of the first tree in the garden that brought forth the need for a second tree which was the Cross of the Lord Jesus Christ who bore the curse for us.

Following the miraculous healing of the waters, God gave the children of Israel His Covenant conditions for healing. He first showed forth His power to heal after they had sinned by grumbling; then He spoke to Moses at Marah on the importance of obedience to His will. Jehowah-Ropheka introduced Himself as the Healer of His people; He was all the physician they would ever need, and He had just proven Himself by giving His children the Branch of healing. Divine healing was made a statute and an ordinance as far back as the wilderness journey. In Psalm 105:37 we read, *"He sent his word, and healed them, and delivered them from their destructions."* God provided not only spiritual healing for us, but also physical healing. We are to give ear to His commandments. The last part of that ordinance should read, *"I, the Lord thy God, am healing thee,"* suggesting a continual exercise of His healing love and power. Sickness in the life of a child of God never originates from Him, but it comes from that old serpent who seeks whom he may devour. Careful study of this passage of scripture is necessary. The casual reader might take the King James Version as law, as many have, and when illness comes, they courageously suggest they are suffering for the Lord. Hebrew manuscripts render this thought in the permissive instead of causative sense. It would sound something like this: "If you obey me and hearken to My voice, and will do that which is right in my sight...I will allow none of the diseases to come upon you that I brought upon the Egyptians." God has made sorrow and wretchedness to be the sure fruit of sin.

God made a covenant of healing with the children of Israel, but it carried with it a condition: we have the promise of divine health, but disobedience of God's laws can bring about a sick body and mind. God led His children to the bitter waters to test what was in their hearts. He knew they had the dust of Egypt still clinging to them, and they would need to be taught. All of God's beautiful promises will be fulfilled in our lives when we counteract the test with words of faith. Temptation in the Bible (Greek) literally means "to be put to the test." We must treat any wilderness experience as God's way of opening our eyes to our own insufficiency and His all-sufficiency. Once this is recognized, obedience and love will follow. Tests in life could easily be labeled: (1) God's Promise for our Inheritance; (2) His conditions must be met; (3) test, and (4) having passed the test, enter into the fullness of those promises. Keep praising His Name, and He will make the bitter waters sweet.

We must not apply verses 25 and 26 merely to their exception from the plagues of Egypt. They had no reason to fear such plagues would come upon them. They had been protected against them while in Egypt, and there was no suggestion that they would now be exposed to them. This has reference to the diseases that were common to the Egyptians they had seen in that land. In Deuteronomy 7:15, this is repeated: *"The Lord will take away from thee all sickness, and will put none of the evil diseases of Egypt which thou knowest upon thee; but will lay them upon all them that hate thee."* And we know that all this was for an example to us today. *"And they came to Elim, where were twelve wells of water, and threescore and ten palm trees; and they encamped there by the waters."* These are types of the times of rest and refreshing that comes after the "bitter" waters experience. Elim was the complement to Marah. We note there were twelve wells of water, for the refreshing of the soul, and Jesus chose for Himself twelve disciples to preach the Word and refresh the people; there were seventy palm trees, the number selected by Christ in sending forth His apostles. There was a well[2] for every tribe. *"He maketh me to lie down in green pastures; he leadeth me beside the still waters. He restoreth my soul; he leadeth me in the paths of righteousness for his name's sake"*(Psalm 23). The branches of the palm trees were often used for festivities, for they were regarded as tokens of joy and triumph.

---

[2]Only 9 of the 12 wells remain; the missing ones have been filled with blowing sand through the years; but the 70 palm trees have multiplied into more than 2,000 (Dakes).

Chapter 6

BREAD AND MEAT FROM HEAVEN

Murmuring For Bread

The children of Israel must be fed and taught from whence would come all their provisions during their journey towards the Promised Land. If they had never had a need, God could not have shown Himself strong in their behalf. Their supply would have to come in a supernatural way for God to receive His Glory, and the wilderness was the perfect place for it afforded no natural supply of food or means of survival.

From Elim the children of Israel proceeded into the desert of Sin. According to Numbers 33:10, they encamped at the Red Sea (Sea of Reeds), between Elim and the desert of Sin; but this is passed over here since nothing of importance took place. The Wilderness of Sin, the modern El Markha, is a dreary, desolate track with a long range of white chalk hills.

"And they took their journey from Elim, and all the congregation of the children of Israel came unto the wilderness of Sin, which is between Elim and Sinai, on the fifteenth day of the second month after their departing out of the land of Egypt. And the whole congregation of the children of Israel murmured against Moses and Aaron in the wilderness; And the children of Israel said unto them, Would to God we have died by the hand of the Lord in the land of the Egyptians when we sat by the flesh pots, and when we did eat bread to the full; for ye have brought us forth into this wilderness, to kill this whole assembly with hunger."

(Exodus 16:1-3

Note their absolute lack of faith as they sighed in despair, and turned on their leaders with murmurings, claiming it would have been better if they had stayed slaves in Egypt, at least there they had enough bread and water to eat. In verse 2, we read that the entire congregation turned against Moses and Aaron. They had traveled form Elim, the place of refreshing, right into the barren desert. This is indeed a very interesting position for the congregation. In this place the children of Israel are seen as the objects of the same grace and mercy which had brought them out of the land of Egypt, and all their murmurings are instantly met by divine supply.

God did not Divinely intervene until all their natural supply was gone. They were in their fifteenth day of the second month of their journey at this point. As their leader, Moses learned a constant lesson day by day. There were times during the exodus that Moses felt the entire reposibility lay upon his own shoulders; but when the Lord God spoke to him, his heart took courage, and he rested "In Himself" as they did under the psalm trees of Elim. We are not called upon to carry the burdens of God's responsibilites in life; if we stay in union with Him, He will lead and direct us to the wells of refreshing. At Marah, Moses received from God a glad, fresh revelation that He was their healer, and that none of the Egyptian diseases would touch them as long as they were obedient to His commands. When there are no psalm trees, the shadow of the Almighty will be our refuge and strength.

"Then said the Lord unto Moses, Behold, I will rain bread from heaven for you; and the people shall go out and gather a certain rate every day, that I may prove them, whether they will walk in my law, or no. And it shall come to pass, that on the sixth day they shall prepare that which they bring in; and it shall be twice as much as they gather daily. And Moses and Aaron said unto all the children of Israel, At even, then ye shall know that the Lord hath brought you out from the land of Egypt. And in the morning, then ye shall see the glory of the Lord; for that he heareth your murmurings against the Lord: and what are we, that ye murmur against us? And Moses said, This shall be, when the Lord shall give you in the evening flesh to eat, and in the morning bread to the full; for that the Lord heareth your murmurings which ye murmur against him: and what are we? your murmurings are not against us, but against the Lord. And Moses spake unto Aaron, Say unto all the congregation of the children of Israel, Come near before the Lord: for he hath heard your mur-

murings. And it came to pass, as Aaron spake unto the whole congregation of the children of Israel, that they looked toward the wilderness, and, behold, the glory of the Lord appeared in the cloud. And the Lord spake unto Moses, saying, I have heard the murmurings of the children of Israel: speak unto them, saying, At even ye shall eat flesh, and in the morning ye shall be filled with bread; and ye shall know that I am the Lord your God. And it came to pass, that at even the quails came up, and covered the camp: And in the morning the dew lay round about the host. And when the dew that lay was gone up, behold, upon the face of the wilderness there lay, And Moses said, This is the thing which the Lord commandeth, Fill an omer of it to be kept for your generations; that they may see the bread where with I have fed you in the wilderness,when I brought you forth from the land of Egypt. And Moses said unto Aaron, Take a pot, and put an omer full of manna therein, and lay it up before the Lord, to be kept for your generations. As the Lord commanded Moses, so Aaron laid it up before the Testimony, to be kept. And the children of Israel did eat manna forty years, until they came to a land inhabited; they did eat manna, until they came unto the borders of the land of Canaan. Now an omer is the tenth part of an ephah." (Exodus 16:4-36)

God told Moses to tell the people that He would rain down food from heaven for them, and that in this, He would test them to see if they would follow His instructions. They were told to gather a certain supply each day; but on the sixth day they were to gather twice as much as usual for the Sabbath was their day of rest, and they were not to gather on that day.

In verses 4 through 13, we have manna promised to perhaps three million Hebrew people in an isolated spot in the wilderness. There is nothing more dishonoring to God than the manifestation of a complaining spirit by His Own people. Over and over Israel lost the sense of being in the hands of God, and this led to still thicker darkness and greater accusations against Him.

We must not fail to recognize the love and tender mercy of God in the midst of their unbelief. They were short of memory. They were only fifteen days into their second month out of Egyptian slavery, and they were longing for its flesh pots where they could eat until full, perhaps they had forgotten the lash of the taskmasters' whip on their backs, the parting of the Red Sea, the healing of the bitter waters, and the rest under the psalms, all supplied supernaturally by the Lord God. At this point, they had failed to recognize the Providence of God behind it all. They failed to see that God had each time let them come to the end of themselves before He worked His miracles to show forth His Glory.

In verses 6 through 12 the promise of "food from heaven" is repeated, along with a rebuke for their unbelief, and murmurings. Every detail in this chapter speaks loudly to us that the manna which the Lord provided for Israel in the wilderness is a beautiful type of the food which God has provided for our souls. This food is His Word; not only His written Word, but His Incarnate Word.

This manna was not a product of the earth. God had said to Moses, *"Behold, I will rain bread from heaven for you . . ."* (verse 4); it was a gift from God. Many and various attempts have been made to explain away the supernatural in this connection; but they cannot explain how it grew in the summer and the winter, how it was attainable in all of the wilderness no matter where the children of Israel camped, and how there was sufficient amounts to feed up to two million Jews for forty years in the desert as they wandered. How very foolish is man when he attempts to reason out the written Word of God, and explain away its miracles. It is equally ridiculous to try to explain manna on a natural plane. This is without question a type of God's provision for His people's deeper need in their Christian life.

Moses spoke to Aaron and instructed him to gather all the congregation together for they would see the glory of the Lord for He had hear their complaints. As Aaron spoke to the people, they looked toward the wilderness, and the glory of the Lord appeared in the cloud. It was at that point the Lord promised to open the windows of heaven, and feed his children with heavenly provisions.

The word "manna" is a transliteration of two hebrew words meaning "What is it?" That was the question the Israelites asked on first seeing this little round thing lying all around them. It is "bread" in this chapter. In Psalms 78:24-25, it is called "the corn of heaven" and "angels' food." In Numbers 21:5, it was called "light bread." It fell for the forty years they wandered, and was preserved in a pot in the Tabernacle. Manna is a type of Christ in humiliation giving His flesh that we might have life everlasting.

As mentioned, manna was a gift from God. Manna came right to where the people were. They did not need to search for it. The need was there, and the Lord met the need. So it is with the Word of God. It is truly accessible to all who will call out in their distress. Note the responsibility that was attached to this provision. They had to gather it, or trample upon it. It was round, and small in size. The Word of God has no rough edges or angles. There is nothing meaningless in Scripture. We are told the manna was white in color, and white stands for purity in the Bible. This speaks of the splotless purity of our Lord as manifested outwardly in His daily walk. He knew no sin; the manna for God's people fell first in the Wilderness of Sin.

The manna was to be eaten. It was for food. Just as this manna was God's daily provision to meet their bodily needs, it is Jesus who is the manna from heaven who meets our needs as we feed upon Him daily. It was gathered in the morning; it was gathered by labor; it was gathered by stooping; what was gathered must by used; it was not anything they recognized; it was despised by the mixed multitudes. This manna was ground and baked; it was preserved on the Sabbath. This manna is now hidden. In Revelation 2:17, we read, *"To him that overcometh will I give to eat of the hidden manna."* In John chapter 6, Jesus fed the five thousand with five barley loaves, and two small fishes. Later He tested their faith, then declared himself to be the "Bread of Life." In verses 32-35, we read, *"Then Jesus said unto them, Verily, verily, I say unto you, Moses gave you not that bread from heaven; but my father giveth you the true bread from heaven. For the bread of God is he which cometh down from heaven, and giveth life unto the world. Then said they unto him, Lord, evermore give us this bread. And Jesus said unto them, I am the bread of life: he that cometh to me shall never hunger; and he that believeth on me shall never thirst.''*

An ''omer'' was to be gathered for everyone of these two million souls, and an ''omer'' is the equivalent of six pints. There would be 12 million pints, or nine million pounds gathered daily, which was 4,500 tons. This would equal ten trains, each having thirty cars, and each car having in it fifteen tons. This would be needed for a single day's supply. Over a million tons of manna were gathered annually by Israel. And remember this continued for forty years! Yet, equally wonderful, miraculous, and Divine is the Lord Jesus Christ who is ''the Bread of Life.''

Chapter 7

THE SMITTEN ROCK

Journey To Rephidim

"And all the congregation of the children of Israel journeyed from the wilderness of Sin, after their journeys according to the commandment of the Lord, and pitched in Rephidim: and there was no water for the people to drink. (Exodus 17:1)*

Note the above scripture points out the fact that they journeyed according to the commandment of the Lord. We get the complete route when we refer to Numbers 33:12-14, *"And they took their journey out of the wilderness of Sin, and encamped in Dophkah. And they departed from Dophkah, and encamped in Alush. And they removed from Alush, and encamped at Rephidim, where was no water for the people to drink."* Here again their faith was tested.

"Wherefore the people did chide with Moses, and said, Give us water that we may drink. And Moses said unto them, Why chide ye with me? wherefore do ye tempt the Lord? And the people thirsted there for water; and the people murmured against Moses, and said, Wherefore is this that thou hast brought us up out of Egypt, to kill us and our children and our cattle with thirst? And Moses cried unto the Lord, saying, What shall I do unto this people? they be almost ready to stone me. (Exodus 17:2-4)*

If we did not know of the humiliating evil of our own hearts, we would be quite at a loss to explain their gross insensibility to all the miracles that the Lord God had already performed in their behalf. Moses, chosen of God, cried out, "What am I going to do, Lord. They are ready to stone me!" Would we have acted differently were we in this situation? Oh, man of faith, look upward!

They had just seen the Lord rain down quail and bread from heaven, yet here they were ready to stone their leader. One writer said, "Nothing can exceed the desperate unbelief and wickedness of the human heart save the superabounding grace of God. In that grace alone can anyone find relief under the growing sense of his evil nature which circumstances tend to make manifest."

If Israel had been directed by God to go from Egyptian bondage, directly to Canaan, they would not have had to view the depravity of thier own hearts. Such was not the case, and they stand as types and examples for us when we endeavor to master our life without the Lord Jesus Christ.

Hear the cry of the Israelites: "What shall we eat? What shall we drink?" The only answer to the what, when, and how of life is Jesus. We are admonished, even warned, in the New Testament that we are to be careful for nothing. We are to rest in the Lord, and depend on Him for our daily quota. *"But my God shall supply all your need according to his riches in glory by Christ Jesus" (Philippians 4:19).*

Water From The Rock

"And the Lord said unto Moses, go on before the people and take with thee of the elders of Israel; and thy rod, wherewith thou smotest the river, take in thine hand, and go. Behold, I will stand before thee there upon the rock in Horeb: and thou shalt smite the rock, and there shall come water out of it, that the people may drink. And Moses did so in the sight of the elders of Israel. And he called the name of the Place Massah, and Meribah, because of the chiding of the children of Israel, and because they tempted the Lord, saying Is the Lord among us, or not? (Exodus 17:5-7)

God had directed Moses to led His children to Rephidim; He knew there was no water for the people to drink. He knew where to find the water. Ofttimes when we reach some particularly hard place, when the streams of creature-comfort are dried up, we blame others, especially our leaders, before we consult the will and ways of the Lord who may have purposed to lead us thusly, to prove what is in our hearts.

Moses was instructed to take his rod in hand, and go to Mount Horeb, one of the mountain ranges of Mount Sinai, and smite the rock; and water would come forth to saitisfy the thirst of the people. God told Moses that His Presence would go before him. Moses did as he was commanded in the sight of the elders. Every murmur brought forth a fresh display of the grace of God to comfort His people.

In I Corinthians 10: 1-4, we read, *"Moreover, brethren, I would not that ye should be ignorant, how that all our fathers were under the cloud, and all passed through the sea; And were all baptised unto Moses in the cloud and in the sea; And did all eat the same spiritual meat; And did all drink the same spiritual drink; for they drank of that spiritual Rock that followed them: And that Rock was Christ."* The "Rock" is one of the titles of Jehovah found frequently in the Old Testament. In Deuteronomy 32:15, Moses laments that Israel forsook God and *". . . lightly esteemed the Rock of his salvation."*

The Living Water from the Smitten Rock is the type of God's provision for our spiritual refreshing through the indwelling and continual influence of the Holy Spirit. Just as the manna represents Christ as the source of our life, so the Holy Spirit is typified by water. The rod in the hand of Moses typified God's authority; the Rock, a type of Christ, coming to a people totally unworthy. He was the "smitten Rock," whose death brought forth the outpouring of the Holy Ghost. In Matthew 16:17-18, we read *"And Jesus answered and said unto him, Blessed art thou, Simon Barjona: for flesh and blood hath not revealed it unto thee, but my Father which is in heaven. And I say also unto thee, That thou art Peter, and upon this rock I will build my church; and the gates of hell shall not prevail against it."* In Psalm 78:15-16, we read, *"He clave the rocks in the wilderness, and gave them drink as out of the great depths. He brought streams also out of the rock, and caused waters to run down like rivers."* And in verse 20, we read, *"Behold, he smote the rock, that the waters gushed out, and the streams overflowed; can he give bread also? can he provide flesh for his people?"*

In John 4:7 we read, *"There cometh a woman of Samaria to draw water: Jesus saith unto her, Give me a drink."* She recognized Him to be a Jew, and questioned Him as to why He was asking her for water since Jews had no dealings with Samaritans. He said to her, *"If thou knewest the gift of God, and who it is that saith to thee, Give me to drink; thou wouldest have aked of him, and he would have given thee living water... Whosoever drinketh of this water shall thirst again: But whosoever drinketh of the water that I shall give him shall never thirst; but the water that I shall give him shall be in him a well of water springing up into everlasting life"* (verses 10-14). In John 7:37-38, Jesus cries out, *"If any man thirst, let him come unto me, and drink. He that believeth on me, as the scripture hath said, out of his belly shall flow rivers of living water."* He spoke of the Spirit which they who believed on Him would receive after He had been glorified.

Conflict With Amalek

Thus far the children of Israel had fought no battles. We are reminded that when the Lord led them out of Egypt, He did not lead them through the land of the Philistines, although that was the most direct route to their destination, the Promised Land. He felt that the people might become discouraged by having to fight their way through the land, even though they had left Egypt well armed. He led them along a route through the Red Sea wilderness. Because of their murmurings, the journey got tougher, and God required more of them. In the early stages of our Christian life, we are exempt from severe conflicts. But when the first battle comes, it is to teach the true meaning of victory, to test our confidence and trust in the Lord God, and to put to final death any active remains of self-sufficiency.

Rephidim was apparently a wide, fertile plain, shut in by mountains, and at the time, held by Amalek, who had gathered around the wells and palms, waiting to attack the enemy as he came up thirsty, weary, and road-worn. Amalek was a type of the flesh. He was a descendant of Esau who represented the carnal nature of man.

"Then came Amalek, and fought with Israel in Rephidim. And Moses said unto Joshua, Choose us out men, and go out, fight with Amalek: tomorrow I will stand on the top of the hill with the rod of God in mine hand. So Joshua did as Moses had said to him, and fought with Amalek: and Moses, Aaron, and Hur went up to the top of the hill. And it came to pass, when Moses held up his hand, that Israel prevailed: and when he let down his hand Amalek prevailed. But Moses' hands were heavy; and they took a stone, and put it under him, and he sat thereon; and Aaron and Hur stayed up his hands, the one on the one side and the one on the other side; and his hands were steady until the going down of the sun. And Joshua discomfited Amalek and his people with the edge of the sword. And the Lord said unto Moses, Write this for a memorial in a book, and rehearse it in the ears of Joshua; for I will utterly put out the remembrance of Amalek from under heaven. And

Moses built an altar, and called the name of it Jeho-vahnissi. For he said, Because the Lord hath sworn that the Lord will have war with Amalek from generation to generation." (Exodus 17:8-16)

The rod of God was used in many miracles; here it is used to bring victory in war. Moses did not call it his rod; rather he called it, "the rod of god." In this war we have conflict and intercession combined with the rod of authority to bring about a complete victory. God through His Word has told us that we do not fight these battles in our own strength. We are to be strong in the Lord and in the power of His might; we have no ability or strength within ourselves against the enemy. The secret of this victory was in the uplifted hands. Moses, Aaron, and Hur (the son of Caleb), went to the top of the hill to pray, while Joshua led the chosen men into battle. The uplifted hands not only represented continued prayer, but also triumph —holding for the rod typified the Lord God as a banner over us: JEHOVAH NESSI, "The Lord is my Banner." In 1 Corinthians 15:57-58, we read, *"But thanks be to God, which giveth us the victory through our Lord Jesus Christ. Therefore, my beloved brethren, be ye stedfast, unmovable, always abounding in the work of the Lord, for as much as ye know that your labour is not in vain in the Lord."* In Joshua we have a type of the Lord Jesus Christ who fought our battles for us and gave us the spoils of war. Very blessed are these words: *"And the Lord said unto Moses, Write this for a memorial in the book, and rehearse it in the ears of Joshua; for I will utterly put out the remembrance of Amalek from under heaven. And Moses built an altar, and called the name of it Je-hovah-Nissi: For he said, Because the Lord hath sworn that the Lord will have war with Amalek from genera-tion to generation"* (verses 14-16). God here promised that He would totally annihilate Amalek.

Water From The Rock

Chapter 8

THE MOSAIC COVENANT

Moses Reunited With His Family

Exodus 18 is parenthetical, and as far as Israel's history is concerned should have been inserted between Numbers 10:10 and 11, because Israel was not yet camped at Sinai, (19:1-2), but when Jethro vistied Moses they were already at Mount Sinai, (18:5); Moses had already received the law.

We have come to the close of a most important division of the Exodus, the second book of Moses. God visited His people in Egypt, and delivered them form the evil Pharaoh, then from the hand of Amalek; He gave them manna in the wilderness, and water from the Rock; He has reunited Moses with his family, and given the Law to the people through him.

When Jethro, Moses' father-in-law, heard all that the Lord had done for Israel, he brought Zipporah, and their two sons, to Moses in the wilderness. Moses met him, bowed to him, and broke bread with him. When Jethro saw Moses as he sat from morning until late in the day judging the people, he gave him wise advice.

Jethro

"And it came to pass on the morrow, that Moses sat to judge the people: and the people stood by Moses from the morning unto the evening. And when Moses' father in law saw all that he did to the people, he said, What is this thing that thou doest to the people? why sittest thou thyself alone, and all the people stand by thee from morning unto even? And Moses said unto his father in law, Because the people come unto me to inquire of God. When they have a matter, they come unto me; and I judge between one and another, and I do make them know the statutes of God, and his laws. And Moses father in law said unto him, The thing that thou doest is not good. Thou wilt surely wear away, both thou, and this people that is with thee: for his thing is too heavy for thee; thou art not able to perform it thyself alone. Hearken now unto my voice, I will give thee counsel, and God shall be with thee, Be thou for the people to God-ward, that thou mayest bring the causes unto God: And thou shalt teach them ordinances and laws, and shalt shew them the way wherein they must walk, and the work that they must do. Moreover thou shalt provide out of all the people able men, such as fear God, men of truth, hating covetousness; and place such over them, to be rulers of thousands, and rulers of hundreds, rulers of fifties, and rulers of tens: And let them judge the people at all seasons: and it shall be, that every great

matter they shall bring unto thee, but every small matter they shall judge: so shall it be easier for thyself, and they shall bear the burden with thee. If thou shalt do this thing, and God command thee so, then thou shalt be able to endure, and all this people shall also go to their place in peace. So Moses hearkened to the vocie of his father in law, and did all that he had said. And Moses chose able men out of all Israel, and made them heads over the people, rulers of thousands, rulers of hundreds, rulers of fifties, and rulers of ten. And they judged the people at all seasons: the hard causes they brought unto Moses, but every small matter they judged themselves. And Moses let his father in law depart; and he went his way into his own land."   *(Exodus 18: 13-27)*

Fifth Despensation: Law

From Rephidim To Sinai

It was the third month after leaving the land of Egypt that the children of Israel arrived at Mount Sinai. This mountainous range bears in Scripture two distinct names: Horeb and Sinai, Horeb provably referring to the whole group, and Sinai to one special mountain in the range. Horeb likely means "mountain of the dried-up ground," and Sinai, "mountain of the thorn." At the present time the whole Sinaitic group is known by the designation of Jebel Musa, (mountain of Moses as named by the Arabs[1]). It forms a huge mountain-block, about two miles in length and one mile in width, with a narrow valley on each side. There is a spacious plain at the northeastern end.

---

[1]*According to a survey the triangle of the Sinaitic Peninsula covers an area of 11,600 square miles.*

"In the third month, when the children of Israel were gone forth out of the land of Egypt, the same day came they into the wilderness of Sinai. For they were depared from Rephidim, and were come to the desert of Sinai, and had pitched in the wilderness; and there Israel camped before the mount."   *(Exodus 19:1-2)*

The Covenant Proposed

(Trip 1, Verses 3-7)

"And Moses went up unto God, and the Lord called unto him out of the mountain, saying, Thus shalt thou say to the house of Jacob, and tell the children of Israel; Ye have seen what I did unto the Egyptians, and how I bare you on eagles' wings, and brought you unto myself. Now therefore, if ye will obey my voice indeed, and keep my covenant, then ye shall be a peculiar treasure unto me above all people: for all the earth is mine: And ye shall be unto me a kingdom of priests, and an holy nation. These are the words which thou shalt speak unto the children of Israel. And Moses came and called for the elders of the people, and laid before their faces all these words which the Lord commanded him."

(Exodus 19: 13-7)

The Covenant Accepted

(Trip 2, Verses 8-13)

And all the people answered together, and said, All that the Lord hath spoken we will do. And Moses returned the words of the people unto the Lord.

When the Lord appeared to Moses at the burning bush He said, *"Certainly I will be with thee; and this shall be a token unto thee, that I have sent thee; When thou hast brought forth the people out of Egypt, ye shall serve God upon this mountain"* (Exodus 3:12). All of the difficulties they had faced along the way had disappeared before the irresistable sovereign will of the God of Abraham, Isaac, and Jacob. In three months they had arrived; three is ever the number of divine manifestation. He was now to give His people a long-awaited manifestation of Himself.

Proposed Meeting Of Israel With God

"And the Lord said unto Moses, Lo, I come unto thee in a thick cloud, that the people may hear when I speak with thee, and believe thee forever. And Moses told the words of the people unto the Lord. And the Lord said unto Moses, Go unto the people, and sancitfy them today and tomorrow, and let them wash their clothes, And be ready against the third day: for the third day the Lord will come down in the sight of all the people upon mount Sinai. And thou shalt set bounds unto the people round about, saying, Take heed to yourselves, that ye go not up into the mount, or touch the border of it: whosoever toucheth the mount shall be surely put to death. There shall not an hand touch it, but he shall surely be stoned, or shot through; whether it be beast or man, it shall not live: when the trumpet soundeth long, they shall come up to the mount. And Moses went down from the mount unto the people, and sanctified the people; and they washed their clothes. And he said unto the people, be ready against the third day: come not at your wives." (Exodus 19:9-15)

The Meeting With God

"And it came to pass on the third day in the morning, that there were thunders and lightnings, and a thick cloud upon the mount, and the voice of the trum-

121

pet exceeding loud; so that all the people that was in the camp trembled. And Moses brought forth the people out of the camp to meet with God; and they stood at the nether part of the mount. And mount Sinai was altogether on a smoke, because the Lord descended upon it in fire: and the smoke thereof ascended as the smoke of a furnace, and the whole mount quaked greatly. And when the voice of the trumpet sounded long, and waxed louder and louder, Moses spake, and God answered him by a voice."   *(Exodus 19:16-19)*

Boundary Set

(Trip 3, verses 20-25)

"And the Lord came down upon mount Sinai, on the top of the mount: and the Lord called Moses up to the top of the mount; and Moses went up. And the Lord said unto Moses, Go down, charge the people lest they break through unto the Lord to gaze, and many of them perish. And let the priests also, which come near to the Lord, sanctify themselves, lest the Lord break forth upon them. And Moses said unto the Lord, The people cannot come up to mount Sinai: for thou chargedst us, saying, Set bounds about the mount, and sanctify it. And the Lord said unto him, Away, get thee down, and thou shalt come up, thou, and Aaron with thee: but let not the priests and the people break through to come up unto the Lord, lest he break forth upon them. So Moses went down unto the people, and spake unto them."
     (Exodus 19:20-25)

Moses was priest and prophet set aside and separated by God Himself to special service. He called Moses apart into Mount Sinai several times to complete His instructions to His chosen people. He prepared the people before He led them into a most solemn covenant. He reminded them Who it was thát led them out of Egyptian bondage, and of His promises to Abraham, Isaac, and Jacob. He speaks of the Hebrew people as a "peculiar treasure," and told them they were called by Him and set aside and, *"ye shall by unto me a kingdom of priests, and an holy nation."* The people agreed to enter into covenant with the Lord and to receive His laws.

One point must be noted at this time. The scholars do not agree just when the "new dispensation" of law actually began. Some feel stongly it was Exodus 12, the Passover night. In fact, the commandments of God started in the garden; God has never left His people without rules and guidelines. The Passover night did indeed mark the beginning of their national history; previous to that night they had no existence as a nation, no corporate existence; they were a disorganized mass of slaves who had all but forgotten the Yahweh of Abraham, Isaac, and Jacob. It was at that time that their calendar was changed by Divine order. Since we do no discredit to the Word by so doing, we will follow our stated outline for clarity. It would be well to also note that the new dispensation (the Mosaic) began by the establishment of a new relationship between Jehovah and His people. They were now His redeemed. Israel was purchased by the Blood of the Lamb, they were delivered from their enemies by His Power. In many of the scriptures already studied, God referred to His commandments, His laws, and His precepts. Up to this point, God had dealt with this people according to the Abrahamic covenant; for now on it would be nationally, according to the terms of the Sinaitic convenant. In Exodus

34: 27-28, we read, *"And the Lord said unto Moses, Write thou these words: for after the tenor of these words I have made a covenant with thee and with Israel. And he was there (on the Mount) with the Lord forty days and forty nights; he did neither eat bread, nor drink water. And he wrote upon the tablets the words of the covenant, THE TEN COMMANDMENTS ."* Returning to Exodus 19, we find that God made the proposal, and Israel accepted it.

How very awesome was the scene described to us in this chapter as God dealt with Moses and His people at the foot of the Mount. The people were to sanctify themselves even to the washing of their clothes. They were to prepare to meet Him on the third day. When God appeared to Abraham, He said, "I will," but here at the Mount, it is, "Thou shalt not!" It was at Mount Sinai that Jehovah's relationship to Israel was placed upon a different basis. When God delivered them from Egypt, He did so on the grounds of His covenant with Abraham. In Exodus 2:24, we read, *"And God heard their groaning, and God remembered His covenant with Abraham, unto Isaac and unto Jacob."* It was on the ground of this covenant that the Lord dealt with Israel up to the time they reached Mount Sinai. The last thing we have recorded before they reach the peninsula was the giving of water from the smitten Rock, and we read in Psalm 105:41-42, how this was done in remembrance of His covenant with Abraham: *"He opened the rock, and the waters gushed out; they ran in the dry places like a river. For He remembered His holy promise to Abraham His servant."* It was a covenant that carried with it no conditions or stipulations.

But here at Sinai, God proposed to make another covenant, a covenant which would include Himself and Israel. This would be a covenant of works; it was covenant that Israel must keep if they were to enjoy the conditional blessings attached to it. In this chapter we read of God's proposal to enter into a legal covenant with them, and they unanimously and heartily accepted it. In verse 8 we are told that they said, *"And all the people answered together, and said, all that the Lord hath spoken we will do."* In Exodus 24:3, the people said, *"And Moses came and told the people all the words of the Lord, and all the judgements: and all the people answered with one voice, and said, All the words which the Lord hath said will we do."* And it was ratified in blood. One writer said, "It suits Him far better to place a fair mitre upon a sinner's head than to put a yoke upon his neck." It is most important for us to realize that Moses laid out all the terms before the people to see if they would accept it or not. They agreed to all its terms, and thereby, obliged themselves to obey the voice of the Lord God at all times. They gave up themselves to be His people. Moses, as their mediator, returned to God and gave Him their answer.

God instructed Moses to go down and see if the people were ready for His visit with them. He was to set bounds around the mount and warned the people not to pass or come up into the mountain; they were not to touch it! They were to stay away from the mountain entirely, until they heard one blast from the ram's horn; then, they could gather at the foot of the mountain. On the third day, they heard a powerful burst of thunder, and saw awesome streaks of lightning flashing, and a huge cloud came down upon the mountain, followed by a long, loud blast from a ram's horn; all the people trembled. Moses led them out to the foot of the mountain, and they saw that Mount Sinai was covered with smoke because God had descended upon it in the form of fire. The smoke took the shape of a smoke screen billowing from a fiery furnace. The entire mountain shook and quaked. Moses spoke to God, and He thundered His reply, and Moses ascended to the top of the mountain to talk with God; but on his way up the Lord commanded that he go back down and warn the people again not to break through the boundaries. They must not try to ascend the mountain to see God, or they would die.

Moses protested that the people had been given their orders, and they would obey them. God said, *"Go back down, and bring Aaron back with you."*

The Ten Commandments
(June 21, 1462 B.C.)

(1) Law Against Polytheism

"And God spake all these words, saying, I am the Lord thy God, which have brought thee out of the land of Egypt, out of the house of bondage. Thou shalt have no other gods before me."   *(Exodus 20:1-3)*

(2) Law Against Idolatry

"Thou shalt not make unto thee any graven image, or any likeness of any thing that is in heaven above, or that is in the earth beneath, or that is in the water under the earth. Thou shalt not bow down thyself to them, nor serve them: for I the Lord thy God am a jealous God, visiting the iniquity of the fathers upon the children

unto the third and fourth generation of them that hate me. And shewing mercy unto thousands of them that love me, and keep my commandments."

(Exodus 20:4-6)

(3) Law Against Profanity

"Thou shalt not take the name of the Lord thy God in vain; for the Lord will not hold him guiltless that taketh his name in vain."   *(Exodus 20:7)*

(4) Law Against Sabbath Breaking

"Remember the sabbath day, and keep it holy. Six days shalt thou labour, and do all thy work; But the seventh day is the sabbath of the Lord thy God: in it thou shalt not do any work, thou, not thy son, not thy daughter, thy manservant, nor thy maidservant, nor thy cattle, nor thy stranger that is within thy gates: For in six days the Lord made heaven and earth, the sea, and all that in them is, and rested the seventh day: wherefore the Lord blessed the sabbath day, and hallowed it."   *(Exodus 20:8-11)*

(5) Law Against Parental Dishonour

"Honour thy father and thy mother: that thy days may be long upon the land which the Lord thy God giveth thee."   *(Exodus 20:12)*

(6) Law Against Murder

"Thou shalt not kill."   *(Exodus 20:13)*

(7) Law Against Adultery

"Thou shalt not commit adultery."

(Exodus 20:14)

(8) Law Against Stealing

"Thou shalt not steal." *(Exodus 20:15)*

(9) Law Against Perjury

"Thou shalt not bear false witness against thy neighbour." *(Exodus 20:16)*

(10) Law Against Covetousness

"Thou shalt not covet thy neighbour's house, thou shalt not covet thy neighbour's wife, nor his manservant, nor his maidservant, nor his ox, nor his ass, nor any thing that is thy neighbour's." *(Exodus 20:17)*

The Effect Upon The People

"And all the people saw the thunderings, and the lightnings, and the noise of the trumpet, and the mountain smoking: and when the people saw it, they removed, and stood afar off. And they said unto Moses, Speak thou with us, and we will hear: but let not God speak with us, lest we die, And Moses said unto the people, Fear not: for God is come to prove you, and that his fear maybe before your faces, that ye sin not." *(Exodus 20:18-20)*

Instructions For An Altar
(Trip 4, Verses 21-26)

"And the people stood afar off, and Moses drew near unto the thick darkness where God was. And the Lord said unto Moses, Thus thou shalt say unto the children of Israel, Ye have seen that I have talked with you from heaven. Ye shall not make with me gods of silver, neither shall ye make unto you gods of gold. An altar of earth thou shalt make unto me, and shalt sacrifice

thereon thy burnt offerings, and thy peace offerings, thy sheep, and thine oxen: in all places where I record my name I will come unto thee, and I will bless thee. And if thou wilt make me an altar of stone, thou shalt not build it of hewn stone: for if thou lift up thy tool upon it, thou hast polluted it. Neither shalt thou go up by steps unto mine altar, that thy nakedness be not discovered thereon.''   *(Exodus 20 21:26)*

We note here several things about this part of the story in way of review: (1) God led the people to the foot of Mount Sinai; (2) He called Moses apart; (3) the people were to prepare themselves, and gather around the base of the Mount on the third day; (4) on the third day the Shechinah appeared upon Mount Sinai, and all were filled with irresistible awe and fear; (5) Moses disappeared in the cloud to talk with God; and (6) the voice of God was heard, and sentence after sentence fell as He gave the mighty law to His peculiar people.

The law was given to Moses three times as follows:

(1) orally as read in chapter 20:1-17, where they received the ten commandments, recorded in Chapter 21: 1-23, plus the directions for the keeping of three annual feasts, chapter 23:20-33;

(2) Moses was then called up to receive the tables of stone as recorded in chapter 24:12-18; and while in the mount he received the instructions for the tabernacle, priesthood, and sacrifice;

(3) Moses came down from the mount and found the people worshipping a golden calf, and he broke the laws (tablets) written by the very finger of God, entered the mount for another 40 days and nights, and received them written again by the Hand of God.

At the foot of Mount Sinai, right after the giving of the law, God gave instructions for the building of His altar. Here we have a beautiful provision for the frailty and sin of the covenant people, and for the very trangressors who were soon to break the law, and need its blessed atonement. It was to be an altar of earth. The poorest could afford this altar for the materials were all around the area. So Christ needs no costly offering from the helpless sinner, but anywhere, everywhere, and whosoever will, may come boldly to the altar of grace. It would not be hewed of stone, which teaches us that it is not the works of our own hands, but the righteousness of our Lord Jesus Christ that delivers us. We are not required to lift a tool to this finished work of Calvary, and there are no steps to this altar. It is not above the humblest and most desperate sinner. The foot of the Cross is level where all meet with the cry, "Just as I am without one plea."

Chapter 21 reveals ten civil laws concerning persons:

(1) Menservants (1-6)

(2) Maidservants and wives (7-11)

(3) Penalty for Murder (12-14)

(4) Death for Parental Dishonour (15)

(5) Death for Kidnapping (16)

(6) Death for Parental Dishonour (17)

(7) Assault and Battery (18-19)

(8) Injuries to Servants (20-21)

(9) Injuries to Pregnant Women (22-25)

(10) Injuries to Servants (26-27)

Chapter 22 reveals civil laws were given concerning property and animals:

(1) Penalties for Larceny (1-4)

(2) Penalty for Loss Through Spite (5)

(3) Penalty for Carelessness (6)

(4) Penalty for Loss of Things (7-13)

(5) Penalty for Loss of Borrowed Things (14-15)

(6) Penalty for Rape (16-17)

(7) Penalty for Being a Witch (18)

(8) Penalty for Beastiality (19)

(9) Penalty for Idolatry (20)

(10) Penalty for Oppression (21-24)

(11) Law against Charging Interest to the Poor (25-27)   (12) Law against Anarchy (28)

(13) Law of Firstfruits (29-30)

(14) Law of Personal Holiness (31)

Chapter 23 deals with various other laws:

(1) Law against Perjury (1)

(2) Law against Following the Crowd (2)

(3) Law against Favoring the Poor (3)

(4) Law of Love (4-5)

(5) Law against Injustice (6-7)

(6) Law against Bribery (8)

(7) Law against Oppression (9)

Six Religious Laws:

(1) Law of the Sabbath Year (10-11)

(2) Law of the Weekly Sabbath (12)

(3) Law of Faithfulness to God (13)

(4) Law of Three National Feasts (14-16)

(5) Law of Assembly of The Males (17)

(6) Law of the Offerings (18-19)

Guidance Promised (20-23)

Law against Idolatry (24)

Blessings for Obedience (25-31)

No Fellowship with the Enemy (32-33)

Ratification of The Covenant
(Trip 5, Verses 9-11)

Order of worship

"And he said unto Moses, Come up unto the Lord, thou, and Aaron, Nadab, and Abihu, and seventy of the elders of Israel; and worship ye afar off. And Moses alone shall come near the Lord: but they shall not come nigh; neither shall the people go up with him."

(Exodus 24:12

In this twenty-fourth chapter of Exodus, God manifested His Glory as never before or after during the whole of the Mosaic economy. God called for Moses to bring his brother Aaron, and Aaron's two sons, Nadab, and Abihu, and seventy of the elders of Israel, and worship Him afar off; they were priviliged to witness the Presence of God. Before they came near to Him, they must worship afar off. Thus we must enter into God's gates with humble and solemn adorations; those who approach God must ascend. Moses alone must come near, being a type of Christ as our Mediator.

By Promise And Monuments

"Moses came and told the people all the words of the Lord, and all the judgments: and all the people answered with one voice, and said, All the words which the Lord hath said will we do. And Moses wrote all the words of the lord, and rose up early in the morning, and builded an altar under the hill, and twelve pillars, according to the twelve tribes of Israel."

(Exodus 24: 3-4)

By Blood and Promise

"And he sent young men of the children of Israel, which offered burnt offerings, and sacrificed peace offerings of oxen unto the Lord. And Moses took half of the blood, and put it in basons; and half of the blood he sprinkled on the altar. And he took the book of the covenant, and read in the audience of the people: and they said, All that the Lord hath said will we do, and be obedient. And Moses took the blood, and sprinkled it onto the people, and said, Behold the blood of the covenant, which the Lord hath made with you concerning all these words." *(Exodus 24:5-8)*

This typifies the covenant of grace between God and believers through Christ Jesus. Moses told the people the words of the covenant; they had all of God's laws laid out before them for their consent and amen. The people were not divided in their acceptance of the covenant. Moses wrote it down. There was to be no mistake. He likely wrote as God dictated to him upon the mount. The people agreed to all the Lord had said, and Moses sealed it with blood. He then built an altar to the honour and worship of God. What a glorious picture in type of Jesus and His church. In Hebrews 9:12-22 we read, *"Neither by the blood of goats and calves, but by his own blood he entered in once into the holy place, having obtained eternal redemption for us. For if the blood of bulls and goats, and the ashes of an heifer sprinkling the unclean, sanctifieth to the purifying of the flesh: How much more shall the blood of Christ, who through the eternal Spirit offered himself without spot to God, purge your conscience from dead works to serve the living God? And for this cause he is the mediator of the new testament, that by means of death, for the redemption of the transgressions that were under the first testament, they which are called might receive the promise of eternal inheritance. For where a testament is, there must also of necessity be the death of the testator. For a testament is of force after men are dead: otherwise it is of no strength at all while the testator liveth. Whereupon neither the first testament was dedicated without blood. For when Moses had spoken every precept to all the people according to the law, he took the blood of calves and of goats, with water, and scarlet wool, and hyssop, and sprinkled both the book, and all the people, Saying, This is the blood of the testament which God hath enjoined you. Moreover he sprinkled with blood both the tabernacle, and all the vessels of the ministry. And almost all things are by the law purged with blood; and without shedding of blood is no remission."*

In His Presence
(Trip 5 Verses 9-11)

"Then went up Moses, and Aaron, Nadab, and Abihu, and seventy of the elders of Israel, And they saw the God of Israel: and there was under his feet as it were a paved work of a sapphire stone, and as it were the body of heaven in his clearness. And upon the nobles of the children of Israel he laid not his hands: also they saw God, and did eat and drink"   *(Exodus 24:9-11)*

The children of Israel had agreed to obey the laws of God, and walk in His statutes and commandments, and God favored their leaders by giving them a special meeting with Him. They saw the God of Israel, and He did not kill them. There they beheld His splendor; there was under His feet as it were a paved work of a sapphire stone, and as it were the body of heaven in clearness. They saw God and did eat and drink. Israel's history continued almost fifteen hundred years after this memorable occasion, but never again did the elders see God, and never again did they eat and drink in His Presence because of their broken vows; the official heads of Israel viewed the Glory of God for a brief moment of time; in Him a way has been opened for us to enter the very thrown room of God where we may commune continually with the Father God.

Forty Days In the Mount
(Trip 6, Verses 12-18)

"And the Lord said unto Moses, Come up to me into the mount, and be there: and I will give thee tables of stone, and a law, and commandments which I have written; that thou mayest teach them. And Moses rose up, and his minister Joshua: and Moses went up into

*the mount of God. And he said unto the elders, Tarry ye
here for us, until we come again unto you: and, behold,
Aaron and Hur are with you: if any man have any mat-
ters to do, let him come unto them. And Moses went up
into the mount, and a cloud covered the mount."*

(Exodus 24:12-18)

Moses Resumes Mediatory Position

*"And the glory of the Lord abode upon mount
Sinia, and the cloud covered it six days: and the seventh
day he called unto Moses out of the midst of the cloud.
And the sight of the glory of the Lord was like devouring
fire on the top of the mount in the eyes of the children
of Israel. And Moses went into the midst of the cloud,
and gat him up into the mount: and Moses was in the
mount forty days and forty nights."*

(Exodus 24:16-18)

*Moses and Joshua fellowshipped in the mount for
six days, but on the seventh day, God called from the
midst of the Glory Cloud for Moses to come up to Him
so he could receive the tables of the law. Moses disappeared into the cloud-covered mountaintop and the
people watched the mountain as it glowed like a raging
forest fire, and there for forty days and nights, God
talked and instructed him.*

Chapter 9

THE TABERNACLE OF MOSES

The tabernacle of Moses in the wilderness is the absolute and perfect type of the excellency of our Lord Jesus Christ in His redemptive work on Calvary as the final sacrifice for a fallen race. Here we enter into a most blessed and Holy study of the sacrifices God made under law; and in the book of Hebrews, Paul warned that they were merely types and shadows of the good things to come.

The best way to begin such an in-depth study would be with these four questions:

(1) *What is a tabernacle?* According to the dictionary, a tabernacle is a temporary dwelling place. The tabernacle in the wilderness was a temporary dwelling place where God met with His children. In way of comparison, it might be noted that the church "ekklesai"

is a called-out company of people who meet together temporarily in a tabernacle of flesh, until the day comes when they take up their abode forever with Him in the city four-square, where the Lamb will be the light. The God who chose to dwell in the tabernacle and temple in the old dispensation tabernacled in the Lord Jesus as He walked this earth. In 2 Corinthians 5:19, we read, *"God was in Christ, reconciling the world unto himself."* In Matthew 1:23, we read, *"Behold, a virgin shall be with child, and shall bring forth a son, and they shall call his name Emmanuel, which being interpreted is, God with us."* In 1 Corinthians 6:16, we read, *"And what agreement hath the temple of God with idols? for ye are the temple of the living God; as God hath said, I will dwell in them, and walk in them; and I will be their God, and they shall be my people."* Jesus spoke of the temple of His body when He said, *"Destroy this temple, and in three days I will raise it up. But he spake of the temple of his body"* (John 2:19, 21).

(2)   *To whom was it given?* The tabernacle in the wilderness was given to a peculiar people chosen by God to occupy a special place in this earth.

(3)   *Why was the tabernacle given to them?* It was given to them because God desired to dwell among them and to be their God; to teach them obedience, and their need for Him as their One True God. He wanted to give the law to show them their sinfulness, and that the way into the Holy of Holies was through sacrifice, the Blood.

(4)   *When was it given?* It was given to them after they had so miserably failed under the covenant of grace which God had given to their forefathers.

The tabernacle in the wilderness was designed by God Himself. This tent became the center of all worship of the children of Israel during their journey into the promised land. It not only pictured for us the Lord Jesus in His Redemptive work and the believer who is complete in Him, but it also depicts a complete picture of the plan of salvation:

(1) Sinners stand on the outside, for they must enter through the one door into the outer court, and once in, they stop at the ALTAR (the cross for us).

(2) At the LAVER, there is separation and daily cleansing, (the Word).

(3) In the HOLY PLACE there is fellowship with the One Who is the Bread of Life.

(4) Darkness is illuminated by the GOLDEN CANDLESTICK.

(5) At the ALTAR OF INCENSE, there is worship and intercession, the highest form of prayer and communion.

(6) With the renting of the veil at Calvary, a way was made for easy access into the Holy of Holies, where the ARK AND MERCY SEAT rest containing Aaron's rod that budded (Resurrection).

(7) In HOLY OF HOLIES the believer beholds the Glory of God (Shekinah).

Names of the Tabernacle

Several different names were used in referring to the tabernacle of Moses in the wilderness. In all, SEVEN names were given to this structure which so clearly prefigures the Person and the work of our Lord Jesus Christ.

139

(1) TENT

The tabernacle is often referred to as the tent. In Exodus 39:32, 33, 40 we read, *"Thus was all the work of the tabernacle of the tent of the congregation finished: and the children of Israel did according to all that the Lord commanded Moses, so did they. And they brought the tabernacle unto Moses, the tent, and all his furniture, his taches, his boards, his bars, and his pillars, and his sockets. . . .his cords, and his pins, and all the vessels of the service of the tabernacle, for the tent of the congregation."* A tent is an outer covering, and because it is a temporary dwelling place, and movable, it suggests a pilgrimage. God wanted to keep His people moving towards the promised land. The church, which is the Body of Christ, is temporarily on this earth, but its ultimate goal is the New Jerusalem mentioned in Revelation 21:22, *"And I saw no temple therein: for the Lord God Almighty and the Lamb are the temple of it."* In Corinthians 5:1, we read, *"For we know that if our earthly house of this tabernacle were dissolved, we have a building of God, and house not made with hands, eternal in the heavens."* In Exodus 36:14, the word "tent" was also used to refer to the tabernacle as a meeting place, *"And he made curtains of goats' hair for the tent over the tabernacle: eleven curtains he made them."* How glorious it is to think that God Almighty would be willing to come down to a lowly tent as it were to establish fellowship with His people. Jesus humbled Himself and took upon Him the tent of flesh that He might walk among men.

(2) SANCTUARY

It was called the sanctuary, which means a consecrated place, a holy place. It was Holy because God chose to put His Name there; it was to be a meeting place between Him and His children. God said, *"Let them make me a sanctuary; that I may dwell among them"* (Exodus 25:8). In Exodus 29:45-46, He said, *"I will dwell among the children of Israel, and will be their God. And they shall know that I am the Lord their God, that brought them forth out of the land of Egypt, that I may dwell among them: I am the Lord their God."* The universal Church which is the mystic Body of the Lord Jesus Christ, is also God's sanctuary upon the earth. In Exodus 15:17, the song of the Redeemed (Song of Moses) was sung out by the children of Israel in praise of their God Who had delivered them from the hand of Pharaoh, and cast their enemies into the depth of the sea: *"Thou shalt bring them in, and plant them in the mountain of thine inheritance, in the place, O Lord, which thou hast made for thee to dwell in, in the Sanctuary, O Lord, which thy hands have established."* They sang of a Sanctuary before a Sanctuary pattern was given.

(3) TABERNACLE

It was from this tabernacle (dwelling place) that God spoke through Moses to His people. In Leviticus 1:1, we read, *"The Lord called unto Moses, and spake unto him out of the tabernacle of the congregation."* In John 14:23, Jesus said, *"If a man love me, he will keep my words: and my Father will love him, and we will come unto him, and make our abode with him."* God desires to fellowship with us. In Revelation 3:20, we read, *"Behold, I stand at the door, and knock: if any man hear my voice, and open the door, I will come in to him, and will sup with him, and he with me."* And believers look forward to the day mentioned in Revelation 21:3: *"Be-*

hold, the tabernacle of God is with men, and he will dwell with them, and they shall be his people, and God himself shall be with them, and be their God.''

(4)   TABERNACLE OF THE CONGREGATION

The name itself indicated that there was a people chosen by God to build a tabernacle where they were to gather in unity and worship the One true God. In Matthew 16:18, Jesus said, *". . . I will build my church; and the gates of hell shall not prevail against it.''*

(5)   TABERNACLE OF THE LORD

In 1 Kings 2:28, the Old Testament tabernacle is referred to as "the tabernacle of the Lord." It is awesome to realize that God Himself actually dwelt among His people in this tabernacle, and that He now tabernacles on the earth in the hearts of born-again believers.

(6)   TABERNACLE OF TESTIMONY

God's dwelling place on the earth was also called the tabernacle of testimony. *"And on the day that the tabernacle was reared up the cloud covered the tabernacle, namely, the tent of the testimony: and at even there was upon the tabernacle as it were the appearnace of fire until the morning" (Numbers 9:15).* Just as the Old Testament tabernacle was a testimony to the surrounding world, so we, the universal body, must be a testimony to the glory of the Lord Jesus.

(7)   TABERNACLE OF WITNESS

The seventh name given to the tabernacle was the tabernacle of witness. In Numbers 17:7-8, it was first called this when the rods of the various tribes were placed within the tabernacle to verify which tribe was distinctly chosen to represent God to the other: *"And Moses laid up the rods before the Lord in the tabernacle of witness. And it came to pass, that on the morrow Moses went into the tabernacle of witness; and, behold, the rod of Aaron for the house of Levi was budded, and brought forth buds, and blossoms, and yielded almonds."* In Acts 7:44, Stephen gave an account of the "tabernacle of witness" just before he was stoned to death by the Jews: *"Our fathers had the tabernacle of witness in the wilderness, as he had appointed, speaking unto Moses, that he should make it according to the fashion he had seen."* The rod represented the authority of God in the Old Testament, and believers today are also endured with His Power from on high. We have authority by using the Name of Jesus Christ.

Heave Offerings

"And the Lord spake unto Moses, saying, Speak unto the children of Israel, that they bring me an offering: of every man that giveth it willingly with his heart ye shall take my offering."   *(Exodus 25:1-2)*

The tabernacle in the wilderness was to be built with the freewill offerings of the people chosen by God to dwell with Him therein. God asked for an offering; it was to be of their own freewill, not forced. The people responded, and brought more than enough offerings to build the sanctuary. They gave so much that Moses instructed them to be restrained. The children of Israel were told to build not with their tithes, but with their offerings. In Exodus 36:5-7, we read, *"And they spake unto Moses, saying, The people bring much more than enough for the service of the work, which the Lord com-*

manded to make. And Moses gave commandment, and they caused it to be proclaimed throughout the camp, saying, Let neither man nor woman make any more work for the offering of the sanctuary. So the people were restrained from bringing. For the stuff they had was sufficient for all the work to make it, and too much.''

We cannot lightly skip over this groundwork for the building of the sanctuary. Where did these Hebrew people get so much gold, silver, brass, spices, and precious stones? God instructed the Egyptians to give up their precious things to the departing slaves, and at the same time, He instructed the children of Israel to accept all that was offered to them. God can work on both ends of the line at the same time. In Genesis 15:13-14, we read, *"And he said unto Abram, Know for a surety that thy seed shall be a stranger in a land that is not theirs, and shall serve them; and they shall afflict them four hundred years; And also that nation, whom they shall serve, will I judge: and afterward shall they come out with great substance.''*

Remembering His Word to Abram, when God brought the children of Israel forth, He fulfilled His prophecy as recorded in Exodus 12:35-36, *"And the children of Israel did according the the word of Moses: and they borrowed of the Egyptians' jewels of silver, and jewels of gold, and raiment: And the Lord gave the people favour in the sight of the Egyptians, so that they lent unto them such things as they required, And they spoiled the Egyptians.''*

One might say this was 400 years of back wages that went into the construction of the tabernacle. The first lesson God would teach His people was how to give. He does not force the issue, therefore, they learn to give willingly and cheerfully. They stood in line to respond to the call. Giving is a privilege, as well as a responsibility. It is a vital part of our worship service. He has given to us that we might give back to Him for the propagation of the gospel. This was a love offering that left no one out. Every man and woman had something to give. It must be noted that the Lord called it His offering; they were to bring it to Him. This was to be a "heave offering" suggestive of something lifted high above the head.

Later on in their history, God accuses them with strong words, *"Even from the days of your fathers ye are gone away from mine ordinances, and have not kept them. Return unto me, and I will return unto you, saith the Lord of hosts. But ye said, Wherein shall we return? Will a man rob God? Yet ye have robbed me. But ye say, Wherein have we robbed thee? In tithes and offerings. Ye are cursed with a curse: for ye have robbed me, even this whole nation. Bring ye all the tithes into the storehouse, that there may be meat in mine house, and prove me now herewith, saith the Lord of hosts, if I will not open you the windows of heaven, and pour you out a blessing, that there shall not be room enough to receive it"* (Malachi 3:7-10). God sounded out a warning to them that they had knowingly robbed Him; they had gotten fat and rich, and had lost their way to the storehouse. He offered a way of return: *"And I will rebuke the devourer for your sakes, and he shall not destroy the fruits of your ground; neither shall your vine cast her fruit before the time in the field, saith the Lord of hosts"* (Malachi 3:11).

145

In Psalm 105:44-45, we read, *"And gave them the lands of the heathen: and they inherited the labour of the people. That they might observe his statutes, and keep his laws. Praise ye the Lord."* In Proverbs 13:22, we learn that the wealth of the sinner (Egypt) is laid up for the just. In our covenant walk with the Lord, He has access to all that we own in the natural, and we have access to all that is His in the supernatural. To place giving on the level of "freewill" offerings is allowing man to exercise his freewill, or choice, for the receiving of a blessing or a cursing in this life. In 2 Corinthians 8 and 9, Paul compliments the church people for their liberal giving. He pointed out that they had first given of themselves, then of their possessions. God loves a cheerful giver for it is His nature and way to bless in the one-hundred-fold return.

Materials for the Tabernacle and Furniture

"And this is the offering which ye shall take of them; gold, and silver, and brass, and blue, and purple, and scarlet, and fine line, and goats' hair, and rams' skins dyed red, and badgers' skins, and shittim wood, Oil for the light, spices for anointing oil, and for sweet incense, onyx stones, and stones to be set in the ephod, and in the breastplate."　　　　　*(Exodus 24:37)*

Metals (3)

(1)　*GOLD:* typifies the deity of our Lord Jesus Christ. In Revelation 3:18, we read, *"I counsel thee to buy of me gold tried in the fire, that thou mayest be rich; and white raiment, that thou mayest be clothed, and that the shame of thy nakedness do not appear; and*

anoint thine eyes with eyesalve, that thou mayest see."
It speaks of Divine Righteousness as in the Mercy Seat in
Exodus 25:17. Of the three metals to be used, gold is men-
tioned first for God is to be first in all things.

(2) *SILVER:* typifies Redemption, as seen in the
atonement money in Exodus 30:12-16: *"When thou takest the sum of the children of Israel after their number,
then shall they give every man a ransom for his soul
unto the Lord, when thou numberest them; that there
be no lague among them, when thou numberest them.
This they shall give, every one that passeth among them
that are numbered, half a shekel after the shekel of the
sanctuary: (a shekel is twenty ge-rahs:) an half shekel
shall be the offering of the Lord. Every one that passeth
among them that are numbered, from twenty years old
and above, shall give an offering unto the Lord. The rich
shall not give more, and the poor shall not give less than
half a shekel, when they give an offering unto the Lord,
to make an atonement for your souls. And thou shalt
take the atonement money of the children of Israel, and
shalt appoint it for the service of the tabernacle of the
congregation; that it may be a memorial unto the children of Israel before the Lord, to make an atonement
for your souls."*

In Numbers 18:16, we read, *"And those that are to
be redeemed from a month old shalt thou redeem, according to thine estimation, for the money of five shekels, after the shekel of the sanctuary, which is twenty ge-
rahs."* (Half a shekel is 32 cents in U.S. money.) In Luke
15:8-10, we have the parable of the lost coin illustrating
Redemption, and the joy that is experienced in heaven
when the lost is found: *"Either what woman having ten*

147

pieces of silver, if she lose one piece, doth not light a candle, and sweep the house, and seek diligently till she find it? And when she hath found it, she calleth her friends and her neighbours together, saying, Rejoice with me; for I have found the piece which I had lost. Likewise, I say unto you, there is joy in the presence of the angels of God over one sinner that repenteth."

(3) *BRASS:* Typifies judgment, (the Brazen altar), the death of Christ. Exodus 27:3 says, *"And thou shalt make his pans to receive his ashes, and his shovels, and his bason, and his fleshhooks, and his firepans: all the vessels thereof thou shalt make of brass."* In Revelation 1:15, we read, *"And his feet like unto fine brass, as if they burned in a furnace; and his voice as the sound of many waters."*

Colors To Be Used In The Tabernacle (4)

(1) *BLUE:* Heavenly; typifies Christ as the spiritual One, or Heavenly Man; Holy, harmless, undefiled, separated from sinners, and made higher than the heavens. This tabernacle is heavenly, therefore heavenly colors are used as opposed to earth-toned colors. in 1 Corinthians 15:47-48, we read, *"The first man is of the earth, earthly: the second man is the Lord from heaven. As is the earthy, such as thy also that are earthy: and as is the heavenly, such are they also that are heavenly."* In Hebrews 7:26, we read, *"For such an high priest became us, who is holy, harmless, undefiled, separate from sinners, and made higher than the heavens;"*

(2) *PURPLE:* Typifies Christ as the sovereign One, the King of Kings and Lord of Lords, who will reign universally: *"And he hath on his vesture and on his*

thigh a name written, KING OF KINGS, AND LORD OF LORDS" (Revelation 19:16). *"And they clothed him with purple, and platted a crown of thorns, and put it about his head"* (Mark 15:17).

(3) *SCARLET:* Typifies Him as the Sacrificed One. This sacrificial color embodies the entire thought of redemption. *"And they sung a new song, saying, Thou art worthy to take the book, and to pen the seals thereof: for thou wast slain, and hast redeemed us to God by thy blood out of every kindred, and tongue, and people, and nation; And has made us unto our God kings and priests: and we shall reign on the earth."* (Revelation 5:9-10).

(4) *WHITE:* Purity and righteousness; He is our righteousness.

Fabrics Used In The Tabernacle (4)

(1) *FINE LINENS:* Typifies righteousness. *"And to her was granted that she should be arrayed in fine linen, clean and white: for the fine linen is the righteousness of saints"* (Revelation 19:8). This is imputed unto us by and through our Lord Jesus Christ. In 1 Corinthians 1:30, we read, *"But of him are ye in Christ Jesus, who of God is made unto us wisdom, and righteousness, and sanctification, and redemption:"*

(2) *GOAT'S HAIR:* Typifies serviceableness. Garments of goat's hair were worn by the prophets of old, so the thought is of serviceableness in the prophetic office.

(3) *RAM'S SKINS, DYED RED:* Typifies devotedness in the priestly office.

(4)   *BADGERS' SKINS:*   Typifies Holiness; repelling every form of evil. These skins speak or illustrate the natural man's view of Christ, having "no form nor comeliness" as outlined in Isaiah 53:2.

Wood To Be Used In The Tabernacle

The only wood mentioned in the building of the tabernacle was acacia (shittim) wood. This speaks of the incorruptibility of the human nature of our Lord Jesus Christ.

Oil To Be Used In The Tabernacle

Oil used in the tabernacle typifies the Holy Spirit. Oil for light is pure oil from ripe olives as mentioned in Leviticus 24:2, *"Command the children of Israel, that they bring unto thee pure olive oil beaten for the light, to cause the lamps to burn continually."* These olives were carefully crushed in mortar; the first drops were especially pure in quality.

"And thou shalt command the childen of Israel, that they bring thee pure oil olive beaten for the light, to cause the lamp to burn always. In the tabernacle of the congregation without the vail, which is before the testimony, Aaron and his sons shall order it from evening to morning before the Lord: it shall be a statute forever unto their generations on the behalf of the children of Israel."   *(Exodus 27:20-21)*

"And the Lord spake unto Moses, saying, Command the children of Israel, that they bring unto thee pure oil olive beaten for the light, to cause the lamps to burn continually. Without the vail of the testimony, in the tabernacle of the congregation, shall Aaron order

it from the evening unto the morning before the Lord continually: it shall be a statute forever in your generations. He shall order the lamps upon the pure candlestick before the Lord continually."

(Leviticus 24:1-4)

"Oil for the light" is one of the things God directed to be brought by the children of Israel so that the seven lamps in the Holy Place might bring forth their light. God referred to this as "oil for the light" and not "oil for the lamps."

As we have already mentioned, oil is one of the emblems of the Holy Spirit. This oil would have many uses in ministering unto the Lord in His Sanctuary. This oil was to be the best golden variety made from olives, and it was to be pure. Every impurity was to be beaten out of it. We take note here that "Gethsemane" means "oil-press." This Holy Oil was compounded from four principal spices; it was designed for food, light, and anointing. There had to be fresh oil at the Candlestick every day. This oil was not to be imitated in any way.

The olive tree is more closely associated with the history and civilization of man than any other tree. When we enter into the deeper walk of the Spirit, we see the similarity between the olive tree, its fruit, and the Christian. As mentioned, great care is taken in gathering the fruit of the olive trees so that the fruit and the boughs of the tree will not be injured. The gathering is done by hand or by shaking off the tree very carefully. We liken this to the gentleness of the Holy Spirit as He gathers the elect into the Kingdom of God.

There are two processes by which the oil is extracted from the fruit. One process is to bruise the olive with a mortar without applying heat. This is a slower process, and the product is known as the "beaten oil" which is the "pure oil." The other method is extraction by great pressure and heat, but the product is an inferior oil. Jesus is the Pure Oil of sacrifice, purity and holiness. The Holy Spirit is the oil which keeps the light burning eternally in the lamps of the believers' hearts. In the Old Testament, this oil was used to anoint the priest, which we will cover later. Jesus, however, is the Holy Anointed One.

"The Spirit of the Lord is upon me; because the Lord hath anointed me to preach good tidings unto the meek; he hath sent me to bind up the brokenhearted, to proclaim liberty to the captives, and the opening of the prison to them that are bound; To proclaim the acceptable year of the Lord, and the day of vengeance of our God; to comfort all that mourn; To appoint unto them that mourn in Zion, to give unto them beauty for ashes, the oil of joy for mourning, the garment of prise for the spirit of heaviness; that they might be called trees of righteousness, the planting of the Lord, that he might be glorified." *(Isaiah 61:1-3)*

"How God anointed Jesus of Nazareth with the Holy Ghost and with power; who went about doing good, and healing all that were oppressed of the devil; for God was with him. *(Acts 10:38)*

It is the anointing of the Holy Spirit that enables us to live lives of sacrifice and love. God has chosen to represent the anointing of the Holy Spirit by a combination of spices and olive oil, which are peculiarly emblematic of the operation of the Spirit upon a purified soul. Though mention has been made previously of the spices, we note here that myrrh has in it the virtue of easing pain, (though bitter to taste), stopping the flow of blood from a wound, and extracting the soreness from a cut or a bruise in the flesh. Sweet cinnamon has in it the property of a sweet, spicy fire. Also, we find that calamus, commonly called flag-root, though much like cinnamon, is noted for its spicy perfume. Its virtue is to ease pains in the stomach area, and to aid digestion or counteract sour acids. It is pleasant to taste, and fragrant to the smell. The cassia is soothing for burns and also very nourishing. All of the spices typify in some way the many offices of the precious Holy Spirit. One writer said that this divine oil takes the rust from the hinges of all the soul's doors, so that like the prison gate when the angel led Peter, they open of their own accord at the approach of God.

To David, the olive tree was an emblem of divine blessing and prosperity, as illustrated in Psalm 52:8 and Psalm 128:3. It was the symbol of beauty, luxury, and strength to the later prophets.

"But I am like a green olive tree in the house of God: I trust in the mercy of God forever and ever."
(Psalm 52:8)

"Thy wife shall be as a fruitful vine by the sides of thine house: thy children like olive plants round about thy table".
(Psalm 128:3)

"The Lord called thy name, A green olive tree, fair, and of goodly fruit . . . "
(Jeremiah 1:16)

Paul wrote in Romans 16:17, *"And if some of the branches be broken off, and thou, being a wild olive tree, were grafted in among them, and with them partakest of the root and fatness of the olive tree;"*

153

Some Uses Of Oil

(1) *Oil in wounds:* Luke 10:30-37: the good samaritan. Though the old life of sin leaves many wounds and open sores, He who was wounded for us will bind all the wounds, pour in the oil and the wine, and set us upright, and be responsible for our lives.

(2) *Oil in a cruse:* I Kings 17:12-16: ". . . And the barrel of meal wasted not, neither did the cruse of oil fail . . ."

(3) *Oil in the pot:* 2 Kings 4:1-7: Same kind of story, but this miracle was performed by the Prophet Elisha.

(4) *Oil on the face:* Psalm 104:15; Psalm 133:1-3; precious ointment of anointing speaks of unity.

(5) *Oil on the parts of the body:* Leviticus 14:10-28, in cleansing of a leper. Leprosy is symbolic of sin in lives. This oil is mingled with the Blood.

Chief Spices Used In The Anointing Oil (4)

"Moreover the Lord spake unto Moses, saying, Take thou also unto the principal spices, of pure myrrh five hundred shekels, and of sweet cinnamon half so much, even two hundred and fifty shekels, and of sweet calamus two hundred and fifty shekels, And of cassia five hundred shekels, after the shekel of the sanctuary, and of olive oil an him: And thou shalt make it an oil of holy ointment, an ointment compound after the art of the apothecary: it shall be an holy anointing oil."

(Exodus 30:22-25)

Thus, we read that there are four principal spices to be used in the anointing oil:

(1) *MYRRH:* This is the sap of the balsam bush. In the Song of Solomon, it is referred to as one of the chief

spices: *"Spinkenard and saffron; calamus and cinnamon, with all trees of frankincense; myrrh and aloes, with all the chief spices:"* In Hebrew, the myrrh means "bitter or free." It is taken from the gum of the dwarf tree; it might flow freely, or have to be cut by a deep incision into the heart of the tree. It was bitter to the taste, but had a fragrant odor. This pure myrrh was a symbol of "meekness" and "temperance." In Galatians 5:22, we read that the fruit of the Spirit is love, joy, peace, longsuffering, gentleness, goodness, faith, meekness and temperance. It is the nature of the Spirit of God to be meek and humble. Jesus was anointed with a double portion of the Spirit of God.

As stated in the Song of Solomon 4:12, the Bride likens her beloved to a bundle of myrrh: *"He is a bundle of gentleness, goodness, and meakness nestling at her side all the night long."* The Hebrew word "bundle" means a parcel, a kernel, bag, or small stone. The western mind cannot grasp this. We must think in terms of the customs and manners of the eastern habits and practices. Women in the western worlds buy the most expensive perfumes and spray lavishly over their person, while the eastern women wore what was called a "sa-sheba" bag between their bosom. This was their way of keeping themselves permeated with fragrances all through the day. The breast of the bride was a symbol of her love and affection for her Bridegroom. Humility is contrary to the natural man; but we are to take this kernel, this seed of humility and meekness, and wear it close to our heart for our Beloved Bridegroom to enjoy its fragrance all the day long and into the night while we sleep.

Myrrh is a product of the land of Canaan. It is sold for medicinal purposes in globules of a white and yellow color. It is also used for embalming purposes. It was used as a valuable gift. It was often used as an anesthetic. In Ester 2:12, it was used for purification before she visited the king. In Proverbs 7:17, we read, *"I have perfumed my bed with myrrh, aloes, and cinnamon."* In Psalm 45:8, we read, *"All thy garments smell of myrrh, and aloes, and cassia, out of the ivory palaces, whereby they have made thee glad."* In Matthew 27:34, it is said they gave Jesus to drink of vinegar mixed with gall, which in Mark 15:23 is called wine mingled with myrrh. Jesus refused to have His senses deadened. The aloes (temperance) was well known to the Greeks and to the Arabians. It is a large tree with lanceolate leaves; the wood contains a resin, and an oil, which furnished the perfume prized in those days. This perfume came from the oil thickening into resin within the trunk. Without knowledge of the God-given spices, we can never understand the Song of Solomon: the bride and His Bridegroom. This was brought by wise men as a present to Jesus (Matthew 2), and used for embalming (John 19:39). In Genesis 37:25 and 43:11, it is mentioned.

(2) *SWEET CINNAMON:* This spice speaks of goodness. It is extracted from the inner bark of a tree. This tree attains the height of perhaps 30 feet (Naves Bible). We are told the oil of cinnamon is obtained from the coarser pieces of bark, and by boiling the ripe fruit, a finer oil is obtained to be used for the burning of incense. According to Strongs Concordance, this word is from an un used root meaning "to erect," or "upright." The beauty of Holiness is the beauty of "goodness." This fragrance of the cinnamon, which the oil for anointing contained, filled the tabernacle day and night. The goodness of the

Spirit is always erect and upright. It never bends or sways. It prefers others in its place.

(3) *CALAMUS:* Speaks of gentleness. What a beautiful fruit and one to be desired above all else. It comes from a Hebrew word meaning "reed." This was a species of sweet cane, and became most fragrant when bruised. Jesus was anointed with the Spirit of gentleness. Even when the enemy came to take Him from the garden, and Peter cut off the man's ear, Jesus in compassion and gentleness reached out and healed the man. We are instructed to be anointed with the oil of sweet calamus. In 2 Timothy we read, *"And the servant of the Lord must not strive; but be gentle unto all men, apt to teach, patient."* We read of this gentleness in James 3:17: *"But the wisdom that is from above is first pure, then peaceable, gentle, and easy to be intreated, full of mercy and good fruits, without partiality, and without hypocrisy."*

(4) *CASSIA:* This word comes from the Hebrew word which means "to bend the neck of the head." It represents surrender. Our blessed Lord set this example of surrender for us all through His ministry. In Isaiah 53:7, we read, *"He was oppressed, and he was afflicted, yet he opened not his mouth: he was brought as a lamb to the slaughter, and as a sheep before her shearers is dumb, so he opened not his mouth"* (Matthew 27:14). In 1 Peter 2:21-23, we read, *"For even hereunto were ye called: because Christ also suffered for us, leaving us an example, that ye should follow his steps: Who did no sin, neither was guile found in his mouth: Who, when he was reviled, reviled not again; when he suffered, he threatened not; but committed himself to him that judg-*

eth righteously:'' Few exist in the churches today who want to be anointed with the oil of cassia, or "surrender."

This anointing oil was to be mixed with the olive oil. This oil had many uses in the Bible, which we have discussed previously. We must stay before the Lord to receive a fresh anointing from Him each day.

Sweet Spices Used At Altar Of Incense

"And the Lord said unto Moses, Take unto thee sweet spices, stacte, and onycha, and galbanum; these sweet spices with pure frankincense: of each shall there be a like weight: And thou shalt make it a perfume, a confection after the art of the apothecary, tempered together, pure and holy: And thou shalt beat some of it very small, and put of it before the testimony in the tabernacle of the congregation, where I will meet with thee: it shall be unto you most holy. And as for the perfume which thou shalt make, ye shall not make to yourselves according to the composition thereof: it shall be unto thee holy for the Lord. Whosoever shall make like unto that, to smell thereto, shall even be cut off from his people.'' (*Exodus 30:34-38*)

(1) STACTE: This word in Hebrew means "to drop or distil." While the PURE MYRRH was secured from a deep incision into the heart of the tree, the stacte was a sap which came from a voluntary giving of the tree itself. The little drops of life just came out and stood like tears upon the trunk of the tree. (Just another form of the myrrh sap flowing from the tree.) JEHOVAH IN THE FLESH came down to this earth, humbled Himself, and took upon Himself the flesh of man. He voluntarily gave His life that we might live.

(2) *ONYCHA:* The Hebrew word means "scale." We are told that it is the operculum of shells of Strombi, and is prepared for use by ROASTING, which evolves an empyreumatic oil, from which its aromatic properties depend. It must also be noted that the onycha derived its perfume or odor from feeding on the spikenard. The spikenard produced in the onycha made it possible for God to use it in the incense for His Golden Altar where worship would continue through the day and through the night. The spikenard mentioned in the Song of Solomon was the third plant, and pictured the third fruit which is PEACE. That adds to our understanding of the use of the onycha in the incense. Jesus is our peace. Onycha was taken from a ground shellfish, or from a perfume crab from the Red Sea. This incense flows from the Spirit of His Son from within. The ROASTING speaks to us of the EXPIATORY work of the Lord Jesus in our behalf. The word expiatory means "the power to make atonement of reconciliation." Precious is the knowledge of the incense. The priest need not fear as he ministered in the Tabernacle if he had the incense on the altar made according to the pattern which God had given to Moses. Nothing could be added or taken away; in this the priest had perfect PEACE. *"Peace I leave with you, my peace I give unto you: not as the world giveth, give I unto you. Let not your heart be troubled, neither let it be afraid"* (John 14:27).

(3) *GALBANUM:* The chief ministry of the galbanum was to increase the perfume of the incense nd to support it, causing it to last longer. Jesus is our STRENGTH and SUPPORT. We are told that this ingredient had an offensive odor used to drive away insects. It is

159

from a Hebrew word meaning "fatty" (Strong Concordance). This speaks of the best part of the sacrifice. It was a sap or gum that came from a broken shrub in the highlands of Syria. Note that one must climb to obtain it. He is the one on whom we can lean for our STRENGTH AND SUPPORT.

(4) *FRANKINCENSE:* In Hebrew this means "white" which stands for purity and righteousness. Some feel that this spice came from a tree having flowers with five petals (grace), and ten (redemption) stamens and fruit with five sides that grew upon the rocks (Isaiah 53:2). This speaks to us of ministry and responsibility. Again, when we compare this seventh plant found in the Song of Solomon with the seventh fruit found in Galatians 5:22, we learn that frankincense and faith go together. Frankincense becomes a picture of faith, wisdom, and UNDERSTANDING for we have had the "eyes of our understanding enlightened" (Ephesians 1). Frankincense also speaks of loneliness. It came from a tree that was pierced during the night, letting the sap flow out during the dark hours. This speaks to us, of course, of Gethsemane or Calvary.

(5) *SALT:* There was yet another ingredient to add to all we have set forth. All this was to be tempered with SALT. Of these four ingredients, it was said that each should be of equal weight or portion, which speaks to us of the evenness and the importance of each part of the revelation of His Name and Ministry. In the salt we note the clue to all that was contained in Him as our SAVIOUR. One writer pointed out to us that these five ingredients came from (1) vegetable kingdom: stacte, galbanum,

frankincense; (2) animal kingdom: onycha; and (3) the mineral kingdom: salt.

Salt was used on all offerings unto the Lord: *"And every oblation of thy meat offering shalt thou season with salt: neither shalt thou suffer the salt of the covenant of thy God to be lacking from thy meat offering: with all thine offerings thou shalt offer salt"* (Leviticus 2:13). The salt of the covenant spoke of purity of friendship and freedom from corruption, or everlasting loyalty. It speaks of covenant.

It is very interesting to note that the "covenant of salt," even to this day, is so highly respected that even a thief who comes in contact with it will adhere to the covenant of loyalty and friendship, and dismiss his purpose or motive of robbing when it is discovered it is a friend. In Numbers, we read of God making a covenant of salt with the family of Aaron: *"And the flesh of them shall be thine, as the wave breast and as the right shoulder are thine. All the heave offerings of the holy things which the children of Israel offer unto the Lord, have I given thee, and thy sons and thy daughters with thee, by a statute forever: it is a covenant of salt forever before the Lord unto thee and to thy seed with thee."* God was saying that with a covenant of salt He promised to feed and give them their portion forever. Jesus said He came to give us life, and give it to us more abundantly. Jesus said that we are the salt of this earth, and that we must not lose our flavor. In Mark 9:49-50, we read,, *"For every one shall be salted with fire, and every sacrifice shall be salted with salt. Salt is good: but if the salt have lost his saltness, witherwith will ye season it? Have salt in yourselves, and have peace one with another."*

In the middle east one might refer to a friend by saying, "There is salt between us." That means they regularly eat together and pass salt. One might also say, "He has eaten my salt." A person brought up in such a covenant environment would never think of "passing salt," then betraying or dealing treacherously (International Standard Bible Encyclopedia).

The salt would keep the incense pure for it has an enduring quality. Salt is used for seasoning; it is used for flavor or seasoning; it irritates the open wound. In Colossians 4:6, we read, *"Let your speech be always with grace, SEASONED WITH SALT, that ye may know how ye ought to answer every man."*

According To Pattern

"And let them make me a sanctuary; that I may dwell among them. According to all that I shew thee, after the pattern of all the instruments thereof, even so shall ye make it. And look hat thou make them after their pattern, which was shewed thee in the mount."

(Exodus 15:8-9; 40)

"Who serve unto the example and shadow of heavenly things, as Moses was admonished of God when he was about to make the tabernacle: for, See, saith he, that thou make all things according to the pattern shewed to thee in the mount." *(Hebrews 3:5)*

We need to be aware of the fact that there are a total of 50 chapters in the Bible furnishing scriptural background for the Tabernacle: Exodus has 13; Leviticus has 18; Numbers has 13; Deuteronomy has 2; Hebrews has 4. The tabernacle was a place where God could dwell with His people; teach them His Holiness; cause them to see

162

Cross-Section of Tabernacle

- ELLIOTT

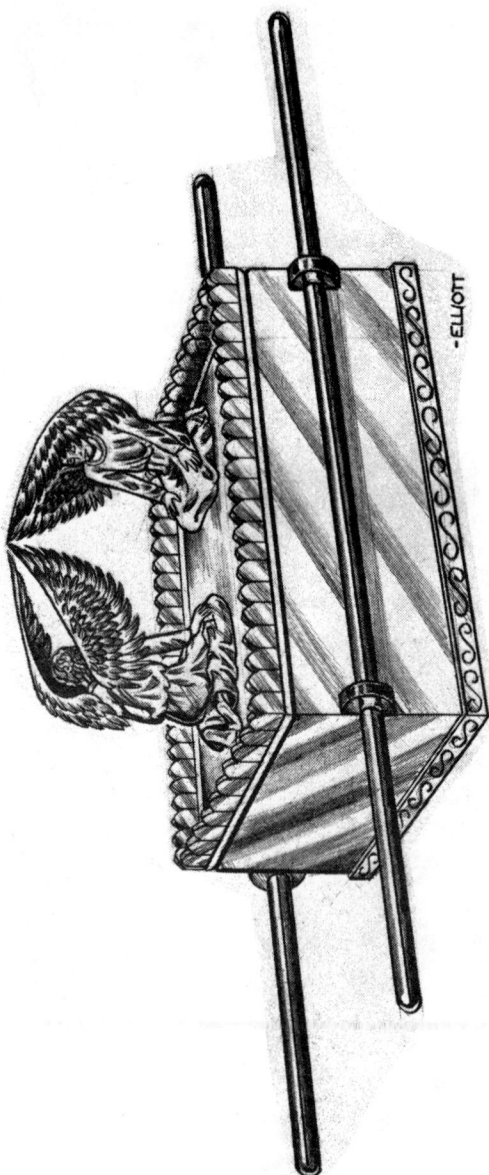

Ark – Mercy Seat – Cherubim

Golden Alter of Incense

Golden Candlestick

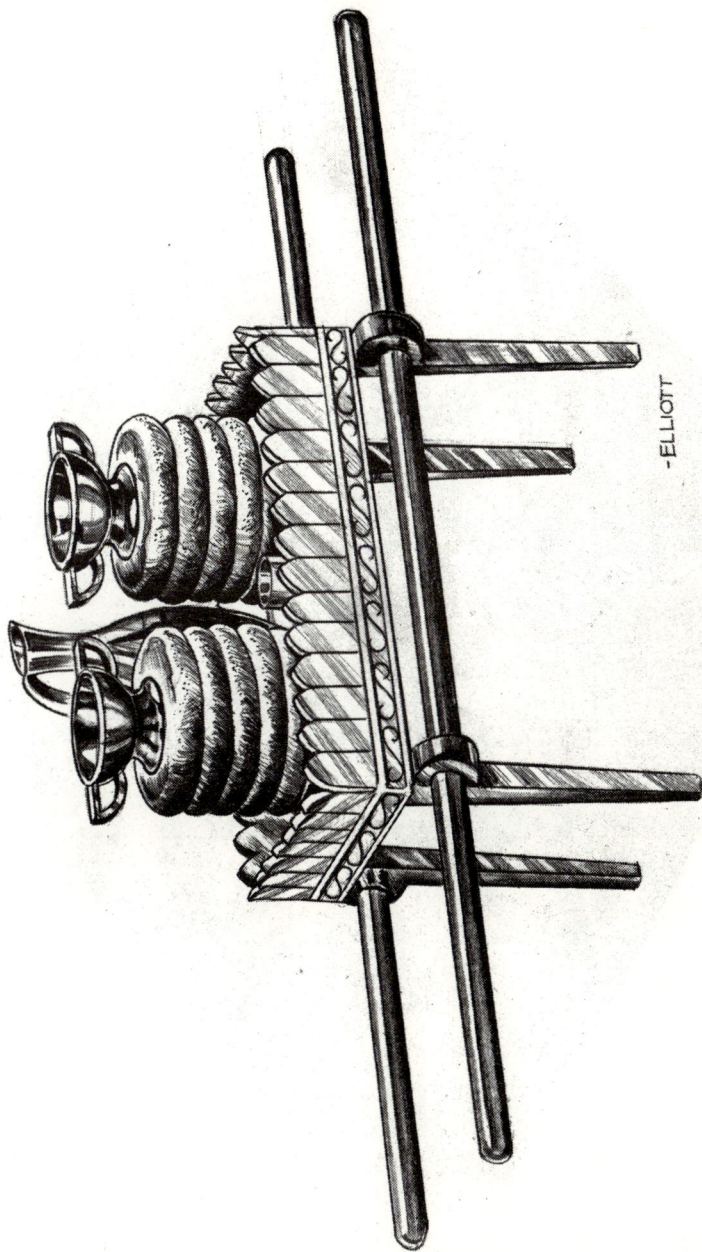

Table of Shrewbread

—ELLIOTT

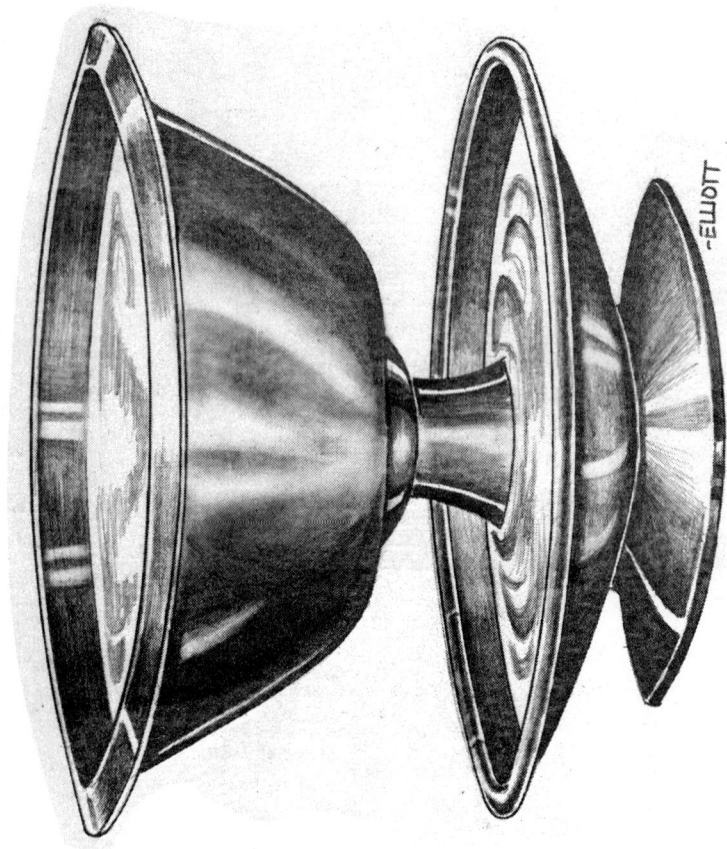

-ELLIOTT-

Brazen Altar

their own sinfulness; and teach His people how to approach Him through sacrifice.

The tabernacle was an oblong structure, 45 feet long, and 15 feet wide and high. It was constructed of boards of shittim wood, which was a peculiarly indestructible material, overlaid with gold, and fastened with sockets and tenons of silver and brass. It was covered with three tiers or layers of skins, and a final interior lining of very costly curtains, embroidered and adorned with symbolical figures of the highest beauty and spiritual significance. The outside covering of the roof was of rough badgers' skins to protect it from the inclemency of the weather. The exact form of the roof is not clear. The tabernacle itself was divided into two unequal chambers by magnificent curtains called "The Veil." We will cover this more in detail as we follow the scriptural outline. The inner chamber was a perfect cube, fifteen feet square. It housed the ark of the covenant, over which was the mercy seat, which was its lid, and consisted of a solid plate of gold. Then, formed of the same piece of solid gold, hovered the cherubim. Between their wings the Lord God met with His people. This was the Holy of Holies, where none but the High Priest entered once a year.

THE FOUR GOSPELS:

Book:	Color:	Written To:	Type:	Symbol:
Matthew	Purple	Jews	King	Lion
Mark	Scarlet	Romans	Servant	Ox
Luke	White	Greeks	Son-Man	Man
John	Blue	Christians	Spirit	Eagle

In Matthew, we see Jesus as the Lion from the tribe of Judah, who has conquered for us. This is the kingdom book. In Mark, we see Him as the suffering servant who carries all our burdens. In Luke, we view Him as the Son of man; the perfect man. The book of John teaches us to soar up into the heavens as the eagle. Jesus is viewed as Deity. In this book He promised the advent of the Holy Spirit after His resurrection.

The Three Sections Of The Tabernacle

    I. THE OUTER COURT—TYPE OF THE FLESH
        A. BRAZEN ALTAR—BURNT OFFERINGS (SACRIFICES)
        B. LAVER—CLEANSING BEFORE ENTERING HOLY PLACE
    II. THE HOLY PLACE—TYPE OF SOULISH MAN
        A. CANDLESTICK—JESUS IS THE LIGHT
        B. TABLE OF SHEWBREAD—JESUS IS THE BREAD
        C. ALTAR OF INCENSE—JESUS OUR INTERCESSOR
    III. THE HOLY OF HOLIES—TYPE OF THE SPIRITUAL MAN
        A. ARK OF THE COVENANT
            (1) law
            (2) manna
            (3) rod
        B. MERCY SEAT—PROPITIATION

The Ark

The first of the Holy vessels described and commanded by the Lord to be made was the Ark, with its cover—the Mercy Seat. Though these two pieces of furniture form one, they are mentioned separately. It is interesting to note that God began with Himself and worked out towards man. Without the Ark, the rest would have been meaningless. This Ark was to be placed in the Holy of Holies, which is symbolic of God's throne room; in the Holy of Holies the Glory of God would be the light. The Ark would rest in the Shekinah-Presence of the Lord. Man could not come to God unless He had first come to man. Throughout all the years that the tabernacle was in existence, until Solomon's Temple was built, this 15-foot cubic room housed the Ark of God.

"And they shall make an ark of shittim wood: two cubits and a half shall be the length thereof, and a cubit and a half the breadth thereof, and a cubit and a half the height thereof. And thou shalt overlay it with pure gold, within and without shalt thou overlay it, and shalt make upon it a crown of gold round about. And thou shalt cast four rings of gold for it, and put them in the four corners thereof; and two rings shall be in the one side of it, and two rings in the other side of it. And thou shalt make staves of shittim wood, and overlay them with gold. And thou shalt put the staves into the rings by the sides of the ark, that the ark may be borne with them. The staves shall be in the rings of the ark: they shall not be taken from it. And thou shalt put into the ark the testimony which I shall give thee."

(Exodus 37:10-16)

"Then verily the first covenant had also ordinances of divine service, and a worldly sanctuary. For there was a tabernacle made; the first, wherein was the candlestick, and the table, and the shewbread; which is called the sanctuary. And after the second veil, the tabernacle which is called the Holiest of all; Which had the golden censer, and the ark of the covenant overlaid round about with gold, wherein was the golden pot that

172

had manna, and Aaron's rod that budded, and the tables of the law covenant; And over it the cherubims of glory shadowing the mercy seat; of which we cannot now speak particularly." (Hebrews 9:1-15)

The heavenly sanctuary is spoken of for the first time in Hebrews 8:2. We have a High Priest who is at the right hand of the Father in Heaven: *"A minister of the sanctuary, and of the true tabernacle, which the Lord pitched, and not man."* He is the Mediator of a new and better covenant. The discussion is then continued in Hebrews chapter 9 where we learn of the peculiar and indescribable value of His sacrifice to take away sin once and for all. To understand fully the book of Hebrews, one must study the tabernacle in the wilderness and see it in type. With the passing of this old economy, we have entered into the Holy of Holies where we are kings and priests unto the Lord. We have had the veil rent (torn) so that we may live in the very presence of the God of our salvation.

God did not add to the Old Covenant; He did not redo the Levitical priesthood and the Mosaic economy; He wrote His laws on the tables of our hearts that we might obey Him and forever reign with Him. The key word in the book of Hebrews is "better." Jesus is the mediator of better things for us. However, the earthly tabernacle, as we have noted, supplied a type representing the Person, work, and ministry of the Lord Jesus. Since the outer court of the tabernacle was accessible to all the people, the book of Hebrews does not include it. It had no roof, and everything connected with it was minutely and completely fulfilled by our Lord Jesus Christ in the days of His flesh, at which time He was openly manifested before all men.

The Ark was the figure of the incarnate, virgin-born Son of God, and the word used for it should have been translated "incorruptible" wood. This typified the perfect and sinless humanity of Jesus. This incorruptible wood was overlaid within and without with pure gold. This in type is the Divine Glory of our Lord—God in flesh. The two materials used for the ark, the wood and the gold united, symbolized the union of God and man in Christ His Son. In 1 Timothy 3:16, we read, *"It is quite true that the way to live a godly life is not an easy matter. But the answer lies in Christ, who came to earth as a man, was proved spotless and pure in his Spirit, was served by angels, was preached among the nations, was accepted by men everywhere, and was received up again to his glory in heaven."* (TLB).

Shittim wood, we understand, is of a very hard, close-grained nature, and in this we are reminded of the lesson of durability in the face of all adversity. Jesus was tempted in all points, as we are, yet He never failed the test. This wood would not rot, swell, or shrink. It was found in the area where the children of Israel were camped. The Lord did not tell them to make the ark of cedars, for they are found in Labanon; He did not say oak, or gopher wood, for they are found in Palestine; He used a wood that was within their reach. In Isaiah 53:2, we read, *"For he shall grow up before him as a tender plant, and as a root out of a dry ground: he hath no form nor comeliness; and when we shall see him, there is no beauty that we should desire him."* When Jesus came to fallen man, He did not come in the form of an angel, but took upon Himself the form of man with a body of flesh that He might prove to be our perfect example. We should note that since this shittim wood grew in the desert, its root went deep down into subterranean waters; it was not dependent upon external sources of moisture for its growth. Jesus declared throughout His earthly ministry that He was dependent upon the Heavenly Father for His life. He said He could do nothing except what was told Him by God. His moisture was from the God of Glory.

Ark Description

(1) It was placed in the Holy of Holies on an earthen flood. This tells us that the whole earth will be filled with the Glory of the Lord. *"For the earth shall be filled with the knowledge of the glory of the Lord, as the waters cover the sea"* (Habakkuk 1:14). In Numbers 14:21, we read, *"But as truly as I live, all the earth shall be filled with the glory of the Lord."*

(2) It was an oblong-shaped chest (box) that measured 3 feet by 9 inches. (Same height as the table of Shewbread, and the grate of the Brazen Altar.) Man is brought to the Blood of the Cross that he might come to the Mercy Seat, and the Table of Communion; (3′ × 9″ L; 2′ × 3″ W; 2′ × 3″ H).

(3) It was made of shittim wood (Incorruptible Word).

(4) It was overlaid with gold; and it was lined from within with gold. We have been told the Jews teach that this box was made in three, and put into one. Two were made of gold, and one was put in between. The GOLD without is the FATHER; the GOLD within is the HOLY SPIRIT, Who dwells within; and the CENTRAL WOOD is

the SON, crucified in the MIDST. *"Where they crucified him, and two other with him, on either side one, and Jesus in the midst"* (John 19:18).

(5) It had a crown of gold (trimming). Three pieces of the furniture were crowned: the Ark, the Golden Altar, and the Table of Shewbread; this speaks of the Kingship and Headship of Jesus. In Hebrews 2:9, we read, *"But we see Jesus, who was made a little lower than the angels for the suffering of death, crowned with glory and honour; that He by the grace of God should taste death for every man.* In Matthew 2:2, we read, *"Saying, Where is he that is born King of the Jews . . .?"* In John 19:14, we read, *". . . and he saith unto the Jews, Behold your King!"* After man had crowned Him with thorns, the Lord God crowned Him with Glory and Honour. This border, or wreathed work, served to "bind together" the Ark and the Mercy Seat lest, during its journey home, the priest stumbled and the Ark was displaced.

(6) It had four rings of gold and two staves of shittim wood overlaid in gold. Four is the universal number indicating a love that will be carried into the entire world; the message will reach to the four corners of the earth. The message is the Life of Christ found in the four gospels. It is the message of the Kingdom of God; the Priesthood of the Lord Jesus forever after the order of Melchisedec. In Hebrews 7:14-17, we read, *For it is evident that our Lord sprang out of Juda; of which tribe Moses spake nothing concerning priesthood. And it is yet far more evident: for that after the similitude of Melchisedec there ariseth another priest, Who is made, not after the law of a carnal commandment, but after the power of an endless life. For he testifieth, Thou art a priest forever*

after the order of Melchisedec.'' The Ark was made to be carried by four priests. The Gold always speaks of Deity. The rings and the staves will help them keep the Ark balanced as they move in their journey towards the Promised Land.

Staves

These two staves were made of shittim wood overlaid with gold. What is contained within the Ark must be carried in balance. Some have written that the rings were justice and holiness, while grace and truth were on each side, with the atoning Blood in–between. These staves were never to be taken from the rings. The Ark was to be ready for moving, for God would not have a permanent dwelling in the desert. However, when the Ark was later brought to Solomon's Temple, the staves were removed, the priests withdrew, and the Shekinah glory came down. Here Israel had established a permanent home. When John saw the Ark in the heavens, there was mention of staves. All of this represents the thrown of God's Glory in the midst of Israel.

"And Bezaleel made the Ark of Shittim wood: two cubits and a half was the length of it, and a cubit and a half the breadth of it, and a cubit and a half the height of it. And he overlaid it with pure gold within and without." (Exodus 35:2)

The Mercy Seat With The Cherubim

"And thou shalt make a mercy seat of pure gold: two cubits and a half shall be the length thereof, and a cubit and a half the breadth thereof. And thou shalt make two cherubims of gold, of beaten work shalt thou

*make them, in the two ends of the mercy seat. And make
one cherub on the one end, and the other cherub on the
other end:even of the mercy seat shall ye make the cherubims on the two ends thereof. And the cherubims shall
stretch forth their wings on high, covering the mercy
seat with their wings, and their faces shall look one to
another; toward the mercy seat shall the faces of the
cherubims be. And thou shalt put the mercy seat above
upon the ark; and in the ark thou shalt put the testimony that I shall give thee. And there I will commune
with thee from above the mercy seat, from between the
two cherubims which are upon the ark of the testimony,
of all things which I will give from above the mercy seat,
from between the two cherubims which are upon the
ark of the testimony, of all things which I will give thee
in commandment unto the children of Israel.''*

(Exodus 25:17-22)

The Mercy Seat was made of a slab of solid gold; the
same size as the Ark; it had no wood in it. This was the lid
or cover for the Ark; in type, it symbolizes the Lord Jesus
as our Propitiation. This Mercy Seat was where the blood
of atonement was applied. The Mercy Seat was made to
completely cover the Ark. It served as a protection for its
contents. An open Ark would signify a place of justice and
judgment. Man would have no hope if he stood before an
open Ark and its contents. God told Moses to place the
Mercy Seat over the Law; and it was sprinkled with the
Blood of the Lamb slain from the foundation of the world.
This golden Mercy Seat is mentioned 27 times in the Old
Testament (3x3x3).

The Hebrew verb "kaphar," from which comes the
noun "kapporeth," means "to cover the sins" or " to rec-

oncile," "to make atonement." Did not Job cry out, "I have found a ransom.."? He declared long before the time of Moses that he had found a covering (Job 33:24). "To make an atonement" is found 77 times in the Old Testament (7x11). God would be represented by the number seven, and man by the number eleven (incomplete).

"And he made the Mercy Seat of pure gold: two cubits and a half was the length thereof, and one cubit and a half the breadth thereof. And he made two cherubims of gold, beaten out of one piece made he them, on the two ends of the Mercy Seat; one cherub on the end of this side, and another cherub on the other end of that side; out of the Mercy Seat made he the cherubims on the two ends thereof. And the cherubims, spread out their winds over the Mercy Seat, with their faces one to another; even to the Mercy Seatward were the faces of the cherubims." (Exodus 37:6-9)

"For there is one God, and one mediator between God and men, the man Christ Jesus; Who gave himself a ransom for all, to be testified in due time."
(Timothy 2:5-6)

"My little children, these things write I unto you, that ye sin not. And if any man sin, we have an advocate with the Father, Jesus Christ the righteous: And He is the propitiation for our sins: and not for ours only, but also for the sins of the whole world." (1 John 2:1-2)

"For all have sinned, and come short of the glory of God; Being justified freely by his grace through the redemption that is in Christ Jesus: Whom God hath set forth to be a propitiation through faith in his blood, to declare his righeousness for the remission of sins that

are past, through for forebearance of God; To declare, I say, at this time his righteousness; that he might be just, and the justifier of him which believeth in Jesus.''
(Romans 3:21-26)

"The Greek word "propitiation" found in Romans 3:35, is the identical one translated "Mercy–Seat" in Hebrews 9:5. God Himself presents Christ before us as the antitypical Mercy-Seat. *"And every priest standeth daily ministering and offering oftentimes the same sacrifices, which can never take away sins: But this man, after he had offered one sacrifice for sins forever, sat down on the right hand of God"* (Hebrews 10:11-12).

"Herein is love, not that we loved God, but that he loved us, and sent his Son to be the propitiation for our sins."
(1 John 4:10)

We need to note that the Mercy Seat was not the place where propitiation was made. It was the place where the high priest placed the blood of the sacrifice. Propitiation was made at the brazen altar; brass being a symbol of God's judgment. The book of Hebrews is written to prove that Jesus has replaced the figures. The verb "to propitiate" signifies to appease, to placate, to make saitisfaction. Thus, in Romans 3, Christ is set forth a Propitiatory, signifying that through the Gospel, God now bears testimony to His blessed Son as the One by whom He was propitiated; the One by whom His holy wrath against sin was pacified; the One by whom the righteous demands of His law were satisfied; the One by whom every attribute of Deity was glorified. We are carefully taught that Christ as "the propitiation for our sins" is the bleeding victim on the altar; the type of Christ as God's resting place or Propitiatory is the Mercy Seat within the veil. Christ has become God's rest, in whom He can now meet poor sinners in all the fullness of His grace because of the propitiation made by Him on the cross.

In the Tabernacle there was a table, but no chair for Aaron or any of the priests to sit on, because their work was never finished; it had to be repeated constantly signifying that the One great Sacrifice was yet to come to bring final rest. The seat (Mercy Seat) was God's throne; He sat there between the Cherubim; one on each end facing the other. They were to guard the holiness and righteousness of God. When God cast Adam and Eve out of the garden after the fall, He placed cherubim with flaming swords to guard the tree of life. Aaron's rod that budded was placed in the Mercy Seat; therefore, the tree of life was still guarded by the cherubim, since this rod is emblamic of resurrection life.

The Bible says "Cherubim, singular because the two were beaten out of one piece of gold. The Cherubim on both ends of the Mercy Seat were not to be seperated; just like the Candlestick, they were beaten out of one piece of gold. God provided special craftmanship for this job. If we separated the Cherubim, we would break the Mercy Seat. They are symbols of power and guardianship. The fact that they looked one to the other and towards the Mercy speaks to us of agreement and harmony. The number two suggests "unity" to us. The beaten work to form the Cherubim pointed towards the suffering of Christ yet to come.

"Give ear, O shepherd of Israel, thou that leadest Joseph like a flock; thou that dwellest between the cherubims, shine forth." *(Psalms 80:1)*

"The Lord reigneth; let the people tremble: he sitteth between the cherubims; let the earth be moved."

(Psalms 99:1)

In the book of Ezekiel the Cherubim are represented as four living creatures everyone having four faces — the face of a man, a lion, an ox, and an eagle; a study too lengthy to be considered at this point. It is impossible to over-estimate the importance of God's satisfaction in the Blood of His Son for the sins of the entire world. He rests between the Cherubim where the Blood has been sprinkled. There we view Blessed Communion between God and man through Christ.

The Contents of The Ark
(Symbolic of the Godhead)
Law: God

We have previously read from Hebrews the contents of the Ark. The Ark being a symbol of protection, care, and preservation, held the law for safekeeping. The law of God was in the heart of Jesus to keep and preserve it; He fulfilled every aspect of it.

"Take this book of the law, and put it in the side of the ark of the convenant of the Lord your God, that it may be there for witness against thee."

(Deuteronomy 31:26)

The moral law was first given to Moses orally (Exodus 19:19). It was then given upon stone tablets prepared by God and written by God. Moses broke these tablets when he saw Israel in idolatry, and God instructed him to hew two tablets like unto the first and come back up the mountain. God wrote the law upon these tablets and they were eventually put into His ark. These moral laws are divided into two parts: our relationship with God, and our relationship with man.

GODWARD:

> Have no other God
>
> Worship no image
>
> Reverence His Name
>
> Keep His Holy Day in Honour of Him

MANWARD:

> Honour parents
>
> Do not kill
>
> Do not commit adultery
>
> Do not steal
>
> Do not lie
>
> Do not covet

Jesus gave a commadment that covered all these laws: *"Jesus said unto him, Thou shalt love the Lord thy God with all thy heart, and with all thy soul, and with all thy mind. This is the first and great commandment. And the second is like unto it, Thou shalt love thy neighbour as thyself. On there two commandments hang all the law and the prophets" (Matthew 22:37-40).*

The law condemned everyone; only Christ could fulfill it. We are kept from the judgment of the law by the blood which had been sprinkled on the golden lid. Paul tells us in Romans 6:14, that sin is not to dominate us: *"For sin shall not have dominion over you: for ye are not under the law, but under grace."*

"Think not that I am come to destroy, but to fulfill."   *(Matthew 5:17)*

"Wherefore the law was our schoolmaster to bring us to Christ, that we are no longer under a schoolmaster."   *(Galatians 3:24-25*

Praise God! The law led us to Jesus Christ when we fled to Him for refuge, and He keeps the demands of the law under lid and cover. He fulfilled the law and set us free that we might reign forever with Him.

The Golden Pot of Manna

The Son

The first mention of manna was in regard to one of the many complaints and murmurings of the children of Israel after God led them out of bondage and into the wilderness. In Exodus 16:14-15, we read, *"And when the dew that lay was gone up, behold, upon the face of the wilderness there lay a small round thing, as small as the hoar frost on the ground. And when the children of Israel saw it, they said one to another, It is manna: for they wist not what it was. And Moses said unto them, This is the bread which the Lord hath given you to eat."*

In Numbers 11:7-9 we read, *"And the manna was as coriander seed, and the colour thereof as the colour of bdellium. And the people went about, and gathered it, and ground it in mills, or beat it in a mortar, and baked it in pans, and made cakes of it; and the taste of it was as the taste of fresh oil. And when the dew fell upon the camp in the night, the manna fell upon it."* This is a most beautiful picture of Christ. In John 6:32-33, Jesus stated, *"Verily, verily, I say unto you, Moses gave you not that bread from heaven. For the bread of God is he which cometh down from heaven, and giveth life unto the world.''* It is beautiful to realize that the dew (Holy Spirit) fell first, and then the manna followed, signifying that the Holy Spirit came to uplift and lead us to Jesus. They were instructed in the wilderness to gather only what they needed for that day; nothing could be stored until the next day. Jesus is our portion from Heaven, and we must feed daily upon Him for He is the Bread of life. This manna was white, which speaks of His purity. It tasted like fresh oil, which speaks of His anointing and suffering for our sake, since oil is brought forth by crushings. The Pot of Manna in the Ark served to remind the children of Israel that God was their Provision.

"He that hath an ear, let him hear what the Spirit saith unto the churches. To him that overcometh will I give to eat of the hidden manna, and will give him a white stone, and in the stone a new name written, which no man knoweth saving he that receiveth it."

(Revelation 2:17)

"And Jesus said unto them, I am the bread of life, he that cometh to me shall never hunger; and he that believeth on me shall never thrist. But I said unto you, That ye also have seen me, and believe not. All that the Father giveth me shall come to me; and him that cometh to me I will in no wise cast out. For I came down from heaven, not to do mine own will, but the will of him that sent me. And this is the Father's will which has sent me, that of all which he hath given me I should lose nothing, but should raise it up again at the last day. And this is the will of him that sent me, that every one which seeth the Son, and believeth on him, may have

*everlasting life: and I will raise him up at the last day.
The Jews then murmured at him, because he said, I am
the bread which came down from heaven. Your fathers
did eat manna in the wilderness, and are dead. This is
the bread which cometh down from heaven, that a man
may eat thereof, and not die. I am the living bread
which came down from heaven: if any man shall live
forever: and the bread that I will give is my flesh, which
I will give for the life of the world."*

(John 6:35-41;49-51)

Aaron's Rod That Budded

Holy Spirit

Resurrection

This rod that came to life speaks of Jesus in resurrection. Aaron's Rod was a dead almond stick that was laid
up before the Testimony and overnight it budded and
blossomed. This speaks of the Messiah Who was dead, but
is now alive forevermore; we will study this story later in
Numbers 16-17. The budding of Aaron's Rod was a supernatural act of God due to rebellion in the camp; they
questioned Aaron's Priesthood. On the ledger side of the
children of Israel, we have: (1) broken law; (2) denied
the manna; and (3) rejected the Priesthood of Aaron. All
three were stored in the Ark. As we have stated, the Rod
that budded is representative of Christ in His Resurrection; the blossoms portray His beauty of character. He is
the Rose of Sharon. We know that almonds in Hebrew
means "the hastener." The almond tree is the first to blossom in the spring, and bears the first fruit of the spring
season. Jesus is referred to as the "firstfruits," in 1 Cor-

inthians 15:20: *"But now is Christ risen from the dead, and become the firstfruits of them that slept."* In John 12:24, we read, *"Verily, verily, I say unto you, Except a corn of wheat fall into the gound and die, it abideth along: but if it die, it bringeth forth much fruit."* God raised up Jesus from the dead. God chose Him to be the High Priest forever after the order of Melchisedec. The Ark dwelt among the children of God to protect them.

Journey Of The Ark

At Mount Sinai

We will only list the history of the ark as revealed in the scriptures, since we will follow the Ark in our narrative of the encampment and wanderings of the children of Israel.

"And he took and put the testimony into the ark, and set the staves on the ark, and put the mercy seat above the ark; And he brought the ark into the tabernacle, and set up the vail of covering, and covered the ark of the testimony; as the Lord commanded Moses."

(Exodus 40:20-21)

a. It was built according to Divine Instructions from God.

b. Built by the enablement of the Spirit of Wisdom which was put within the heart of Bezaleel (Exodus 37:1-9).

c. The Ark was anointed by God with the Holy Oil (Exodus 30:26; 40:9, Acts 10:38).

d. The Ark was covered previous to each March (Numbers 4; 4-5).

e. The Lord always went before the Ark as He always goes before us. If this Ark moved without Divine directions it resulted in disaster and failures.

KADESH BARNEA — Numbers 14.
CROSSING THE JORDAN —Joshua 3:4
JERICHO TAKEN — Joshua 6.
AI — Joshua 7:2-5
SHILOH — I Samuel 1:3
DAGON OF ASHDOD — I Samuel 5:2
GATH THEN TO EKRON
BETH — SHEMESH — I Samuel 6:19
THE HOUSE OF ABINADAB (KIRJATH — JEARIM)
    I Samuel 7:1-2
NACHON'S THRESHINGFLOOD — II Samuel 6:6
HOUSE OF OBED — EDOM — II Samuel 6:10
JERUSALEM — II Samuel 6:12-19
DAVID PLACES THE ARK IN A TENT — II Samuel 7:2
THE ARK IN HEAVEN — Revelation 11:19

The Table Of Shewbread

"Thou shalt also make a table of shittim wood: two cubits shall be the length thereof, and a cubit the breadth thereof, and a cubit and a half the height thereof. And thou shalt overlay it with pure gold, and make thereto a crown of gold round about. And thou shalt make unto it a border of an hand breadth round about, and thou shalt make a golden crown to the border thereof round about. And thou shalt make for it four rings of gold, and put the rings in the four corners that are on the four feet thereof. Over against the border shall the rings be for places of the staves to bear the ta-

ble. And thou shalt make the staves of shittim wood, and overlay them with gold, that the table may be borne with them. And thou shalt make the dishes thereof, and spoons thereof, and covers thereof, and bowls thereof, to cover withall: of pure gold shalt thou make them. And thou shalt set upon the table shewbread before me alway." (Exodus 25:23-30)

"And thou shalt take fine flour, and bake twelve cakes thereof: two tenth deals shall be in one cake. And thou shalt set them in two rows, six on a row, upon the pure table before the Lord. And thou shalt put pure frankincense upon each row, that it may be on the bread for a memorial, even an offering made by fire unto the Lord. Every sabbath he shall set it in order before the Lord continually, being taken from the children of Israel by an everlasting covenant. And it shall be Aaron's and his sons'; and they shall eat it in the holy place: for it is most holy unto him of the offerings of the Lord made by fire by a perpetual statute."

(Leviticus 24:5-9)

We have now come to the third piece of furniture as we move from the Holy of Holies into the Holy Place; after we have become familiar with all seven pieces of furniture and their location in the tabernacle, we will, of course, study the tabernacle from the aspect of body, soul, and spirit (manward), as opposed to spirit, soul and body (Godward).

The table for the shewbread was made of shittim wood and ovelaid with gold. Again, this speaks of the humanity and the deity of the Lord Jesus Christ. In the complete Tabernacle we see the two-fold nature of our Lord

189

painted through the wood and the gold, or the wood and the brass. This shows us the measure of the stature of the Lord Jesus in that He was both human and Divine. In Ephesians 4:11-13, we read, *"And he gave some, apostles; and some, prophets; and some, evangelists: and some, pastors and teachers; For the perfecting of the saints, for the work of the ministry, for the edifying of the body of Christ: Till we all come in the unity of the faith, and of the knowledge of the Son of God, unto a perfect man, unto the measure of the stature of the fullness of Christ:"*

This table of shewbread was a picture of Jesus, who in His grace guarantees to us security in this life and the life hereafter. He has provided a means whereby we may come into the measure of the full stature of Him. This table is called "the pure table" and is mentioned twenty-one times by Moses: three times seven speaks of divine perfection. This table was made of acacia wood and covered with pure gold. After God gave Moses specific directions as to its measurements, He said that this table was to be made of "pure gold." Here it is easy to identify our Lord in His true humanity and, at the same time, in His true Godhead. We have already discussed the meaning of gold. Its measurements were: 3' L × 18" W × 27" H. The height is the same as the Ark. It is on the north side of the room, opposite the golden Candlestick (the table and the bread cannot be separated, any more than the Ark and its lid can be separated).

The same materials were used in the Ark as were used in the table. The word "shewbread" we are told really means "bread of His Presence," "Bread of Faces," "Bread of Orderings," or the "Continual Bread." The Crown of gold or decorative ornament all around the top kept the bread from falling off and becoming defiled. The four golden *rings,* two on each side, were for the *staves* which were wood overlaid with gold. The staves were passed through the rings in order to carry the Table when they traveled.

We must keep in mind that while these articles of furniture first and foremost speak to us of our Lord, they also include the Church. We cannot separate the body from the Head. God, then as now, set food on the table for us to be nourished as we journey in this life. This was a communion table.

Two Crowns

The crown was made of pure gold: all of God. The Crowns mentioned in the furniture find fulfillment in John 17, where our Lord offered up His intercessory prayer, and asked to be glorified with the glory that He had with the Father before the world took Him away. The Crown finds further fulfillment in 2 Timothy 1:12: *"For the which cause I also suffer these things: nevertheless I am not ashamed: for I know whom I have believed, and am persuaded that he is able to keep that which I have committed unto him against that day."* Paul was thoroughly convinced that the Crown was well able to keep him safe through the journey.

The Shewbread

One might easily say that the Bread was the fulfillment of God's provisions for His children. We must feed upon Him if we are to enter into the Holy of Holies for true worship. This Bread is the Body of Christ in type. The

Bread was made from fine flour which came forth after a grinding process; "fine flour" denoting there must be no imperfection found in it. This type is two-fold. It is Christ who maintained His sinless perfection in spite of the extreme sufferings He allowed while on this earth. *"This is my beloved Son, in whom I am well pleased"* (Mathew 3:17). Judas said, *"I have sinned in that I have betrayed the innocent blood"* (Matthew 27:4). Pilate said, *"I find no fault at all"* (John 18:38).

It also symbolizes the church (Christian) who keeps the faith though the enemy relentlessly stalks his prey. This Bread was baked, which means it was exposed to extreme heat. Our Lord suffered the fires of hell when He agonized in the garden before His crucifixion.

Twelve Cakes
(Two layers-six to each layer)

The word cakes, "challoth," actually means "pierced cakes." They were pierced to allow quick and thorough baking. This was all done in an extremely hot oven. At Calvary our Lord was pierced, and passed through the fires of God's judgment, then He became the Bread of Life, the sustainer and justifier of all.

On the table were: *dishes, spoons, bowls,* and *covers.* The dishes were for holding or conveying the bread; the spoons were for the incense, or the frankincense; the covers (to pour with) and bowls (cups) were for the wine, or drink offering. On the march, the Table was wrapped in a blue cloth, the utensils and bread wrapped in a scarlet cloth, and then there was a final covering of badger skins. Right in the midst of "no-man's land," God had provided a most delicious and satisfying meal for His children. He wanted to come and sit at the communion with them.

"Thou preparest a table before me in the presence of mine enemies." (Psalms 23:5)

May we make note of the word "also" used at the beginning of the text. This word is found only once in connection with the holy vessels and furnishings of the tabernacle. It suggests close link of connection with what has gone before. Previously God had said, *"And there will I meet with thee, and I will commune with thee from above the Mercy-seat,"* and then we are told, *"Thou shalt also make a table . . ."* and that is where He will fellowhsip with us.

"Ye cannot drink the cup of the Lord, and the cup of devils: ye cannot be partakers of the Lord's table, and of the table of devils." (1 Corinthians 10:21)

"For I have received of the Lord that which also I delivered unto you. That the Lord Jesus the same night in which he was betrayed took bread: And when he had given thanks, he brake it, and said, Take eat: this is my body, which is broken for you: this do in remembrance of me. After the same manner also he took the cup, when he had supped, saying, This cup is the new testament in my blood: this do ye, as oft as ye drink it, in remembrance of me. For as often as ye eat this bread, and drink this cup, ye do shew the Lord's death till he come. Wherefore whosoever shall eat this bread, and drink this cup of the Lord, unworthily, shall be guilty of the body and blood of the Lord. but let a man examine himself, and so let him eat of that bread, and drink of that cup. For he that eateth and drinketh unworthily, eateth and

drinketh damnation to himself, not discerning the Lord's body. For this cause many are weak and sickly among you, and many sleep.''

(1 Corinthians 11:23-30)

God gave Moses specific instructions (in later study) of how the priests were to minister at the table of communion. By reading the scriptures we have quoted above from the New Testament, we must allow the Holy Spirit to teach us the seriousness of the Table of the Lord. He said that the bread showed forth His presence. *''. . . Shewbread before Me always.''* How beautiful is the parallel between the Table in the Old Testament, and the Table in the New Testament.

Pure frankincense was put upon each row of the bread for a memorial unto the Lord. Frankincense is derived from a Hebrew root meaning ''to be pure and white.'' Every Sabbath these cakes were renewed so they would be continually before the Lord. Note that it is the frankincense that is burned before the Lord, and not the Bread. The frankincense of the Lord ever rises to the thrown on high through his anointed ones on this earth. We have value before the Lord because of Jesus. *''For we are the sweet fragrance of Christ (which exhales) unto God, (discernible alike) among those who are being saved and among those who are perishing''* (2 Corinthians 2:15, Amplified Bible). We are accepted in the beloved, according to Ephesians 1:6.

The Golden Lampstand

''And thou shalt make a candlestick of pure gold: of beaten work shall the candlestick be made: his shaft, and his branches, his bowls, his knops, and his flowers,

194

shall be of the same. And six branches shall come out of the sides of it; three branches of the candlestick out of the one side, and three branches of the candlestick out of the other side: Three bowls made like unto almonds, with a knop and a flower in one branch; and three bowls made like almonds in the other branch, with knop and a flower: so in the six branches that come out of the candlestick. And in the candlestick shall be four bowls made like unto almonds, with their knops and their flowers. And there shall be a knop under two branches of the same, and a knop under two branches of the same, and a knop under two branches of the same, according to the six branches that proceed out of the candlestick. Their knops and their branches shall be of the same: all it shall be one beaten work of pure gold. And thou shalt make the seven lamps thereof: and they shall light the lamps thereof, that they may give light over against it. And the tongs thereof, and the snuff-dishes thereof, shall be of pure gold. Of a talent of pure gold shall he make it, with all these vessels. And look that thou make them after their pattern, which was shewed thee in the moment.'' (Exodus 25:31-40)

"And he made the candlestick of pure gold: of beaten work made he the candlestick; his shaft, and his branch, his bowls, his knops, and his flowers, were of the same. And six branches going out of the sides thereof; three branches of the candletick out of the one side thereof, and three branches of the candlestick out of the other side thereof: Three bowls made after the fashion of almonds in one branch, a knop and a flower; and three bowls made like almonds in another branch, a knop and a flower: so throughout the six branches

going out of the candlestick. And in the candlestick were four bowls made like almonds, his knops, and his flowers: And a knop under two branches of the same, and a knop under two branches of the same, and a knop under two branches of the same, according to the six branches going out of it. Their knops and their branches were of the same: all of it was one beaten work of pure gold. And he made his seven lamps, and his snuffers, and his snuffdishes, of pure gold. Of a talent of pure gold made he it, and all the vessels thereof."

(Exodus 37:17-24)

The Easterners called lamps on a stand, "a candlestick." The Western mind thinks of it as a "lampstand" because oil is used in a lamp for the flame. Of course, the candle as we know it today was unknown to them. The Hebrew word "menorah" is brought into English as "candlestick," but it could be more correctly called, "a place of light," of pure gold. We note that this fourth piece of furniture has no wood; it is beaten out of pure gold. It stood on the south side of the Tabernacle. No dimensions are given for this article in the Tabernacle. It weighed around 125 pounds; today this Candelabra would probably cost close to half a million dollars. This Lamp is referred to in a personal, masculine pronoun—"His Shaft; His branches." It was beaten out of one bar of solid gold, which is a feat considered humanly impossible by today's craftsmen. God put wisdom in the heart of Bezaleel to do this work. All of the beauty of the interior of the Holy Place could only be seen by the light of this Lampstand. Nothing outside must penetrate this room. This was a chamber that only the priest and his family could enter. Each of the three vessels in this quarter of the Tabernacle stood for communion. There were no windows in the Tabernacle, for God was the Light within. In the New Testament, Jesus is called "the light" twenty-one times; as before stated, three times seven adds up to God's Perfection.

"And he said, It is a light thing that thou shouldest be my servant to raise up the tribes of Jacob, and to restore the preserved of Israel: I will also give thee for a light to the Gentiles, that thou mayest be my salvation unto the end of the earth."   *(Isiah 49:16)*

"As long as I am in the world, I am the light of the world."   *(John 9:5)*

"The word is a lamp unto my feet, and a light unto my path."   *(Psalms 119:105)*

"God is light, and in Him is no darkness at all."
                                               (1 John 1:5)

"That was the true light, which lighteth every man that cometh into the world."   *(John 1:9)*

We must remember that "beaten gold" tells of gold that has gone through the fire. This Lamp was not fashioned from a mold, but beaten, fashioned, and shaped according to the Wisdom of God. Christ is the Lampstand; He is the light of the world. We are the light of the world according to Matthew 5:14-16: *"Ye are the light of the world. A city that is set on a hill cannot be hid. Neither do men light a candle, and put it under a bushel, but on a candlestick; and it giveth light unto all that are in the house. Let your light so shine before men, that they may see your good works, and glorify your Father which is in heaven."*

197

"We have mentioned that gold is symbolic of Deity; here we have the Lampstand made of "beaten gold" which points directly at the Deity of our Lord being "beaten" and "hammered," yet He came through "pure" and "undefiled." (Leave the "L" out of gold, and we have GOD.) Here we do not have the shittim wood, which pointed to His humanity, but the gold of His Deity. In Hebrews 8:5, we read, *"Though he were a son, yet learned he obedience by the things which he suffered."* Jesus learned obedience in a two-fold way, for He was a son in a two-fold way: He was the Son of God (Deity); and He was the Son of man (flesh). In Matthew 1-4, we have related to us the beginning of this beating, this suffering, this obedience, that staggers and overwhelms us. Here we have the Living Word, the Son of God, being taunted and tempted by the devil. *"If thou be the Son of God command these stones be made bread,"* (Matthew 4:3). Then the devil took him up into the Holy City, and he said, *"If thou be the Son of God cast thyself down . . ."* There is no way that we can really imagine the depth of His humiliation; yet He endured this and more. The Jewish people said, "He makes himself God," and yet as the Son of God, He was willing to endure this submission and humiliation even though He need only speak and "things that be not would appear." Note that He never discussed His Deity as Satan. He knew He only had to exhale, and demon forces would have to bow down to Him.

Only the Holy Spirit can enlighten us to fully understand Philippians 2:3-11: *"Let nothing be done through strife or vainglory; but in lowliness of mind let each esteem other better than themselves. Look not every man on his own things, but every man also on the*

198

things of others. Let this mind be in you, which was also in Christ Jesus: Who, being in the form of God, thought it not robbery to be equal with God: but made himself of no reputation, and took upon him the form of a servant, and was made in the likeness of men: And being found in fashion as a man, he humbled himself, and become obedient unto death, even the death of the cross. Wherefore God also hath highly exalted him, and given him a name which is above every name: That at the name of Jesus every knee should bow, of things in heaven, and things in earth, and things under the earth; And that every tongue should confess that Jesus Christ is Lord, to the glory of God the Father."

Only the Spirit of God can show us how Jesus, the Living Word, and co-equal with the Father, could take the low place for us, and never use His Deity to overcome His sufferings. In the garden, the Son of God cried, "My soul is exceedingly SORROWFUL, EVEN UNTO DEATH:" In the midst of His anguish, he asked the disciples to tarry a while with Him; but their eyes were heavy and they slept (Matthew 28:38). We are told that the word "sorrowful" comes from a Greek word which means to "pierce through and through, even to the dividing asunder, or to the dissolving." He was about to drink the cup of death. He was so completely in subjection to the Father, that not even here did He use His deity to strengthen Himself.

Only by Holy Spirit illumination can we enter into this suffering of the "Beaten Gold." Without the aid of the Comforter, we tend to view Him at that hour as the Son of God, and we fail to fully comprehend His walk as the Son of Man subject to pain and grief. The Jews cried out for His death because, *"We have a law, and by our law he ought to die, because he made himself the Son of God"* (John 19:7). Hammer blow after hammer blow on the pure Gold, yet He opened not His mouth, not even on the Cross while He suffered unimaginable pain and sufferings: *"And they that passed by reviled him, wagging their heads, And saying, Thou that destroyest the temple, and buildest it in three days, save thyself, If thou be the Son of God, come down from the cross:"* (Matthew 27:39-40). Again the devil was saying, "Prove your Deity." But Jesus knew that He was chosen by God to be that Beaten Gold, and that He would be fashioned into a glorious Candlestick to Light the way of the Gentiles.

One Shaft

This candlestick was to have a central shaft out of which the six branches would proceed, and be extended to and from the base or pedestal of the Candlestick. We must note that in Genesis 24:2 the word "shaft" was translated "thigh," and in Genesis 46:26 it is translated as "lion." The shaft, along with the six branches, ended in seven sockets that were to hold seven lamps. In Revelation 4:5, we read, *"And out of the throne proceeded lightnings and thunderings and voices: and there were seven lamps of fire burning before the throne, which are the seven Spirits of God."*

Here is the Candlestick with its seven lamps before the throne of God, declared to be the seven Spirits of God found in Isaiah 11:2: (1) the Spirit of the Lord; (2) the Spirit of Wisdom; (3) the Spirit of Understanding; (4) the Spirit of Counsel; (5) the Spirit of Might; (6) the Spirit of Knowledge; and (7) the Spirit of Fear.

Branches

The seven-fold lampstand was the perfect picture of Christ in His complete fullness of Wisdom, Knowledge and Understanding. The six branches that proceeded out of the main shaft, the main loin, presented a most beautiful picture of the believer and his union with the Lord Jesus. Six is the number of man. There were to be three branches proceeding out of each side of the Lampstand; as these six branches are joined together with the main shaft, the number is changed from six to seven. We are complete in Him. In Colossians 2:10, we read, *"And ye are complete in Him, which is the head of all principality and power:"* In John 15:5, Jesus referred to us as the branches: *"I am the vine, ye are the branches: He that abideth in me, and I in him, the same bringeth forth much fruit: for without me ye can do nothing."*

The six branches[1] were to come out of the side of the shaft, not the top, bottom, or back, but "his side."

Bowls-Knops-Flowers

The pattern of the Lampstand is described in our text; it consisted of one central stem, with three lateral branches springing from each side, looking upward. This sevenfold Candelabra was wrought in a three-fold decoration: (1) bowls, or cups like almonds; with (2) knops; and (3) flowers. This Candlestick had 22 sets of oranaments; each set had 3 parts totaling 66 ornaments on it which represents the Word of God. Although most candlesticks made in Israel have all the center shafts the same height, it seems that this seven-branched candlestick had a middle shaft that was taller than the other six.

---

[1]Verse 31, a translation error which is corrected in Exodus 37:17: "his branches" to singular "his branch."

There were to be four of these sets of decorations on the main shaft, the loin, the vine. We are also reminded that these decorations were also hammered out of the same piece of gold. There were three of these sets of decorations found on each branch. This speaks of the perfection that God has planned for each branch that comes out of the vine. This BOWL was to be fashioned like unto an almond. We must remember that the almond had been used in Scripture to picture the quickening power of the Word of God. In Numbers when the children of Israel questioned the authority of the priesthood of Aaron, God required that each tribe of Israel bring a rod along with Aaron. They laid those sticks in the Holy Place before the Lord so He might show His choice for the priesthood; the next day, the rod of Aaron had budded, bloomed real blossoms, and yielded almonds. Here, a dead piece of wood was laid before the Lord under the Candlestick, and overnight it became alive.

"Moreover the word of the Lord came unto me, saying, Jeremiah, what seeth thou? And I said, I see a rod of an almond tree. Then said the Lord unto me, thou hast well seen: for I will hasten my word to perform it." (Jeremiah 1:11-12)

The almond tree is the first tree to blossom, which speaks to us of the resurrection, new life, or spring. The Hebrew word for almond means "watch, alert or expectation." The blossoms are pure white.

As for the knops, it is difficult to define. Joephus renders the word "pomegranate." In any case, the pomegranate is an emblem of "peace," and it was seen on the hem of the Priest's robe, in the adornment of Solomon's temple, and found in the beautiful garden of love in the Song of Solomon. The promegranates speak of Christ in His life of productiveness. It is the emblem of fruitfulness. We might view these as opening buds from out of which the branches likely sprouted. Each almond bowl was to be crowned with a knop; and out of the knop proceeded a flower.

The flowers were provably "lilies." The lilies speak of Christ in His Life of purity. He was holy, separated, and undefiled. In the Song of Solomon, He is spoken of as the "lily of the valleys."

"I went down into the garden of nuts to see the fruits of the valley, and to see whether the vine flourished, and the pomegranates budded."
(Song of Solomon 6:11)

In the Song of Solomon we read of the growth of the Bride in her relationship with her Bridegroom. We learn by the sixth chapter that She has learned to maintain unbroken communion with her lover, her Bridegroom. In the above verse we read of the three things the Bridegroom was looking for in His garden, which are none other than the three-fold pattern of perfection we are outlining in the Candlestick. He was searching to see how the Word was growing in His garden (the almonds).

"Thy plants are an orchard of pomegranates, with pleasant fruits; camphire, with spikenard, Spikenard and saffron; calamus and cinnamon, with all trees of frankincese; myrrh and aloes, with all the chief spices."
(Song of Solomon 4:13-14)

"But the fruit of the Spirit is love, joy, peace, longsuffering, gentleness, goodness, faith, Meekness, tem-

perance: against such there is no law."

(Galatians 5:22-23)

Tongs and Snuffdishes

These articles were pure gold; the lamps would need to be trimmed. The word "tongs" means snuffers or tweezers. These were used to snuff off the burnt part of the wick and to hold the coal of fire from the Brazen Altar to light them again when they were ordered or prepared. The snuffdishes were used to carry off the refuse of the wicks, and for bringing in fire from the Brazen Altar from which the Candlestick was to be lighted.

Seven Lamps

The seven lamps that were to be placed on the six branches and the shaft were to be vessels for the oil, that the lamp might give light for the Holy Place. Without these vessels there would be no light. Jesus is the light of the world; and today His light continues to shine through us, the branches. These seven lamps which stood on the shaft and branches of the lampstand were probably like those used by the Egyptians and other nations. Usually, they were a shallow, covered vessel, perhaps more of an oval form, with a mouth at one end from which the wick protruded. These lamps were to burn continually. This Lampstand was given for the express purpose of providing light for the priest of God to minister in the Holy Place in the things of God. It is of great interest for us to know that only twice is reference made to the Lampstand after the Pentateuch is passed, but in each case the connection is a beautiful one. First, In Samuel 3:3, the Word tells us that Jehovah revealed Himself to young Samuel in the Temple or Tabernacle *"ere the lamp of God went out."*

In Daniel 5:5, we read, *"In the same hour came forth fingers of a man's hand and wrote over against the Lampstand upon the plaister of the wall."*

"And the child Samuel ministered unto the Lord before Eli. And the word of the Lord was precious in those days; there was no open vision. And it came to pass at that time, when Eli was laid down in his place, and his eyes began to wax dim, that he could not see; And ere the lamp of God went out in the temple of the Lord, where the ark of God was, and Samuel was laid down to sleep; That the Lord called Samuel: and he answered, Here am I."   *(Samuel 3:1-4)*

A woman named Hannah was his mother; she prayed before the Lord that if He would bless her with a man child she would indeed vow to give him back to His service as soon as he was weaned. When the child Samuel was born, and in accordance with her promise, she took him to the temple to live with the old prophet, Eli, whose sons knew not the Lord, being a child, girded with a linen ephod. This child grew and found favour in the sight of God and men. And the time came when Jehovah revealed Himself to the child, *"ere the lamp of God went out in the temple of the Lord, where the ark of God was,"* because of the sins of Eli's sons, who were desecrating the Holy Place with their acts of immorality with the women who assembled at the door of the tabernacle. Certainly, the Glory of the Lord was departed from Israel. Here we observe a very low religious state of Israel, the corruption of the priesthood, and the final fate of the Ark of God. From the time of his childhood, until his death, Samuel was faithful to the Lord in the priestly office. And long before Israel was taken into captivity, "I-chabod," "no glory", had been written upon her doorposts.

In Daniel we read of Israel's captivity, and the downfall of those who marched into Jerusalem, desecrated the temple, and took the sacred vessels;

"Belshazzar the king made a great feast to a thousand of his lords, and drank wine before the thousand. Belsahzzar, whiles he tasted the wine, commanded to bring the golden and silver vessels which his father Nebuchadnezzar had taken out of the temple which was in Jerusalem; that the king, and his princes, his wives, and his concubines, might drink therein. Then they brought the golden vessels that were taken out of the temple of the house of God which was at Jerusalem; and the king, and his princes, his wives, and his concubines, drank in them. They drank wine, and praised the gods of gold, and of silver, of brass, of iron, of wood, and of stone. In the same hour came forth fingers of a man's hand, and wrote over against the candlestick upon the plaster of the wall of the king's palace: and the king saw the part of the hand that wrote. Then the king's countenance was changed, and his thoughts troubled him, so that the joints of his loins were loosed, and his knees smote one against another. The king cried aloud to bring in the astrologers, the Chaldeans, and the soothsayers. And the king spake, and said to the wise men of Babylon, Whosoever shall read this writing, and shew me the interpretation thereof, shall be clothed with scarlet, and have a chain of gold about his neck, and shall be the third ruler in the kingdom. Then came in all the king's wise men: but they could not read the writing, nor make known to the king the interpretation

thereof. Then was king Belshazzar greatly troubled, and his countenance was changed in him, and his lord were astonied. Now the queen, by reason of the words of the king and his lords, came into the banquet house: and the queen spake and said, O king, live forever: let not thy thoughts trouble thee, not let thy countenance be changed. There is a man in thy kingdom, in whom is the spirit of the holy gods; and in the days of thy father light and understanding and wisdom, like the wisdom of the gods, was found in him; whom the king Nebuchasnezzar thy father, the king, I say, thy father, made master of the magicians, astrologers, Chaldeans, and soothsayers; Forasmuch as an excellent spirit, and knowledge, and understanding, interpreting of dreams; and shewing of hard sentences, and dissolving of doubts, were found in the same Daniel, whom the king named Belteshazzar now let Daniel be called, and he will shew the interpretation."　　(Daniel 5:1-12)

Feasts were a part of the Babylonian culture; but the feast of Belshazzar was no ordinary event. This feast was the turning point in the history of Babylon; it marked the end of the reign of Belshazzar and the transition from the head of gold to the arms and breast of silver in the image of Nebuchadnezzar's dream. To show his contempt for the armies outside the walls of Babylon, and his defiance of the God who had assigned Himself to Israel, he gave this fabulous feast where the wine flowed freely, and they praised the gods of gold, silver, brass, iron, wood, and stone. Needless to say, it was a feast of drunkenness, idolatry, and licentious debauchery. They drank from the Holy vessels that Nebuchadnezzar had taken from the temple many years ago. Then the finger of Almighty God wrote their doom over against the candlestick upon the plaster of the wall. Though the light from that Lamp had long since gone out, it was still, nonetheless, made of beaten gold, and belonged to the house of God.

The Golden Altar of Incense

"And thou shalt make an altar to burn incense upon: of shittim wood shalt thou make it. A cubit shall be the length thereof, and a cubit the breadth thereof; foursquare shall it be: and two cubits shall be the height thereof: the horns thereof shall be of the same. And thou shalt overlay it with pure gold, the top thereof, and the sides thereof round about, and the horns thereof; and thou shalt make unto it a crown of gold round about. And two golden rings shalt thou make to it under the crown of it, by the two corners thereof upon the two sides of it thou make it; and they shall be for places for the staves to bear it withal. And thou shalt make the staves of shittim wood, and overlay them with gold. And thou shalt put it before the veil that is by the ark of the testimony, before the mercy seat that is over the testimony, where I will meet with thee. And Aarom shall burn thereon sweet incense every morning: when he dresseth the lamps, he shall burn incense upon it. And when Aaron lighteth the lamps at even, he shall burn incense before the Lord throught out your generations. Ye shall offer no strange incense thereon, nor burnt sacrifice, nor meat offering; neither shall ye pour drink offering theron. And Aaron shall make an atonement upon the horns of it once in a year with the blood of the sin offering of atonements once in the year shall he make atonement upon it throughout your gernerations: it is most holy unto the Lord."

(Exodus 30:1-10)

There were two altars connected with the Tabernacle. Both were made of wood, but coverered with a different metal: one with brass, and so named "the brazen altar," and the other with gold, called "the golden altar" (altar of incense). This altar was placed within the Holy Place, near to and in front of the inner veil, in line with the Ark of the covenant; while the other altar was in the outer court. The cross is clearly formed with five pieces of furniture. It is again seen in the completion of the seven pieces of furniture.

This piece of furniture was the narrowest yet the tallest of the seven, (18"x18"x36" four-square). Its purpose was to burn incense. In the morning when Aaron went into the Holy Place to dress the lamps by trimming the wicks and pouring fresh oil, he was to order the lamps again, for they were ordered in the morning and in the evening. He was to light the incense on the altar that stood before the Holy of Holies. This altar speaks to us of prayer and intercession. It was the place of worship.

"Giving thanks always for all things unto God and the Father in the name of our Lord Jesus Christ."
(Ephesians 5:20)

"And whatsoever ye do in word or deed, do all in the name of the Lord Jesus, giving thanks to God and the Father by him." *(Colossians 3:17)*

Jesus is our great High Priest who has entered the Holy of Holies in heaven to make intercession for the saints. He is the ALTAR, HE IS THE INCENSE, HE IS THE ALL IN ALL. The first altar suggests the work of Jesus on the earth in behalf of sinners, while the second altar speaks to us of His present-day ministry as He intercedes for the saints. The incense which was to be offered on this gold-covered piece of furniture is a symbol of prayer. This altar reminds us of the wonderful love and devotion of the son to the Father. In Psalm 141:2, we read, *"Let my prayer be set forth before thee as incense; and the lifting up of my hands as the evening sacrifice."*

Sweet incense was put upon the golden altar in the morning and in the night, lit by a coal from the Brazen Altar whose fire was started by God. This meant a constant column of smoke ascended to God day and night; this is a type of the prayers of the saints.

We are not told if there were two rings of gold or four. The Ark was so small that if properly placed, one ring on each side would have been sufficient to carry and balance it. The two staves of the same incorruptible wood, covered with gold, were for carrying it when the camp was called to march on through the desert.

The Horns of The Altar

Horns always speak of power in the Word of God. By grasping the horns of the altar we learn the fulfillment of the prayers that Paul prayed in Ephesians 1 and 3. We are told that the more literal Hebrew translation would have been, "Of itself shall be its horns." All that Christ is in His wondrous person gives Him power with God; how very beautifully this is typified in John 17. We must also note the number of horns is not given here. Most say it had one at each corner, as had the brazen altar. Since there is nothing in Scripture without spiritual significance, even this omission is significant. Four is the number of earth (universal), and the Golden Altar speaks to us of

210

Christ's priestly ministry in Heaven; thus, we realize that the mention of the "four horns" would have cast a blemish on the perfection of its type. (We believe it had four).

Crown and Staves of Pure Gold

The Golden Altar of Incense had a crown of gold around it. Three of the seven pieces of the tabernacle's furniture had a "crown upon it." This speaks of the CROWNED ONE OF GOD.

"For thou hast made him a little lower than the angels, and hast crowned him with glory and honour. Thou madest him to have dominion over the works of thy hands; thou hast put all things under his feet."
(Psalms 8:5-6)

"Thou settest a crown of pure gold on his head."
(Psalms 21:3)

"But we see Jesus, who was made a little lower than the angels for the suffering of death, crowned with glory and honour." *(Psalms 2:9)*

The object of this rim of gold around the top of the altar was to prevent coals of fire, or the holy perfume being displaced or scattered. When the children of Israel marched, the coals and the incense stayed in tact. The fire and perfume were supposed to remain burning on it, even during the march. Therefore, the golden crown would hold an important office; it would prevent any displacement of these holy things when the Altar was borne on the shoulders of the Levites. In spite of the rugged paths they traveled through the wilderness, the children of Israel had the ceaseless aroma of the ever-burning incense; their flesh would groan and complain, and they would encounter many difficulites along the way, as the corruption of the flesh manifested. This speaks to us of the need we have for the sweet savour of Christ ever before the throne of God on our behalf making endless intercession, and taking the place of our own groanings and failures so that all that reaches the nostrils of God is the "sweet smell of incense." We are presented faultless in the presence of His Glory.

The Brazen Laver

"And the Lord spake unto Moses, saying, Thou shalt also make a laver of brass, and his foot also of brass, to wash withal: and thou shalt put it between the tabernacle of the congregation and the altar, and thou shalt put water therein. For Aaron and his sons shall wash their heads and their feet there at: When they go into the tabernacle of the congregation, they shall wash with water, that they die not; or when they come near to the altar to minister, to burn offering made by fire unto the Lord: So they shall wash their hands and their feet, that they die not: and it shall be a statute for ever to them, even to him and to his seed throughout their generations."   *(Exodus 30:17-21)*

Now we have arrived outside the tabernacle door as we view this sixth piece of furniture. As we have observed, gold was condined to the inside of the tabernacle. In this courtyard, we find the use of brass which typifies judgment. This laver was for the priest alone. God had selected the nation of Israel to be a kingdom of priests. In Exodus 19:6, we read, *"And ye shall be unto me a kingdom of priests, and an holy nation. These are the words which thou shalt speak unto the children of Israel."*

This laver was a great bowl (no dimesions given) or basin of polished BRASS, thus giving the effect of a mirror. It contained water for cleansing, thus adding to the mirror effect. This laver was located to the west of the Brazen Altar, which is the seventh piece of furniture we will cover before we go into the construction of the tabernacle. This laver stood upon a brazen foot. The material for this laver was obtained from the "looking glasses" of the women who assembled by the door of the tabernacle (highly polished copper plates).

"And he made the laver of brass, and the foot of it of brass, of the looking glasses of the women assembling, which assembled at the door of the tabernacle of the congregation." *(Exodus 38:8)*

As we have seen, BRASS meant judgment, and a looking glass speaks of self-scrutiny. The Hebrew word "kiyor" indicates something round. Jesus Christ, the Living Word, took upon Himself our judgment. He is, therefore, qualified to be our sanctifier. If we come to the Living Word (Laver) it is like coming to a mirror in that it reveals to us all the spots and blemishes of our minds and hearts. In James 1:22-25, we read, *"But be ye doers of the word, and not hearers only, deceiving your own selves. For if any be a hearer of the word, and not a doer, he is like unto a man beholding his natural face in a glass: for he beholdeth himself, and goeth his way, and straightway forgetteth what manner of man he was. But whosoever looketh into the perfect law of liberty, and continueth therein, he being not a forgetful hearer, but a doer of the work, this man shall be blessed in his deed."*

It has been pointed out that the laver could not cleanse, but it contained a water that could cleanse the priest of God. Jesus, through the Word, cleanses and washes all sin away. The fact that the Laver and the Candlestick have no dimensions given portrays to us a most beautiful and precious truth from the Word. This reveals that there is no limit with God as to His cleansing power, nor in the amount of light that He will bestow upon His children who walk in His ways.

This laver was for the washing of the hands and the feet of the priests. The hands speak of service; and the only kind of service acceptable to God is a clean and pure service. We all need to see the importance of living in the pure Word, and washing many times a day in the pure waters of the laver. Hands also speak in the natural of the tender touch. With the hands we are able to gently reach out and minister help to others. The feet speak to us of man's ways, or direction. Here we would want to remember that Jesus girded Himself and washed the feet of His disciples.

"Now before the feast of the passover, when Jesus knew that his hour was come that he should depart out of this world unto the Father, having loved his own which were in the world, he loved them unto the end. And supper being ended, the devil having now put into the heart of Judas Iscariot, Simon's son, to betray him; Jesus knowing that the Father had given all things into his hands, and that he was come from God, and went to God; He riseth from supper, and laid aside his garments; and took a towel, and girded himself. After that he poureth water into the basin, and began to wash the disciples' feet, and to wipe them with the towel where-

with he was girded. Then cometh he to Simon Peter: and Peter saith unto him, Lord, doest thou wash my feet? Jesus answered and said unto him, What I do thou knowest not now, but thou shalt know hereafter. Peter saith unto him, Thou shalt never wash my feet. Jesus answered him, If I wash thee not, thou hast no part with me. Simon Peter saith unto him, Lord, not my feet only, but also my hands and my head. Jesus saith to him, He that is washed needeth not save to wash his feet, but is clean every whit: and ye are clean, but not all. For he knew who should betray him; therefore said he, Ye are not all clean. So after he had washed their feet, and had taken his garments, and was set down again, he said unto them, Know ye what I have done to you? Ye call me Master and Lord: and Ye say well; for so I am. If I then, your Lord and Master, have washed your feet; ye also ought to wash one another's feet. For I have given you an example, that ye should do as I have done to you. Verily, Verily, I say unto you, The servant is not greater than his lord; neither he that is sent greater than he that sent him." (John 13:1-17)

Jesus knew that the Father had given all things unto him, and that He had come from God and was on His way back to the Glory He had with Him before the world was. He was gathered with His disciples before the feast of the passover celebration, and after supper, he laid aside His garments of glory, and girded himself with a simple towel; he poured water into a basin, and He washed the feet of His disciples, and wiped them with the towel. When Peter objected to going to the LAVER, the Lord told Him that without the washing of the water, he would have no part of Him. Peter then offered to allow Him to wash not only his feet but all him, but Jesus said only the feet would be needful. Jesus was giving them instructions in humility and compassion one for the other.

The Brazen Altar

"And thou shalt make an altar of shittim wood, five cubits long, and five cubits broad; the altar shall be foursquare: and the height thereof shall be three cubits. and thou shalt make the horns of it upon the four corners thereof: his horns shall be of the same: and thou shalt overlay it with brass. And thou shalt make his pans to receive his ashes, and his shovels, and his basons, and his fleshhooks, and his firepans: all the vessels thereof thou shalt make of brass. And thou shalt make for it a grate of network brass; and upon the net shalt thou make four brasen rings in the four corners thereof. And thou shalt put it under the compass of the altar beneath, that the net may be even to the midst of the altar. And thou shalt make staves for the altar, staves of shittim wood, and overlay them with brass. And the staves shall be put into the rings, and the staves shall be upon the two sides of the altar, to bear it. Hollow with boards shalt thou make it: as it was shewed thee in the mount, so shall they make it." (Exodus 27:1-8)

We have reached the seventh piece of furniture in our particular path of study. This brazen altar was the biggest of the Tabernacle's furniture. It was almost large enough to hold all the other vessels. Its size indicated its importance. It was placed "before the door" just inside the outer court. It would be the first object to meet the eye when the worshipper entered the Tent of the Congregation. It was also called the "altar of burnt offering." The Brazen Altar was the basis of the Levitical system. There was a fire which burned upon this altar day and night, and the sinner came to it with his Divinely-appointed victim for a sacrifice of sin. The daily sacrifice was renewed each morning. What a magnificent picture of salvation as the fires of the sacrifice roared and the blood stains covered the altar. It was always open to any guilty Hebrew who might wish to approach it.

At the Brazen Altar sin was judged and sacrifice was made. This Brazen Altar starts us out on our journey with Jesus as our Burnt Offering. In Hebrews 9:11-14, we read, *"But Christ being come an high priest of good thing to come, by a greater and more perfect tabernacle, not made with hands, that is to say, not of this building. Neither by the blood of goats and calves, but by his own blood he entered in once into the holy place, having obtained eternal redemption for us. For if the blood of bulls and goats, and the ashes of an heifer sprinkling the unclean, sanctified to the purifying of the flesh: How much more shall the blood of Christ, who through the eternal Spirit offered himself without spot to God, purge your conscience from dead works to serve the living God?'*

God set forth the principle that without the shedding of blood there would be no remission for sin. The life of the flesh is in the blood.

We have dealt with the wood and the brass already. The Hebrew word for "Altar" means to "Slay or Slaughter." This Altar was four-square; it measured 5 x 5 x 3[1]

---

[1]Assuming 18″ was their cubit.

cubits or $(7\frac{1}{2}' \times 7\frac{1}{2}' \times 4')$. (5 = grace; 3 = God the Father, God the son, and God the Holy Spirit.) The pans were for removing the ashes. The shovels were used for feeding the fire, collecting the ashes, or for placing coals into the censers for the Golden Altar. The basins were used to contain the blood which was poured out at the base of the Altar or sprinkled. The fleshhooks were used for arranging and placing the pieces of the animal's body until it was completely consumed. The firepans were used to carry coals from the Brazen Altar to the Goden Altar. We will cover this ground again as we go back through the Tabernacle fromthe outside into the Holy of Holies.

First Covering or Inner Curtains

The Curtained Ceiling (Linen)

God begins his instructions for its building with the ceiling and the roof, and works down. God comes down from heaven to earth:

"Moreover thou shalt make the tabernacle with ten curtains of fine twined linen, and blue, and purple, and scarlet: with cherubims of cunning work shalt thou make them. The length of one curtain shall be eight and twenty cubits, and the breadth of one curtain shall be eight and twenty cubits, and the breadth of one curtain four cubits: and every one of the curtains shall have one measure. The five curtains shall be coupled together one to another; and other five curtains shall be coupled one to another. And thou shalt make loops of blue upon the edge of the one curtain from the selvedge in the coupling; and likewise shalt thou make in the uttermost edge of another curtain, in the coupling of the second. Fifty loops shalt thou make in the one curtain, and fifty

loops shalt thou make in the edge of the curtain that is in the coupling of the second; that the loops may take hold one of another. And thou shalt make fifty taches of gold, and couple the curtains together with the taches: and it shall be one tabernacle."

(Exodus 26: 1-6)

We are told that the Hebrew word to "tabernacle" in this text is "mishkan." It is taken from another Hebrew word, "shakan," meaning "to dwell." All of this connects with the Jewish word, "Shekinah," which means "The Presence and Glory of God." We will note that the taberancle was covered with ten (redeemed) curtains, of fine twined linen, (righteousness); and the colors present the Lord Jesus Christ to us as the Lord from Heaven, who is to reign according to the divine counsels, but whose royalty is to be the result of His sufferings. These materials were not only used for the "curtains," but also for the "vail," the hangings "for the door of the tent," the hanging for the "gate of the court," including the cloths for service, and the holy garments of Aaron. By this we may readily see that it is Christ through and through.

It is important for us to realize that these coverings were the first thing made; they were the first thing put in place; all the peices of the furniture remained covered until the COVERINGS were in place. These curtains completely covered the framework of boards. This demonstrates the Biblical teachings on COVERINGS. In this study of the curtains and coverings, we come to the point where we see displayed all the beauty, wisdom, strength, patience, and much more, of our Lord Jesus Christ. The inside of this tabernacle was a most beautiful sight to behold; while the outside was a slaughter house. This tabernacle was a picture of something earthly; symbolic of something that was heavenly, not made with hand. There were seven beautiful pieces of furniture showing forth the perfection and completion of God; here we will see four coverings for the tabernacle, as we work from the inside out.

The Tabernacle (Mishkan) was to be covered with fine twined linen. "Fine" denotes spotlessness or fault-lessness as we see in Christ. He is the righteousness of God; He is our righteousness. He is our Jehovah "Tsid-kenu," our Saviour and Lord. Twined linen refers to the work of bleaching the linen in ancient Egypt. "Sedinim" is a Hebrew word meaning "fine lining." It is mentioned In Judges 14:12-13, as a part of the gift which Samson offered to any one who guessed his riddle. There it is ren-dered "sheets." It also occurs in Proverbs 31:24, in Sol-omon's description of a "virtuous woman." The "sedinim" were inner garments or tunics.

The Glory of God is hidden to all who stand outside of Jesus. These elaborate curtains were to hide the sacred furniture and services of the sanctuary from all outsiders. The natural man cannot understand the things of God. Some writers believe that the ceiling covers were white sheets, and the cherubim were of blue, purple, and scar-let threads woven into the curtains. Nevertheless, there were ten curtains of two sets of five joined together with blue loops and gold taches. We have studied the colors elsewhere; we might add that as a symbol of consecration, the Israelites wore blue ribbons in the fringes of the four quarters or wings of their garments. The woman who suf-fered an infirmity for twelve years "reached for the hem of His garment." The "five joined" together suggests the unity of the church; fifty speaks of Pentecost. The clasps of gold coupled the curtains together and made them as one.

The Second Covering: Curtains of Goat's Hair

"And thou shalt make curtains of goats' hair to be a covering upon the tabernacle: eleven curtains shalt thou make. The length of one curtain shall be thirty cubits, and the breadth of one curtain four cubits: and the eleven curtains shall be all of one measure. And thou shalt couple five curtains by themselves, and shalt double the sixth curtain in the forefront of the tabernacle. And thou shalt make fifty loops on the edge of the one curtain that is outmost in the coupling, and fifty loops in the edge of the curtain which coupleth the second. And thou shalt make fifty taches of brass, and put the taches into the loops, and couple the tent together, that it may be one. And the remnant that remaineth of the curtains of the tent, the half curtain that remaineth, shall hang over the backside of the tabernacle. And a cubit on the one side, and a cubit on the other side of that which remaineth in the length of the curtains of the tent, it shall hang over the sides of the tabernacle on this side and on that side, to cover it."

(Exodus 26:7-13)

The second covering from the inside view was goat's hair. It is not known for sure whether this was black or white. Black goats were plentiful while white goats were a rarity. In Leviticus 9:3, we read, *"Take ye a kid of the goats for a sin offering:"* Since He was the spotless One, it is easier to believe that white–haired goats were used for this covering. It is said that the goats of the East grew beautiful long silken hair which could be woven into gorgeous materials. Eleven curtains were to be made: five for grace; six the number of man. This speaks to us of the grade of God that was manifested in the man Christ Jesus. By keeping our figures in cubits here, we see these curtains were to be thirty cubits in length and four cubits in breadth. Thirty speaks to us again of the numbers five and six ($5 \times 6 = 30$). This curtain hung over the tabernacle as a witness of the truth of the results of the humanity and sacrifice of Jesus Christ. We have already discussed that the number four is the number of earth or universal. Five of the curtains were to be coupled together, then six were to be coupled together, and the sixth curtain was to be doubled in front of the door of the tabernacle. This would be man's invitation to enter into the "Door." Jesus secured for man the right to stand in the Presence of God as if he had never sinned. We will study more on the goat sacrifice in Leviticus.

Note that the joining was to be accomplished with fifty loops on the one section and fifty loops on the other section and these loops were to be coupled together with BRASS taches. Fifty is the number of Pentecost, or the descent of the Spirit of God.

The word for curtains is "yerioth" from a root meaning "to tremble or wave," as suspended curtains do.

"For then must he often have suffered since the foundation of the world: but now once in the end of the world hath he appeared to put away sin by the sacrifice of himself." *(Hebrews 9:26)*

The Third Covering: Rams' Skins

The Fourth Covering: Badgers'' Skins

"And thou shalt make a covering for the tent of rams' skins dyed red, and a covering above of badgers' skins."   *(Exodus 26:14)*

Rams were used in sacrifice as a substitute offering. A ram became a substitute to die in the place of Abraham's son, Isaac. Since our God is a God of order, He likely used the ram to cover the sin of Adam and Eve, although we are not told which animal He used for their covering. Jesus became God's substitutionary Ram for everyone's sins.

"For Christ also hath once suffered for sins, the just for the unjust, that he might bring us to God, being put to death in the flesh, but quickened by the Spirit:"
                    (1 Peter 3:18)

The ram in Scripture is used as a substitute in the consecration offerings. When a sinner comes to Jesus, we know that Jesus comes into the heart and begins the ministry of substitution by replacing the old desires with His new ones. The color red, of course, speaks to us of the Blood that He shed to become our substitute.

The final covering was exposed to the wind, sun and rain; and there was no beauty attached to it. To behold the true beauty of the Christian life, one must look from the inside out. In Ezekiel 16:10, we read, *"I clothed thee also with embroidered work, and shod thee with badger's skin."*

Boards And Sockets

The framework of the tent was to be made from acacia wood; each frame piece would be 5 feet high, and 2¼ feet wide, standing upright. It would have grooves so that each piece could be jointly fit together. Twenty of these frames would frame the south side of the sacred tent, and forty silver bases for the frames would fit into the two bases under each piece of the frame.

On the north side there would be twenty of the same frames; on the west side there would be six frames, and two frames at each corner. These corner frames were to be connected at the bottom and top with clasps.

Outside Bars

These bars were of acacia wood and were to run across the frames, five bars on each side of the Tabernacle. Also, there would be five bars for the rear of the building, facing westward. These frames and the bars were overlaid with gold.

The Inner Veil

"And thou shalt make a veil of blue, and purple, and scarlet, and fine twined linen of cunning work: with cherubims shall it be made: And thou shalt hang it upon four pillars of shittim wood overlaid with gold: their hooks shall be of gold, upon the four sockets of silver. And thou shalt hang up the veil under the taches, that thou mayest bring in thither within the veil the ark of the testimony: and the veil shall divide unto you between the holy place the the most holy. And thou shalt put the mercy seat upon the ark of the testimony of the most holy place. And thou shalt set the table without the veil, and the candlestick over against the table on the side of the tabernacle toward the south: and thou shalt put the table on the north side."

(Exodus 26:31-35)

This was the veil which would divide the Holy of

Holies from the Holy Place. It was from blue, purple, and scarlet cloth, the fine-twined or twisted linen; and it would have cherubim embroidered into the cloth. It was to be hung upon four acacia pillars overlaid with gold, with four golden hooks. These pillars were to rest in four silver bases. Behind the curtain was the Ark containing the stone tablets, Aaron's rod, and a pot of manna. As we have pointed out, the Holy place contained the lampstand, the table of shewbread, and the altar of incense. The lampstand and the table of shewbread were across the room from each other: lampstand on the south side, table of shewbread on the north side of the room.

The word that is used for veil here comes from the Hebrew word "poreketh," which means to break, rend, or separate. This beautiful veil separated the Holy Place from the Most Holy Place. This veil speaks to us of the body of Jesus which was rent (torn) in two, or pierced through by the spear when He hung on the cross. At the time of His crucifixion, the veil in the temple ws rent in two from top to bottom revealing the Most Holy Place, where the priest at that moment was ministering. *"And behold, the veil of the temple was rent in twain from the top to the bottom; and the earth did quake, and the rocks rent"* (Matthew 27:51). For centuries the ordinary priest never saw what was behind the veil and the high priest never discussed it. Jewish tradition claims that the high priest was placed behind that veil supernaturally, since it had no door.

It was a sight to behold in the city of Jerusalem when the veil in the temple tore from the top to the bottom, and many graves were opened after His resurrection, and those saints walked among the people of the city. Now all believers have access to the throne of grace. In Hebrews 10:19-21, we read, *"Having therefore, brethren, boldness to enter into the holiest by the blood of Jesus, By a new and living way, which he hath consecrated for us, through the veil, that is to say, his flesh: And having an high priest over the house of God."* We now live daily in the Holy of Holies, in the Shekinah Glory of our Lord.

It is generally agreed that the four pillars mentioned here represent the four gospels: MATTHEW, MARK, LUKE, and JOHN.

The Door Of The Tabernacle (Outer Veil)

This door was made of the same material as the veil, but the veil had the cherubim work upon it. We know, of course, that all three entrances are Christ as the WAY, the TRUTH, and the LIGHT.

"And thou shalt make an hanging for the door of the tent, of blue, and purple, and scarlet, and fine twined linen, wrought with needlework. And thou shalt make for the hanging five pillars of shittim wood, and ovelay them with gold, and their hooks shall be of gold: and thou shalt cast five sockets of brass for them."

(Exodus 26:36-37)

"Verily, verily, I say unto you, He that entereth not by the door into the sheepfold, but climbeth up some other way, the same is a thief and a robber. But he that entereth in by the door is the shepherd of the sheep. To him the porter openeth; and the sheep hear his voice; and he calleth his own sheep by name, and leadeth them out . . . Then said Jesus unto them again, Verily, verily, I say unto you, I am the door of the sheep. I am the door: by me if any man enter in, he shall be saved, and shall go in and out, and find pasture." *(John 10:1-3, 7, 9)*

The Court

"And thou shalt make the court of the tabernacle: for the south side southward there shall be hangings for the court of fine twined linen of an hundred cubits long for one side: And the twenty pillars thereof and their twenty sockets shall be of brass; the hooks of the pillars and their fillets shall be of silver. And likewise for the north side in length there shall be hangings of an hundred cubits long, and his twenty pillars and their twenty sockets of brass; the hooks of the pillars and their fillets of silver. And for the breadth of the court on the west side shall be hangings of fifty cubits: their pillars ten, and their sockets ten. And the breadth of the court on the east side eastward shall be fifty cubits. The hangings of one side of the gate shall be fifteen cubits: their pillars three, and their sockets three. And on the other side shall be hangings fifteen cubits: their pillars three, and their sockets three."   *(Exodus 27:9-15)*

Moses was instructed to make a courtyard for the Tabernacle, and it was to be enclosed with curtains made from the fine twisted linen. On the south side the curtains were to stretch for 150 feet, and be held up by 20 posts, fitting into 20 bronze post holders. God told Moses several times to see to it that he constructed the tabernacle according to the pattern given to him in the Mount. The curtains were to be held up by silver hooks attached to silver rods, attached to the posts. The same measurements for the north side of the court as seen on the south side—150 feet—to be held up by 20 posts fitted into bronze sockets, with silver hooks and rods. The west side of the tabernacle court would be 75 feet wide, with 10 posts and 10 sockets. The east side of the court of the tabernacle would also be 75 feet wide. On each side of the entrance would be 22½ feet of curtain, held up by three posts embedded in the three sockets.

The Gate Hangings

"And for the gate of the court shall be an hanging of twenty cubits, of blue, and purple, and scarlet, and fine twined linen, wrought with needlework: and their pillars shall be four, and their sockets four. All the pillars round about the court shall be filleted with silver; their hooks shall be of silver, and their sockets of brass. The length of the court shall be an hundred cubits, and the breadth fifty every where, and the height five cubits of fine twined linen, and their sockets of brass. All the vessels of the tabernacle in all the service thereof, and all the pins thereof, and all the pins of the court, shall be of brass."   *(Exodus 27:16-19)*

"Make a joyful noise unto the Lord, all ye lands. Serve the Lord with gladness: Come before his presence with singing. Know ye that the Lord he is God: It is he that hath made us, and not we ourselves; we are his people, and the sheep of his pasture. Enter into his gates with thanksgiving, and into his courts with praise: Be thankful unto him, and bless his name. For the Lord is good; his mercy is everlasting; and his truth endureth to all generations."   *(Psalms 100)*

Chapter 10

THE PRIESTHOOD

"And take thou unto thee Aaron, thy brother, and his sons with him, from among the children of Israel, that he may minister unto me in the priest's office, even Aaron, Nadab and Abihu, Eleazar and Ithamar, Aaron's sons. And thou shalt make holy garments for Aaron, thy brother, for glory and for beauty."

(Exodus 28:1-2)

Aaron and his family were chosen by God for the priesthood. They were consecrated and set apart by Him. A priest was someone who could approach God through the blood and intercede for himself and members of his own family. But when God gave the law to Moses, He instituted the Aaronic priesthood, and He gave the ministry of the priesthood to the family of Aaron. Aaron, the high priest, was a beautiful type of the Lord Jesus Christ, our High Priest in Heaven. However, Jesus was not called after the order of the Aaronic priesthood, for the order of this priesthood was temporary, and upon his death, his priesthood ministry passed on to his oldest son. But Jesus Christ was made an high priest after the order of Melchisedec, who had neither beginning of days, nor end of life. Though Jesus did not come after the order of the Aaronic priesthood, He ministered according to the pattern of the Levitical priesthood for it was made according to a pattern of the heavenly; therefore, it is an eternal pattern in the economy of God.

"Now of the things which we have spoken this is the sum: We have such an high priest, who is set on the right hand of the throne of the Majesty in the heavens; A minister of the sanctuary, and of the true tabernacle, which the Lord pitched, and not man. For every high priest is ordained to offer gifts and sacrifices: wherefore it is of necessity that this man have somewhat also to offer. For if he were on earth, he should not be a priest, seeing that there are priests that offer gifts according to the law: Who serve unto the example and shadow of heavenly things, as Moses was admonished of God when he was about to make the tabernacle: for See, saith he, that thou make all things according to the pattern shewed to thee in the mount." (Hebrews 8:1-5)

We need to note that we have three terms used of the priestly office which we need to understand: (1) Priests: these were the members of the Aaronic family. The only claim for this office was sonship. Their work was to minister in holy things. (2) High Priests: Aaron was the first one, and he was succeeded by his son, and so on down the line. There was only one High Priest in office at a time. According to Josephus, something more than eighty men officiated in this capacity between Aaron, the first, and Christ; the only reason for change being death. (3) Great High Priest: of which there was One and only One, the Lord Jesus Christ. He inherited His Priesthood from no one, and passed it on to no one. He ever lives to make intercession for the church today. He was forever a Priest after the order of Melchisedec. Let us clarify the question so often asked, "Who was this Melchisedec? Was he a superhuman being or a visitation from the Lord to Abraham after battle?" He was just what the scriptures state him to be in Genesis 14:18-20, *"And Melchizedek, king of Salem, brought forth bread and wine; and he was the priest of the most high God. And he blessed him, and said, Blessed be Abram of the most high God, possessor of heaven and earth: And blessed be the most high God, who hath delivered thine enemies into thy hand. And he gave him tithes of all."*

Melchisedec was the king of Salem, meaning Peace (Jerusalem). He was the king of the Most High God. He brought bread and wine out to Abram after he had rescued Lot, who had been taken captive in battle. This statement about Melchisedec in no way indicates that he is an angel, or super-human; when we read the entire account, we have a battle, a defeat, a victory, and a blessing. Salem could be found on any map of that period of time as the ancient name for Jerusalem, which was at that time Canaanitish. We know where he lived, that he was a priest in a godless place at that time, and that he was priest of the Most High God. Note that he held two offices: King and Priest, which was never known or heard of under the old economy. Paul gave the historical account, then the rest of his statements are doctrinal. Our Lord came from the tribe of Judah, and Moses said nothing concerning priesthood from that tribe. Jesus was a Priest forever after the order of Melchisedec. The priesthood of Melchisedec was unique; it was universal. He came before Jews and Gentiles existed as separate people. When the Greater than Melchisedec came, he made Jew and Gentile one again in Himself.

Garments For The Priesthood

It is interesting to note that the garments for Aaron which were for "glory and for beauty" were eight in number. His dress was the symbol of authority. His ministry was twofold: to make atonement for the people, (and for himself); and to teach the law, the Word of the Lord. We must recognize that the tabernacle without the priesthood would be barren and void. The best of quality was used, such as fine linens, pure gold, precious stones, costly ointments, and cunning workmanship, all used by wise hearts. This was because it was all a type of the Lord Jesus, and His character, all of which are carefully and beautifully intertwined. We are His workmanship created in Christ Jesus.

"And thou shalt speak unto all that are wise hearted, whom I have filled with the spirit of wisdom, that they may make Aaron's garments to consecrate him, that he may minister unto me in the priest's office. And these are the garments which they shall make: a breastplate, and an ephod, and a robe, and a broidered coat, a mitre, and a girdle: and they shall make holy garments for Aaron thy brother, and his sons, that he may minister unto me in the priest's office." (Exodus 28:3-4)

As we study the garments of Aaron and his sons, we will see Jesus and His Church in ministry. This will be easier to understand if we comment on it as we move on in the study. We have the same ministry today in Christ Jesus.

"Ye also, as lively stones, are built up a spiritual house, an holy priesthood, to offer up spiritual sacrifices, acceptable to God by Jesus Christ . . . But ye are a chosen generation, a royal priesthood, a holy nation, a peculiar people; that ye should shew forth the praises of him who hath called you out of darkness into his marvelous light. Which in time past were not a people, but are now the people of God: which had not obtained mercy, but now have obtained mercy."

(1 Peter 2:5, 9-10)

The sons of Aaron ministered with him each day with the exception of the Day of Atonement; Jesus atoned for our sins alone; now we have the ministry of reconciliation along with Him. In Leviticus 8:7-9, we read the order in which the garments were put on: *"And he put upon him the coat, and girded him with the girdle, and clothed him with the robe, and put the ephod upon him, and he girded him with the curious girdle of the ephod, and bound it unto him therewith. And he put the breastplate upon him: also he put in the breastplate the Urim and the Thummin. And he put the mitre upon his head: also upon the mitre, even upon his forefront, did he put the golden plate, the holy crown: as the Lord commanded Moses."*

The Coat

Certainly we see that there was nothing plain or ordinary in the things which God planned; everything around us declares it. The root word used for "embroider" gives us the same idea as our modern "damask," which is an embroidery not worked on, but skillfully worked into the material. One writer said it was woven in diaper work; the threads of one color were diapered in checkers by the ordinary weaver. In Revelation 1:12-16 we read, *"And I turned to see the voice that spake with me. And being turned, I saw seven golden candlesticks; And in the midst of the seven candlesticks one like unto the Son of man, clothed with a garment down to the foot, and girt about the paps with a golden girdle. His head and his hairs were white like wool, as white as snow; and his eyes were as a flame of fire; And his feet like unto fine brass, as if they burned in a furnace; and his voice as the sound of many waters. And he had in his right hand seven stars: and out of his mouth went a sharp two-edged sword: and his countenance was as the sun shineth in his strength."*

This coat was made of fine white linen which speaks of the righteousness of Christ. In Revelation 19:7-8, we read, *"Let us be glad and rejoice, and give honour to him: for the marriage of the Lamb is come, and his wife hath made herself ready. And to her was granted that she should be arrayed in fine linen, clean and white: for the fine linen is the righteousness of saints."* This coat is most certainly symbolic of the holiness and the righteousness that God requires of His servants and His ministers. *"But we are all as an unclean thing, and all our righteousnesses are as filthy rags; and we all do fade as a leaf; and our iniquities, like the wind, have taken us away"* (Isaiah 64:6). But we know that the righteousness of Christ is like unto the pure, white, fine linen coat, and He has adorned us with it. This coat was to reach to the bottom of the feet of the priest so that his nakedness or flesh would be completely covered.

We will compare the eight pieces of clothing that the high priest wore with the eight things Paul instructed us to put on in Colossians 3:12-14: *"Put on therefore, as the elect of God, holy and beloved, bowels of mercies, kindness, humbleness of mind, meekness, long-suffering; forbearing one another, and forgiving one another, if any man have a quarrel against any: even as Christ forgave you, so also do ye. And above all these things put on charity, which is the bond of perfectness."* This is the nature and character of our Lord, and it is to be our nature and character as we follow Him. We can wear this coat only as we have been washed (Leviticus 8:7).

The Fine Twined Linen Girdle

"And a girdle of fine twined linen, and blue, and purple, and scarlet, of needlework; as the Lord commanded Moses."   *(Exodus 39:29)*

The priest, along with the high priest, was to put on the coat and then put on the girdle of the coat which was different from the CURIOUS GIRDLE OF THE EPHOD. This true girdle (avneht) for the coat was to be made of fine linen, of blue, purple, and scarlet needlework. It was to be made according to the pattern that God commanded Moses to follow. In Isaiah 11:5, we read, *"Righteousness shall be the girdle of his loins, and faithfulness, the girdle of his reins."* In Isaiah 22:21, we read, *"And I will clothe him with thy robe, and strengthen him with thy girdle, and I will commit thy government into his hand: and he shall be a father to the inhabitants of Jerusalem,*

235

and to the house of Judah." The object of the girdle was
to strengthen the loins for service. We are told it was the
Oriental custom that anyone must gird himself before entering active service. This speaks to us of the "towel-
girded" Lord Jesus Christ as He declared that He came to
minister to others, and not to be ministered unto as stated.
Mark 10:45 states, *"For even the Son of man came not
to be ministered unto, but to minister, and to give his
life a ransom for many."* The girdle was to be made of
the same material as the outer veil of the sanctuary. We
have often discussed the meaning of the fine linen. Jesus
girded Himself and served mankind. *"He riseth from supper, and laid aside his garments; and took a towel, and
girded himself. After that he poureth water into a basin,
and began to wash the disciples' feet, and to wipe them
with the towel wherewith he was girded"* (John 13:4-5).
Note again the "service" of seven.

We are told to *"Gird thyself and serve me"* (Luke
17:8). In Ephesians 6:13-17, we read, *"Wherefore take
unto you the whole armor of God, that ye may be able
to withstand in the evil day, and having done all, to
stand. Stand therefore, having your loins girt about
with truth, and having on the breastplate of righteousness; And your feet shod with the preparation of the gospel of peace; Above all, taking the shield of faith,
wherewith ye shall be able to quench all the fiery darts
of the wicked. And take the helmet of salvation, and the
sword of the Spirit, which is the word of God:"* As spiritual soldiers of Jesus, we see that the "girdle" represents
"truth." If we go into battle without girding up our loins,
we will experience total disaster.

*"Blessed are those servants, whom the Lord, when
He cometh shall find watching: verily I say unto you,*

*that He shall gird Himself, and make them sit down to
meat, and will come forth and serve them."*

(Luke 12:37)

*"Wherefore gird up the loins of your mind, be
sober, and hope to the end for the grace that is to be
brought unto you at the revelation of Jesus Christ."*

(1 Peter 1:13)

Here we are addressed as "strangers and pilgrims"
passing through the wilderness of this world on our way
to the land of Promise. We are admonished to keep our
minds upon Christ; to put on the whole armour of God;
keep our loins girt about with "truth;" and with this full
armour of equipment, we are ready to withstand the at-
tacks of the devil. The priests in those days would never
presume to perform before God without the entire set of
clothing prescribed by God. Ephesians 6 is our fulfillment of these garments.

The Robe Of The Ephod

*"And he made the robe of the ephod of woven work,
all of blue. And there was an hole in the midst of the
robe, as the hole of an habergeon, with a band round
about the hole, that it should not rend. And they made
upon the hems of the robe pomegranates of blue, and
purple, and scarlet, and twined linen. And they made
bells of pure gold, and put the bells between the pomegranates upon the hem of the robe, round about between the pomegranates. A bell and a pomegranate, a
bell and a pomegranate, round about the hem of the
robe to minister in; as the Lord commanded Moses."*

(Exodus 39:22-26)

This robe was worn only by the High Priest; it was to be woven in one piece, indicating the completeness of his spiritual integrity. It was BLUE. It stood in contrast to the veil, the door hangings, and the coat, which were all white linen with blue, purple and scarlet interwoven. A robe speaks to us of an office, position, and authority to respect.

There was an opening at the top for the head, and it was bound to a habergeon, a metal plate, to prevent rending of this priestly ROBE. Again, the ROBE SPEAKS OF ROYALTY. Scripture after scripture tells us that Jesus Christ is the only rightful KING OF KINGS. Many man-appointed emperors and rulers have assumed such a title, but they have long since passed from the scene; men mocked our Lord by placing a purple robe on Him and a crown. His scorners have fallen, their kingdoms disappeared, but our Lord has a kingdom that will forever reign in this earth. *"And he hath on his vesture and on his thigh a name written, KING OF KINGS, AND LORD OF LORDS"* (Revelation 19:16).

In 1 Samuel 24, we have an interesting story of a robe. King Saul is in pursuit of David's life. He is wearing his robe of authority and kingship as he enters a cave to rest. David and his men were already hiding in the cave. After the king has gone soundly to sleep, we read, *"And the men of David said unto him, Behold the day of which the Lord said unto thee, Behold, I will deliver thine enemy into thine hand, that thou mayest do to him as it shall seem good unto thee"* (verse 4). It was then that David arose and cut off the skirt of Saul's robe, signifying the loss of authority and kingship. David was quick to repent for he knew that only God could remove a king from his office.

Pomegranates—Bells

At the hem of this BLUE ROBE were pomegranates in purple and scarlet, with little gold bells between each one. Whenever the High Priest was behind the veil, in the Holy of Holies, all was quiet except for the tinkling of the little bells as he moved around in the room. This speaks to us of Divine witness; if the bells were silent, it meant death—separation. These bells were always silent at the death of the sacrifice; they rang again when the atonement was completed.

The Ephod and Curious Girdle

"And they shall take gold, and blue, and purple, and scarlet, and fine linen. And they shall make the ephod of gold, of blue, and of purple, of scarlet, and fine twined linen, with cunning work. It shall have the two shoulder pieces thereof joined at the two edges thereof; and so it shall be joined together. And the curious girdle of the ephod, which is upon it, shall be of the same, according to the work thereof; even of gold, of blue, and purple, and scarlet, and fine twined linen. And thou shalt take two onyx stones, and grave on them the names of the children of Israel: Six of their names on one stone, and the other six names of the rest on the other stone, according to their birth. With the work of an engraver in stone, like the engravings of a signet, shalt thou engrave the two stones with the names of the children of Israel: thou shalt make them to be set in ouches of gold. And thou shalt put the two stones upon the shoulders of the ephod for stones of memorial unto the children of Israel: and Aaron shall bear their names before the Lord upon his two shoulders for a memorial." *(Exodus 28:5-12)*

239

The ephod means the shoulder piece. It was upon the shoulders that the burden of the office rested. *"And the key of the house of David will I lay upon his shoulder; so he shall open, and none shall shut; and he shall shut, and none shall open"* (Isaiah 22:22). In Isaiah 9:6, we read, *"For unto us a child is born, unto us a son is given: and the government shall be upon his shoulder: and his name shall be called Wonderful, Counsellor, the mighty God, the Everlasting Father, the Prince of Peace."*

We see that the ephod of the High Priest had also two onyx stones, one on each shoulder which carried the names of the twelve tribes of Israel; six on each side. He bore the responsibility of the nation of Israel. This ephod was to be held in place by the curious girdle that was upon it, which matched the ephod in material, colors, and work. In Psalm 45:13-14, the picture of the bride and her clothing speaks to us of the ephod of the high priest: *"The king's daughter is all glorious within: her clothing is of wrought gold. She shall be brought unto the king in raiment of needlework: the virgins her companions that follow her shall be brought unto thee."*

The Breastplate of Judgment

"And thou shalt make ouches of gold; And two chains of pure gold at the ends; of wreathen work shalt thou make them, and fasten the wreathen chains to the ouches. And thou shalt make the breastplate of judgment with cunning work; after the work of the ephod thou shalt make it; of gold, of blue, and of purple, and of scarlet, and of fine twined linen, shalt thou make it. Foursquare it shall be being doubled; a span shall be

the length thereof, and a span shall be the breadth thereof. And thou shalt set in it settings of stones, even four rows of stones: the first row shall be a sardius, a topaz, and a carbuncle: this shall be the first row. And the second row shall be an emerald, a sapphire, and a diamond. And the third row a ligure, an agate, and an amethyst. And the fourth row a beryl, and an onyx, and a jasper: they shall be set in gold in their enclosings. And the stones shall be with the names of the children of Israel, twelve, according to their names, like the engravings of a signet; every one with his name shall they be according to the twelve tribes."

"And thou shalt make upon the breastplate chains at the ends of wreathen work of pure gold. And thou shalt make upon the breastplate two rings of gold, and shalt put the two rings on the two ends of the breastplate. And thou shalt put the two wreathen chains of gold in the two rings which are on the ends of the breastplate. And the other two ends of the two wreathen chains thou shalt fasten in the two ouches, and put them on the shoulder pieces of the ephod before it. And thou shalt make two rings of gold, and thou shalt put them upon the two ends of the breastplate in the border thereof, which is in the side of the ephod inward. And two other rings of gold thou shalt make, and shalt put them on the two sides of the ephod underneath, toward the forepart thereof, over against the other coupling thereof, above the curious girdle of the ephod. And they shall bind the breastplate by the rings thereof unto the rings of the ephod with a lace of blue, that it may be above the curious girdle of the ephod, and that the breastplate be not loosed from the ephod."

"And Aaron shall bear the names of the children of Israel in the breastplate of judgment upon his heart, when he goeth in unto the holy place, for a memorial before the Lord continually. And thou shalt put in the breastplate of judgment the Urim and the Thummim; and they shall be upon Aaron's heart, when he goeth in before the Lord: and Aaron shall bear the judgment of the children of Israel upon his heart before the Lord continually." (Exodus 28:13-30)

We are to keep in mind that the breastplate, ephod, girdle, and shoulder-stones are all united to make one garment. This in type is our Lord Jesus Christ in His Deity, Divinity, Humanity, Mediatorialship, and Righteousness. The name BREASTPLATE OF JUDGMENT, meant THE ORNAMENT OF DECISIONS. Its sole purpose was to house the URIM AND THUMMIM. The Scriptures are silent as to the form or shape of these two properties. We know they were put inside the breastplate, and it was a means whereby God gave the High Priest wisdom when he was in doubt about a situation. He would simply reach in and touch the Urim and Thummim. The breastplate was folded over in the form of a pocket or bag, foursquare to contain them. We have the Urim and Thummim in the gifts of the Holy Spirit today. These two words mean LIGHT AND PERFECTION.

"And he shall stand before Eleazar the priest, who shall ask counsel for him after the judgment of Urim before the Lord: at his word shall they go out, and at his

*word they shall come in, both he, and all the children
of Israel with him, even all the congregation."*

(Numbers 27:21)

The Mitre and the Bonnet

*"And thou shalt embroider the coat of fine linen,
and thou shalt make the mitre of fine linen, and thou
shalt make the girdle of needlework. And for Aaron's
sons thou shalt make coats, and thou shalt make for
them girdles, and bonnets shalt thou make for them, for
glory and for beauty."* *(Exodus 28:39-40)*

Not much is said about the MITRE. We must observe
that there was a distinction made between the headdress
of the High Priest and that of the priests. The Mitre was
for the High Priest, and the bonnets were for the priests.
The Mitre seemed to be formed like a turban or bonnet.
The word "mitre" means "to wrap" or "to roll around,"
a diadem. It was also made of fine linen. This would speak
to us of the purity of the mind. The head, of course, denotes authority. It is the head that controls the whole
body. The word "bonnet" is derived from a word that
means "to elevate," or "lift up."

Holiness unto the Lord

The Holy Crown

On the front of the Mitre was placed a diadem of gold
or a thin plate of gold on which was engraved HOLINESS
TO THE LORD. We will note the following about the
golden plate:

(1)   It was pure gold plate.

(2)   It was in the form of a crown.

(3)   It had letters inscribed into it.

(4)   It said: *"Holiness unto the Lord."*

(5)   It was attached to a ribband of blue.

(6)   It was to be on the forehead of Aaron.

(7)   Aaron was to bear the iniquity of the holy things.

(8)   It was always to be worn on his forehead.

Linen Breeches

"And thou shalt make them linen breeches to cover their nakedness; from the loins even unto the thighs they shall reach. And they shall be upon Aaron, and upon his sons, when they come in unto the tabernacle of the congregation, or when they come near unto the altar to minister in the holy place; that they bear not iniquity, and die: it shall be a statute for ever unto him and his seed after him."   *(Exodus 28:42-43)*

When we compare these scriptures with Leviticus 8:13, we discover a strict moral code set down by God before Israel. When we read verse 13, we might see an omission of this garment. Moses was commanded to put the coats, girdles, and bonnets upon Aaron's sons, but he was not told to put the breeches or trousers on them. The breeches would be put on first, before they came to him to be formally invested with the other garments; for they must not appear before him in their nakedness. Much could be said along this line but time and space will not allow it.

These linen breeches speak to us of the perfect provision which God has made for His people in Christ Jesus, and that Jesus by His sacrifice put an end to all flesh. We stand before the Father knowing that the old man has been crucified with Christ. This also tells us that all that is fleshly must be kept out of sight in the priestly office. The whole strength of nature is to be hidden; that power of indwelling evil, which ever opposes God and seeks to mar our walk, must be covered.

Consecration of the Priests

There are five great offerings which we will study in the book of Leviticus; after the priests were washed, clothed, and anointed, they were directed to offer up four of these five great sacrifices before they were considered wholly consecrated to the Lord. In this consecration, because the priests were sinners, they had to start with the sin offering, then the whole burnt offering, and next was the peace offering and the meat offering. Through the sacrifice of our Lord, He has made a way whereby we can come to God; He is the fulfillment of all offerings.

Food for the Priests

"And thou shalt take the breast of the ram of Aaron's consecration, and wave it for a wave offering before the Lord: and it shall be thy part."

(Exodus 29:26)

Continual Burnt Offerings

Each day they were to offer two yearling lambs upon the altar, one in the morning and the other in the evening. Each time they were to offer with them three quarts of finely ground flour mixed with 2½ pints of oil pressed from olives, and 2½ pints of wine, as a libation. This was for a fragrant burnt offering to the Lord.

245

Atonement Money

As stated in Exodus 30:11-16, Moses was instructed to take a census of the people of Israel, and each man that was numbered was to give a ransom to the Lord for his soul so that there would be no plague among them. All who had reached the age of twenty would give this offering. This would be 32 cents in U.S. money. The money collected was for the upkeep of the tabernacle.

We read that all were to pay the same amount whether rich or poor. In the matter of atonement, all would have to stand on one common platform. The *"Precious Blood of Jesus"* not works, devotedness, or fruitfulness, is the basis for every man's salvation. This is the believer's rest; this is the solid ground upon which we all may stand to inherit everlasting life. Jesus Christ is our Ransom money; we need not pay the price for it has been paid for us. He finished the work of atonement upon the Cross, and when the veil in the temple was rent from top to bottom, we were invited to come in and continually worship the King of Kings. Sweet and Precious is the Blood of Jesus that satisfies the longing of every thirsty soul; *"The courts of heaven will ever resound with the glorious doctrine of the blood."* (C. H. MacKintosh).

We must keep in mind that the book of Exodus is the book of REDEMPTION. From the very beginning we saw that they were in need of redemption from bitter Egyptian bondage. We read of the might and Holiness of the Redeemer Himself as He brought the plagues upon Egypt, and told Moses to instruct the people to kill the Passover Lamb and place the blood upon the door posts, for without the Blood there would be no deliverance. The duty of those who were redeemed by the Blood was obedience to the Lord who had delivered them. Thus, we see that the numbering of Israel is connected with ransom money. The thing suggested to us about "numbering" is ownership. Isaiah 40:26: *"Lift up your eyes on high, and behold who hath created these things that bringeth out their host by number, He calleth them all by names by the greatness of his of His might, for that He is strong in power; not one faileth."* In Daniel 5:26, we read, *"Men, God hath numbered thy kingdom and finished it."* In numbering the children of Israel, it was Jehovah dealing with His own redeemed people in the way He chose. God guards His right to do with His own as He so chooses. We see this in His dealings with David when he numbered the people and forgot God's glory, and sought after his own way. *"And Satan stood up against Israel and provoked David to number Israel. And David said to Joab and to the rulers of the people, Go, number Israel from Beersheba even to Dan; and bring the number of them to me, that I may know it . . . and God was displeased with this thing; wherefore He smote Israel . . ."* (1 Chronicles 21). This ransom money sets forth God's people as redeemed and set aside unto their God. The true meaning of our type is ever so clear to us as we observe how the Holy Spirit sets it aside once the antitype has come in.

The Golden Calf and Broken Law

Chapter 11

THE GOLDEN CALF

"And when the people saw that Moses delayed to come down out of the mount, the people gathered themselves together unto Aaron, and said unto him, Up, make us gods, which shall go before us; for as for this Moses, the man that brought us up out of the land of Egypt, we wot not what is become of him. And Aaron said unto them, Break off the golden earrings, which are in the ears of your wives, of your sons, and of your daughters, and bring them unto me. And all the people brake off the golden earrings which were in their ears, and brought them unto Aaron. And he received them at their hand, and fashioned it with a graving tool, after he had made it a molten calf: and they said, These be thy gods, O Israel, which brought thee up out of the land of Egypt. And when Aaron saw it, he built an altar before it; and Aaron made proclamation, and said, Tomorrow is a feast to the Lord." *(Exodus 32:1-5)*

249

(August 1, 1462 B.C. Chronological Bible)

"And they rose up early on the morrow, and offered burnt offerings, and brought peace offerings; and the people sat down to eat and to drink, and rose up to play."
(Exodus 32:6)

Israel's rejection of God was most complete at this point. When they saw that Moses delayed his coming back to them, they went to Aaron and demanded that he make a god for them to follow. They brought their golden earrings to him, and he fashioned and molded a golden calf for them. Aaron built an altar for the idol to stand upon, and declared that on the morrow they would have a feast "unto the Lord." This was putting aside the Lord who had delivered them out of the hand of their oppressors, and putting a calf in His stead. How quickly they turned aside from the ways of the Lord God who had provided water when they were thirsty, and food to satisfy their hunger. With a calf before him, Aaron proclaimed a feast day unto the Lord! God was displaced by an idol; a golden calf fashioned by one of their holy leaders. Israel had served false gods in Egypt, according to Joshua 24:14, and we see the flesh was yet unchanged: *"Now therefore fear the Lord, and serve him in sincerity and in truth: and put away the gods which your fathers served on the other side of the flood, and in Egypt; and serve ye the Lord."*

Covenant Broken

There is a break in our narrative; God and Moses have spent forty days and nights in the Mount together in behalf of the children of Israel, and we find it most difficult to contrast the scene in the mount with that of the sinning people right below the GLORY. For some time now we

250

have been occupied with the Holiness of God and His precepts, now we must go down the mountain and again witness the depravity of the human heart.

"And the Lord said unto Moses, go, get thee down; for the people, which thou broughtest out of the land of Egypt, have corrupted themselves: They have turned aside quickly out of the way which I commanded them: they have made them a molten calf, and have worshipped it, and have sacrificed thereunto, and said, These be thy gods, O Israel, which have brought thee out of the land of Egypt. And the Lord said unto Moses, I have seen this people, and, behold it is a stiffnecked people: Now therefore let me alone, that my wrath may wax hot against them, and that I may consume them: and I will make of thee a great nation." (Exodus 32:7-10)

God told Moses to let Him alone so that His anger could blaze out hot against the children of Israel to totally destroy them. He was ready to turn to Moses and make a great nation come from him.

Intercession

The subject of idolatry is a most solemn one. God said to Moses, *"Go, get thee down; for thy people, which thou broughtest out of the land of Egypt, have corrupted themselves:"* Those sinning Israelites now belonged to Moses. He in turn becomes the TYPICAL MEDIATOR for them. If it had not been for Moses, they would have been lost forever. How awesome were the words, *"Let me alone . . ."*

Moses, as the typical mediator, gave the people back to God when he said, *". . . Lord, why doth they wrath wax hot against THY PEOPLE, which thou hast brought*

251

forth out of the land of Egypt with great power, and with a mighty hand" (verse 11)? Let us view this same kind of prayer in John 1:2-3, when our Lord prayed for His own: *"As thou hast given him power over all flesh, that he should give eternal life to as many as thou hast given him. And this is life eternal, that they might know thee the only true God, and Jesus Christ, whom thou has sent (verses 2-3) . . . And now, O Father, glorify thou me with thine own self with the glory which I had with thee before the world was. I have manifested thy name unto the men which thou gavest me out of the world: thine they were, and thou gavest them me, and they have kept thy word (verses 5-6) . . . I pray for them: I pray not for the world, but for them which thou hast given me; for they are thine"* (verse 9).

Here we have a perfect example of the "effectual, fervent prayers of a righteous man" mentioned in James. Moses besought the Lord as to His anger. He reminded Him that it was He who had brought them out of Egypt with great power and with a mighty hand. "If you do this evil, Lord, the Egyptians will laugh and say their god brought them out into the desert to kill them. Lord, turn Yourself from Your fierce anger, and REPENT."

Moses continued to reason with the Lord: "Keep in mind Abraham, Isaac, and Israel, your servants, to whom you swore by your Own Self that you would multiply their seed as the stars of heaven; and You, Lord promised them you would give them this land as their inheritance forever."

The Lord turned back from the Evil He was set on doing to the children of Israel. With that, Moses turned and went down the mountain with the two tablets of stone in his hand. They were the work of God; the writing was the writing of God graved upon both sides of the tablets. As Moses approached Joshua who had been waiting in the mount for him, He said to Moses, "Sounds like those people are preparing for war." But Moses replied, "No, I hear singing. It is not the victory song, but the noise of sin in the camp." As they reached the camp, Moses saw the golden calf, and the dancing; in anger he threw the tablets to the ground, and they lay broken at the feet of the people. This sin would be charged to them. He melted the calf in the fire, then grounded it to powder—put it in their water, and made them drink. In this we may readily see that God loves because He wants to love; He gives because He chooses to give, and not because of any good thing within us. Therefore, we bow down before our Sovereign Lord, and let Him have His way in our lives. It is He who knows what is best for us. Yet, as we stand to make fervent intercession, we are reminded that we, too, may remind the Lord of His promises and His Word.

In Deuteronomy 9:21, we read more detail of the burning of the calf: *"And I took your sin, the calf which ye had made, and burnt it with fire, and stamped it, and ground it very small, even until it was as small as dust: and I cast the dust thereof into the brook that descended out of the mount."* In Exodus 17:6, we are reminded of the brook that "descended out of the mount."

Moses turned on Aaron, his brother, who had been left in charge of the camp. He demanded to know what the people could have done to him to cause him to lead them into such a gross sin as idolatry. Aaron claimed he threw the gold earrings into the fire and out jumped a calf.

253

Moses saw that the people were committing adultery, not only at the encouragement of Aaron, but also to the amusement of their enemies. He stood at the camp entrance and shouted for those who were on the side of the Lord to join him. All the Levites stood with him.

"And Moses stood in the gate of the camp, and said, Who is on the Lord's side? Let him come unto me. And all the sons of Levi gathered themselves together unto him. And he said unto them, Thus saith the Lord God of Israel, Put every man his sword by his side, and go in and out from gate to gate throughout the camp, and slay every man his brother, and every man his companion, and every man his neighbour. And the children of Levi did according to the word of Moses: and there fell of the people that day about three thousand men. For Moses had said, Consecrate yourselves today to the Lord, even every man upon his son, and upon his brother; that he may bestow upon you a blessing this day." *(Exodus 32:26-29)*

Second Intercession By Moses To Make Atonement For The People

(Trip 7, Verses 30-32)

"And it came to pass on the morrow, that Moses said unto the people, Ye have sinned a great sin: and now I will go up unto the Lord; peradventure I shall make an atonement for your sin. And Moses returned unto the Lord, and said, Oh, this people have sinned a great sin, and have made them gods of gold. Yet now, if thou wilt forgive their sin—; and if not, blot me, I pray thee, out of thy book which thou hast written."

(Exodus 32:30-32)

"At the close of this chapter, Jehovah asserts His rights in moral government, in the following words: 'Whosoever hath sinned against Me, him will I blot out of My book. Therefore now go, lead the people unto the place of which I have spoken unto thee: behold, Mine Angel shall go before thee: nevertheless, in the day when I visit I will visit their sin upon them.' This is God in government, not God in the gospel. Here he speaks of blotting out the sinner; in the gospel He is seen blotting out sin. A wide difference!" (MacIntosh)

These people were sent forward under the mediatorship of Moses, by the hand of an angel. They had forfeited their rights and claims to Jehovah.

Israel Plagued

"And the Lord plagued the people because they made the calf, which Aaron made." *(Exodus 32:35)*

"And the Lord said unto Moses, Depart, and go up hence, thou and the people which thou hast brought up out of the land of Egypt, unto the land which I sware to Abraham, to Isaac, and to Jacob, saying, Unto thy seed will I give it: And I will send an angel before thee; and I will drive out the CANAAN-ite, the AMORITE, and the HITTITE, and the PERIZZITE, the HIVITE, and the JEBUSITE. Unto a land flowing with milk and honey: for I will not go up in the midst of thee; for thou art a stiffnecked people: lest I consume thee in the way."

(Exodus 33:1-3)

God had declared that He would not go with them for they were a stubborn, and unruly people, and He would be tempted to destroy them along the way. When they heard His Words, they went into mourning and stripped themselves of all their jewelry and ornaments.

Temporary Tabernacle

"And Moses took the tabernacle, and pitched it without the camp, afar off from the camp, and called it the Tabernacle of the congregation. And it came to pass, that every one which sought the Lord went out unto the tabernacle of the congregation, which was without the camp. And it came to pass, when Moses went out unto the tabernacle, that all the people rose up, and stood every man at his tent door, and looked after Moses, until he was gone into the tabernacle. And it came to pass, as Moses entered into the tabernacle, the cloudy pillar descended, and stood at the door of the tabernacle, and the Lord talked with Moses. And all the people saw the cloudy pillar stand at the tabernacle door; and all the people rose up and worshipped, every man in his tent door. And the Lord spake unto Moses face to face, as a man speaketh unto his friend. And he turned again into the camp: but his servant Joshua, the son of Nun, a young man, departed not out of the tabernacle."

(Exodus 33:7-11)

Moses took the temporary tent (Ohel) and pitched it outside the camp. This action on the part of Moses revealed three things: (1) It was an act of submission in that he was bowing to the righteous verdict of God. While they were a stiffnecked people, God would not dwell in their midst. While they remained unrepentant, He would not own them as His people. (2) It was an act of faith on the part of Moses. Moses had been hearing the Word of God while he was in the mount, and he knew God would no longer dwell where the golden calf had been, so he pitched the tent outside the camp, or made a place for it outside the camp, and called it "the tabernacle of the congregation." (3) This was also an act of grace on the part of Moses. Before God smote His people, He would give them room for repentance. As another has said, "He who pronounced judgment upon the people for their sins, provided a way for their escape." Those who "sought the Lord" were not only spared, but permitted to go forth unto the tent. Thus, "where sin abounded, grace did much more abound." Grace made it possible for the people to meet Him outside.

"Let us go forth therefore unto him without the camp, bearing his reproach."　　　(Hebrews 13:13)

When Moses went into the tent, all the people would rise and stand in their tent doors watching until he reached its entrance. As he entered, the pillar of cloud would come down and stand at the door and God would talk to Moses face to face like one would talk with his best friend. The people bowed down to the ground in their tent doors and worshipped the Lord.

Third Intercession

Moses reminded the Lord that He had a people, and that He had promised to carry them into the Promised Land; but He had not told him who would go with him. Moses asked the Lord for clear-cut guidance along the way.

"And he said, My presence shall go with thee, and I will give thee rest. And he said unto him, if thy presence go not with me, carry us not up hence. For wherein shall it be known here that I and thy people have found

*grace in thy sight? Is it not in that thou goest with us?
So shall we be separated, I and thy people, from all the
people that are upon the face of the earth. And the Lord
said unto Moses, I will do this thing also that thou hast
spoken: for thou has found grace in my sight, and I
know thee by name.''* (Exodus 33:14-17)

God gave Moses full assurance that he had found favor in His sight, and that He would do what he asked of
Him. We note that the Presence of the Lord brings rest to
the heart. Moses stepped out on faith when He asked God
to show forth His Glory in the face of all that has just tran-
spired between God and His people.

*"And he said, I will make all my goodness pass be-
fore thee, and I will proclaim the name of the Lord before thee; and will be gracious to whom I will be
gracious, and will shew mercy on whom I will shew
mercy. And he said, Thou canst not see my face: for
there shall no man see me, and live. And the Lord said,
Behold, there is a place by me, and thou shalt stand
upon a rock: And it shall come to pass, while my glory
passeth by, that I will put thee in a clift of the rock, and
will cover thee with my hand while I pass by: and I will
take away mine hand, and thou shalt see my back parts;
but my face shall not be seen.''* (Exodus 33:19-23)

New Revelation of God

(Trip 8, Verses 5-29)

In chapter 34 Moses was instructed by the Lord to
hew two tables of stone just like the first ones which he
broke, and come back into the mount with Him and there
He would write upon them the commandments. He spent

another forty days and forty nights in the Mount alone with God.

"And the Lord descended in the cloud, and stood with him there, and proclaimed the name of the Lord. And the Lord passed by before him, and proclaimed, The Lord, The Lord God, merciful and gracious, longsuffering, and abundant in goodness and truth. Keeping mercy for thousands, forgiving iniquity and transgression and sin, and that will by no means clear the guilty; visiting the iniquity of the fathers upon the children, and upon the children's children, unto the third and to the fourth generation." *(Exodus 34:5-7)*

The Lord descended in the mount in the form of a CLOUD, and stood with Moses, and passed in front of him, and introduced Himself as Jehovah, the merciful and gracious God. Moses bowed his head to the ground in haste and worshipped the Lord, and listened as the Lord renewed the covenant and commandments.

God spoke with Moses for forty days and forty nights giving him the moral, civil, and ceremonial laws which we will note in more detail in the rest of the books of Moses.

"And the Lord said unto Moses, Write thou these words: for after the tenor of these words I have made a covenant with thee and with Israel. And he was there with the Lord forty days and forty nights; he did neither eat bread, nor drink water. And he wrote upon the tables the words of the covenant, the ten commandments." *(Exodus 34:27-28)*

Descent of Moses

"And it came to pass, when Moses came down from mount Sinai with the two tables of testimony in Moses' hand, when he came down from the mount, that Moses

wist not that the skin of his face shone while he talked
with him.''   (Exodus 34:29)

When Aaron and the children of Israel saw that
Moses' face shone, they were afraid to let him come near
them. Moses called them to him, they came near, and he
gave them the commandments and all the Lord had
spoken unto him. Until he had finished speaking to them,
he wore a veil over his face; but when he went into the
tent to talk with the Lord he took off the veil. We read in
2 Corinthinians 3:12-17, *"Seeing then that we have
such hope, we use great plainness of speech: And not as
Moses, which put a vail over his face, that the children
of Israel could not steadfastly look to the end of that
which is abolished: But their minds were blinded: for
until this day remaineth the same vail untaken away in
the reading of the old testament; which vail is done
away in Christ. But even unto this day, when Moses is
read, the vail is upon their heart. Nevertheless when it
shall turn to the Lord, the vail shall be taken away. Now
the Lord is that Spirit: and where the Spirit of the Lord
is, there is liberty.''*

Completion of the Tabernacle

It was at this point that Moses gave the final instructions for the children of Israel to construct the tabernacle.
The anointed workers were brought forth; the materials
were all delivered to the workers in abundance; and the
Tabernacle in the Wilderness was erected.

Coverings Put In Place

*"Thus did Moses: according to all that the Lord
commanded him, so did he. And it came to pass in the
first month in the second year, on the first day of the*

month, that the tabernacle was reared up. And Moses reared up the tabernacle, and fastened his sockets, and set up the boards thereof, and put in the bars thereof, and reared up his pillars. And he spread abroad the tent over the tabernacle, and put the covering of the tent above upon it; as the Lord commanded Moses."

(Exodus 40:16-19)

Furniture Placed in Holy of Holies

"And he took and put the testimony into the ark, and set the staves on the ark, and put the mercy seat above upon the ark: And he brought the ark into the tabernacle, and set up the veil of the covering, and covered the ark of the testimony; as the Lord commanded Moses." *(Exodus 40:20-21)*

Furniture Placed in Holy Place

"And he put the table in the tent of the congregation, upon the side of the tabernacle northward, without the veil. And he set the bread in order upon it before the Lord; as the Lord had commanded Moses. And he put the candlestick in the tent of the congregation, over against the table, on the side of the tabernacle southward. And he lighted the lamps before the Lord; as the Lord commanded Moses. And he put the golden altar in the tent of the congregation before the veil: And he burnt sweet incense thereon; as the Lord commanded Moses." *(Exodus 40:22-27)*

Court Furniture Placed

"And he set up the hanging at the door of the tabernacle. And he put the altar of burnt offering by the door of the tabernacle of the tent of the congregation,

and offered upon it the burnt offering and the meat of-fering; as the Lord commanded Moses. And he set the laver between the tent of the congregation and the al-tar, and put water there, to wash withal. And Moses and Aaron and his sons washed their hands and their feet thereat: When they went into the tent of the congrega-tion, and when they came near unto the altar, they washed; as the Lord commanded Moses. And he reared up the court round about the tabernacle and the altar, and set up the hanging of the court gate. So Moses fin-ished the work."   *(Exodus 40:28-33)*

The Glory of God

"Then a cloud covered the tent of the congregation, and the glory of the Lord filled the tabernacle. And Moses was not able to enter into the tent of the congre-gation, because the cloud abode thereon, and the glory of the Lord filled the tabernacle. And when the cloud was taken up from over the tabernacle, the children of Israel went onward in all their journeys. But if the cloud were not taken up, then they journeyed not till the day that it was taken up. For the cloud of the Lord was upon the tabernacle by day, and fire was on it by night, in the sight of all the house of Israel, throughout all their journeys."   *(Exodus 40:34-38)*

Summary: Exodus

Jesus, The Fulfillment Of The Tabernacle Types: Book of John

The GATE of the Tabernacle in the wilderness always faced the East. We must keep our eyes turned toward the east from whence the Lord will make His appearence. Jesus said, *"As the lightning cometh out of the east, and shineth even unto the west; so shall also the coming of the Son of man be"* (Matthew 24:27). We must also note that the tribe of Judah was stationed in front of the east gate. Judah means "praise" and we have discussed previously that we are to enter His gate with thanksgiving. This is the only WAY into the courtyard; there is no other way. This was a most beautiful gate, leading to the brazen altar and the laver in the outer court; there the troubled soul found rest.

This gate points us to our Lord Jesus. Even though the fence and the curtains would keep out the curious, he was most welcome to come through the gate and participate in the outer court activities.

Jesus said, *"Enter ye in at the strait gate: for wide is the gate, and broad is the way, that leadeth to destruction, and many there be which go in thereat: because strait is the gate, and narrow is the way which leadeth unto life, and few there be that find it"* (Matthew 7:13, 14). This is the Way which leads into the outer court and to the brazen altar which speaks to us of salvation through Jesus.

"Wherefore when he cometh into the world, he saith, Sacrifice and offering thou wouldest not, but a body thou prepared me: In burnt offerings and sacrifices for sin thou hast had no pleasure. Then said I, Lo, I come (in the volume of the book it is written of me,) to do thy will, O God." (Hebrews 10:5-7)

Jesus said, *"I am the door: by me if any man enter in, he shall be saved"* (John 10:9).

The outer court with its brazen altar was a "slaughter house" full of blood. Without the shedding of blood there is no remission for sin; this is the CROSS. The fire upon this altar was lit by God. The purpose of this altar was to lift up the sacrifices unto the Lord God day and night. This altar was just inside the gate, and accessible to all. We do not linger here, but quickly move to the brazen laver full of water. One writer called this "God's wash basin." Since Christ is the tabernacle, we are in Him the minute we step through the gate and approach the first altar to partake of our sacrifice.

Water is symbolic of the Word; thus, we approach the water and are cleansed of our sins. Here we enter into self-judgment as we look into the "mirror of the word." In John 15:3, we read, *"Now ye are clean through the word which I have spoken unto you."* Jesus said in John 17:17, *"Sanctify them through thy truth: thy word is truth."* Here at the laver we are sanctified through the Word of the Lord, and kept clean from the defilements of this world. The Word teaches us that we are saved by faith in the shed Blood of the Lord Jesus Christ, as the Spirit of the Lord draws us; the Word and the Spirit work together to convict of sin, then the Word, as mentioned, keeps us.

Symbolism of Furniture

FURNITURE: CHRIST

(1) The Ark	The Presence of God
(2) The Mercy Seat	Propitiation
(3) The Altar Of Incense	Intercessor
(4) The Golden Lampstand	The True Light
(5) The Table Of Shewbread	Bread Of Life
(6) The Laver	The Word Of God
(7) The Alter Of Sacrifice	Christ, The Final Sacrifice

MEASUREMENTS:

10 cubits = 15 feet
20 cubits = 30 feet
30 cubits = 45 feet
50 cubits = 75 feet
100 cubits = 150 feet

The height of the Tabernacle, Holy of Holies, and the Holy Place was 15 feet. The linen fence of court was 5 cubits or 7-½ feet.

The measurements used are according to the Hebrew cubit which is 18 inches, or 1-½ feet.

12 Precious Stones Used in the Breastplate of Decision Representing the 12 Tribes of Israel
(Exodus 28)

STONE	HEBREW	TRIBE	MEANING
Sardius–brownish red	Odem	Judah	Praise
Topaz–yellow lustre	Pitdah	Issachar	Bought with a price
Emerald–green	Nohpech	Zebulum	Dwelling
Carbuncle–red garnet	Barketh	Reuben	Look! A Son!
Sapphire–deep blue	sappeer	Simeon	Hearing
Diamond–white	Yah-ghalohim	Gad	A Troop
Ligure–bright yellow	Leh-Sham	Ephaim	Doubly Fruitful
Agate–light blue	Shvoo	Manasseh	Causing
Amethyst–violet	Agh-lah-mah	Benjamin	Forgetfulness
Beryl—green-yellow	tarshish	Dan	Son of My Strength
Onyx–bright yellow	shoh-ham	Asher	God Will Judge
Jasper–clear	jahsh-peh	Naphtali	Happy, Joyous Wrestling

Basic Bible Numbers and Meanings

ONE	GODHEAD	Deuteronony 4:6; John 17;
TWO	WITNESS	Amos 3:3; Matthew 18:16;
THREE	TRINITY	Matthew 28:19
FOUR	UNIVERSAL	Isaiah 11:12; Luke 12:54
FIVE	GRACE	Matthew 14:17,21; 25:15; I Samuel 17:40
SIX	MAN	Exodus 20:9; Revelation 13:18
SEVEN	PERFECTION	All through the tabernacle and the book of Revelation
EIGHT	NEW ORDER	I Peter 3:20; Genesis 17:12
NINE	GIFTS	I Corinthians 12; Galatians 5
TEN	REDEMPTION	Exodus 20:1-17; Luke 15:8-10
ELEVEN	INCOMPLETE	Genesis 35:22; Matthew 12:1
TWELVE	JUDICIAL	Genesis 11; Acts 1:26
FORTY	PROBATION	Exodus 24:18; Matthew 4:2
FIFTY	PENTECOST	(Fifty days after the Passover-Acts 2)
ONE-HUNDRED	FRUITFULNESS	100 -fold

Blow The Trumpet In Zion

SEVEN TRUMPETS OF REVELATION:

(1)   The first TRUMPET (Revelation 8:7)
      hail — fire — blood

(2)   The Second TRUMPET (Revelation 8:8-9)
      A burning mountain

(3)   The third TRUMPET (Revelation 8:10-11)
      The star wormwood

(4)   The fourth TRUMPET (Revelation 8:12)
      The sun, moon, and stars are affected.

THE THREE WOES OF THE LAST THREE TRUMPETS:

(5)   The fifth TRUMPET (Revelation 9:1-12)
      (1st woe) The plague of demon locusts out
      of the abyss

(6)   The sixth TRUMPET (Revelation 9:13-21)
      (2nd woe) The plague of demon horsemen
      out of the abyss

(7)   The seventh TRUMPET (Revelation 11:14-
      13:18)
      (3rd woe) The casting out of satan to earth

LEVITICUS

THE THIRD BOOK OF MOSES

HOLY LIVING

High Priest Garments

Chapter 12

HOLY LIVING

The book of Leviticus is the third book of the Torah or the Pentateuch. In Latin it is known as *Liber Leviticus;* in the Greek *Leuitike Biblos* or "Levitical Book." The Hebrew title is "Wayyiqra" meaning "And he called." It has more to do with the Priests than the Levites themselves.

It contains only four narratives as follows:

(1)   The consecration of Aaron to the Priesthood (Leviticus 8-9).

(2)   Divine punishment of Nadab and Abihu, two of Aaron's four sons. (Leviticus 10:1-7). Although the Priests could not mourn their deaths, the whole house of Israel could (Leviticus 10:4-7).

The specific lesson in the episode of Aaron's sons being killed before a just and holy God is that even priests can sin if given over to the flesh.

It was believed the sons had indulged in liquor before going into the Holy Place because of the passage following their death. God exhorted Aaron in Leviticus 10:8-11: *"Do not drink wine or strong drink, thou, nor thy sons with thee, when ye go into the tabernacle of the congregation, lest ye die: it shall be a statute forever throughout your generations . . ."* This story is also evaluated with other Bible incidents of spirit versus flesh where all seems godly; then sin comes in to cause destruction. Examples are:

(a)   Adam and Eve in the Garden of Eden; then temptation, disobedience and expulsion from the Garden.

(b)   Noah and his family escaped the Flood in the Ark; (Noah, a type of the Jew being kept through the Tribulation; Enoch, a type of the Church in Rapture). Noah offered sacrifice to God; he got drunk and cursed Ham, which in turn became the father and progenitor of the Canaanite nations and flesh enemies of the Israelites.

(c)   Moses received the Law on Mt. Sinai and when he returned to the camp, the Israelites were worshipping the Golden Calf. The flesh had overcome God's spiritual intention for His people and they died because of sin.

(3)   The ritual error of Aaron's remaining sons, Eleazar and Ithamar when they failed to eat the res-

idue of the Sin Offering as commanded by God (Leviticus 10:12-20).

(4)   The last narrative in the Book of Leviticus is the stoning of a blasphemer (Leviticus 24:10-14; 23).

All the rest of the Book is devoted to the Law. The character and function of Hebrew Law as found in the Old Testament is often expressed by Bible scholars in the German term HEILSGESETZ, meaning "sacred and saving law." Both Jewish and Christian theologians recognize HEILSGESETZ as a record and revelation of divine order of a society which was meant to be established throughout Israel. The themes of the Levitical Law are:

(1)   Worship and Sacrifice—Leviticus 1-7 (People's response to the revelation of God)

(2)   Ministry of the Priesthood—Leviticus 8-10 (Consecration and conduct of the Priests)

(3)   Purifying of Israel's Lifestyle—Leviticus 11-15 (Discernment between the clean and unclean and how to choose the clean)

(4)   Israel's Annual Atonement—Leviticus 16 (The High Priest's yearly visit into the Holy of Holies to atone for sins of people; escape of the Scapegoat, a type of the Crucifixion and the Resurrection)

(5)   Holiness of God and Israel—Leviticus 17-22; 24 (Relationship of a holy God and a sanctified, holy nation to be in one accord)

(6)   Dedication of time, life and property—Leviticus 23;25 (Tithes, offerings and alms desired by God from Israel)

(7)   Preaching—Leviticus 26-27 (Blessings for the obedient; curses for the disobedient)

Sacrifices and Offerings

These sacrifices and offerings were a command of God spoken through Moses to the Israelites in the wilderness following their exodus from Egypt. (Leviticus 1:1-6, 7). Bible scholars have noticed that the rituals were not accompanied by spoken liturgy or exposition, so it has been assumed they were conducted in silence. But by studying the Psalms, some have concluded that reading or chanting the Psalms was practiced during the performance of the sacrifice. An example would be: on the Day of Atonement, as the scapegoat was led off into the wilderness bearing the sins of the people, the High Priest might have said Psalms 103:12, *"As far as the east is from the west, so far hath he removed our transgressions from us."*

As we study the typology of the sacrifices and offerings, we see the parallel to the life of Jesus Christ in His character, His manner and His attributes, as well as the same qualities of being a just and Holy God.

This third book of Moses is primarily devoted to instructions for holy living. *"Ye shall be holy for I am holy"* is a key statement for the entire book (Leviticus 11:44-45). The Hebrew word "qodesh," meaning "holy" or "holiness," occurs more than 150 times. These instructions were given during Israel's one-year encampment at Mount Sinai. With the building of the tabernacle, instructions were given concerning the offering of sacrifices. We will deal mostly with the offerings and feast days in outline form. May we keep in mind that the observance of this covenant relationship with God was vitally important for the Israelites. Through the offering of sacrifices it was possible for them individually as well as collectively to approach God repeatedly in worship, expressing their thanksgiving. It is equally important for us to realize that these provisions for guidance to holy living were made in the context of mutual love between God and man, and the second commandment issued out of this relationship, *"Thou shalt love thy neighbor as thyself"* (Leviticus 19:18). In John 13:34, Jesus gave us that commandment as the new and greatest commandment, *"A new commandment I give unto you, That ye love one another; as I have loved you, that ye also love one another."*

Leviticus 1:

(1) BURNT OFFERING
SWEET SAVOUR: VOLUNTARY
CATTLE: A male bullock without blemish had to be given by the head of the household. He brought it of his own voluntary will to the door of the tabernacle where he put his hand on its head transferring his sins as well as the sins of his family to make atonement for them. Next, the priests took the slain animal and sprinkled the blood upon the altar of sacrifice.

TEACHING: Identification with Christ. Christ offered Himself without spot to God. In Ephesians 5:2, we read, *"And walk in love, as Christ also hath loved us, and hath given himself for us an offering and a sacrifice to God for a sweet-smelling savour."* This symbolizes consecration for the Christians (Romans 12:1). The blood sprinkled upon the altar of sacrifice signified the remission of sins (Matthew 26:28).

The head, after being surrendered, was cut off and placed on the altar to be burned along with the fat which had been separated from the meaty parts. The fat is hard to digest and is a type of unconfessed sin. Both were consumed in the fire of the Lord upon the altar with the body.

The body of the animal was flayed and cut into pieces (John 1:29; Isaiah 53:5; Luke 22:63-65), (John 19:1-16) and laid upon the altar along with the head and the fat. Only the inward parts and the legs were washed in water. The inward parts signified the intent of the heart or the inward man (Romans 8:1-17), and the legs personified the willingness to take the gospel into all the world, (Romans 10:14-15). Both parts had to be clean, then laid upon the altar with the other parts of the body, and the whole sacrifice was burned by fire causing a sweet-smelling savour to rise into the nostrils of a Holy God. The sacrifice of the bullock is a type and shadow of the living sacrifice required of us in Romans 12:1-21. The sweet-smelling savour is the spiritual relationship the believer has with the Father.

SHEEP OR GOATS: Made in the same order as the bullock and had the same relationship except they were slain on the north side of the altar (Leviticus 1:10-13). Since nearly all of Israel's enemies usually attacked from the east and the south, they carried their captives off to the north. The north always signified the returning from captivity. When a person's sins are forgiven him, he is free from captivity (Romans 6:8; Isaiah 61:1-3; Luke 4:18). The sacrifices of bulls and goats were given by the affluent people.

FOWLS, TURTLEDOVES, OR YOUNG PI-
GEONS: Usally given by the poor people or
those who could not afford a bullock or goat
(Leviticus 1:14-17). The fowl, although small,
was sacrificed the same way, except the feath-
ers were cast on the side of the altar where the
ashes were to be burned outside the camp later.
The burned sacrifice made a sweet-smelling savour unto the Lord.

Leviticus 2:

(2)   MEAT OFFERING: (MEAL OR GRAIN)
      SWEET SAVOUR: VOLUNTARY

This offering was given by the poorest people who
could not afford live animals or fowls to be sacrificed.
Their offerings consisted of three parts:

(1)   fine flour
(2)   oil
(3)   frankincense

TEACHING: In this we see tripartite man:
spirit, soul, and body. This speaks to us of
Christ in His human perfection, tested by suffering (Isaiah 28:28; 53:4; Hebrews 5: 8-9).

FRUIT OFFERING: The meat offering of the
Firstfruits was to be the first ears of green corn
which were to be dried by fire; then the kernals
beaten (Leviticus 2:14-17). Oil and frankincense were to be laid upon it and the priest was
to burn it as a memorial to the Lord. He was to
use a part of the beaten corn, a part of the oil,
and all of the frankincense was to be burned as

an offering before the Lord. Our firstfruits are to be given in portions (tithes and offerings) (body and spirit) with all (soul) our consent of our will, mind and emotions (frankincense) to the Lord (Exodus 22:29; Deuteronomy 18:4; Romans 11:16; Romans 8:23; James 1:18; Revelations 14:4-5; I Corinthians 15:20).

Leviticus 3:

(3)   PEACE OFFERING

SWEET SAVOUR: VOLUNTARY

PEACE OFFERING OF THE HERD, THE SHEEP AND GOATS: Jesus Christ is the perfect offering for our peace: (Levitius 3:1-16; Isaiah 53:5; John 16:33; John 14:1, 27-28; Luke 24:36; John 20:19-21; Romans 1:7; Romans 15:33; Philippians 4:7).

PERPETUAL LAW FORBIDDING CONSUMPTION OF THE FAT OR BLOOD OF A SACRIFICE: The fat of the animal is hard to digest and symbolized unconfessed sin; the life is in the blood (Leviticus 3:17; John 6:54-56; Acts 15:20, 29).

TEACHING: Jesus is our Peace.

Leviticus 4:

(4)   SIN OFFERING

NON-SWEET SAVOUR: INVOLANTARY

If a person in the congregation, a priest, or a king sinned in ignorance against the commandments of the Lord, they were to offer up a sin offering and they were

276

not to omit anyone. The blood was sprinkled seven times before the Lord before the veil of the sanctuary (Holy of Holies); then the priest applied some to the horns of the altar of incense (Holy Place); then he poured the rest of the blood at the bottom of the brazen altar (Outer Court) making atonement for the tabernacle of man as a whole (spirit, soul, and body).

If the whole congregation sinned without knowledge, the elders of the congregation laid their hands upon the bullock and the blood was applied as before except the atonement was made for the whole congregation and their sins forgiven them.

When a king or ruler sinned in ignorance, he was to bring an offering from the male goats without blemish; if the people sinned because of ignorance, they could bring a kid, male or female, from the goats, and without blemish. If they brought a lamb, it was to be female without blemish. No one was omitted from atoning for their sins.

> TEACHING: Jesus is Our Atonement for Sin
> (John 3:16; Romans 2:11; 3:23).

Leviticus 5:

> (5)   TRESPASS OFFERING
> NON-SWEET SAVOUR: INVOLUNTARY
> This offering is closely connected with the sin offering.
>
> TEACHING: Christ took our guilt.) 1 John 1:7-9).
> GUILT OFFERING MADE FOR SIN THROUGH IGNORANCE IN "THE HOLY THINGS" (Leviticus 5:14-16; 1 John 1:8-10).

TRESPASS OFFERING FOR UNCLEAN THINGS (Leviticus 5:1-16; 1 John 1:6-7).

UNKNOWN SINS (Leviticus 5:17-19; 1 John 2:1-6; Romans 8:31-34).

CRIMES AGAINST A NEIGHBOR (Leviticus 6:1-7; 19:15-19; Matthew 5:43; 19:19; 22:39; Mark 12:31; Romans 13:9; Galiatians 5:13-14).

Leviticus 8

SACRIFICE OF THE BULL OF THE SIN OFFERING: forgiveness of sins of the priest (Leviticus 8:14-17).

SACRIFICE OF THE RAM OF THE BURNT OFFERING: the Priest's total consecration to his office (Leviticus 8:18-21).

SACRIFICE OF THE RAM OF ORDINATION: a peace offering expressing fellowship of God and Israel through the Priesthood (Leviticus 8:22-30).

SPECIAL ANOINTING BY MOSES UPON AARON: (Leviticus 8:23)

(a) Blood applied to tip if Aaron's right ear—hearing the Word of the Lord (Spirit)

(b) Blood applied upon the thumb of his right hand—service unto the Lord (Soul)

(c) Blood applied upon the great toe of his right foot—his walk in the Lord (Body)

Seven Days of Ordination
(Leviticus 8:31-36)

Aaron and his sons were sprinkled anew by the Anointing Oil and then told to boil the flesh of a ram and eat it with unleavened bread that was in the basket of consecration. This was to be done at the door of the Tabernacle of the congregation. What they did not eat, they were to burn with fire. They were to stay at the door day and night for seven days for the Lord to consecrate them "so they would not die." This was known as the "charge of the Lord" (Leviticus 8:35; Numbers 3:7, 9:19; Deuteronomy 11:1; I Kings 2:3).

"And keep the charge of the Lord thy God, to walk in his ways, to keep his statutes, and his commandments, and his judgments, and his testimonies, as it was written in the law of Moses, that thou mayest prosper in all that thou doest, and whithersoever thou turnest thyself." *(I Kings 2:3)*

OFFERING OF ATONEMENT FOR HIMSELF: (Leviticus 9:7-14). Just as the High Priest offered himself as the atonement for sin, Jesus Christ became our High Priest on the Cross (Hebrews 5:1-3; 7:27; 9:7).

ATONING OFFERING FOR THE PEOPLE: (Leviticus 9:15-21; Hebrews 2:17; Isaiah 52:11).

BLESSING OF THE NATION OF ISRAEL: (Leviticus 9:22).

THEN CAME THE GLORY OF THE LORD UNTO ALL THE PEOPLE: (Leviticus 9:23-24).

Rite Of The Day Of Atonement
(Leviticus 16:2)

Aaron the High Priest was to go into the Holy of Holies once a year to atone for the sins of the people. There he was to meet with God before the Mercy Seat in the Ark of the Covenant. God appeared in the cloud above the Mercy Seat (Hebrews 9:7-28).

Jesus Christ is our High Priest of the New Covenant. A "covenant" is to cut a contract between two or more people (God and man). Hebrews 8:10-13, says: *". . . This is the covenant that I will make with the house of Israel after those days, saith the Lord; I will put my laws into their mind, and write them in their hearts: and I will be to them a God, and they shall be to me a people . . . For I will be merciful to their unrighteousness, and their sins and their iniquities will I remember no more . . . A new covenant, he hath made the first old. Now that which decayeth and waxeth old is ready to vanish away."* God has always had mercy upon His people and desired mercy. The purpose of the Mercy Seat in the tabernacle was to show His mercy and compassion in forgiving their sins.

Aaron's Entry Into The Tabernacle
(Leviticus 16:3-15)

Aaron attired himself in his priestly garments, washed himself at the laver, and took with him a bullock for a sin offering for himself and his household. A priest must not have sin in himself if he is to minister for or in behalf of anyone else. He then took two goats, one for the Lord and one for the people. He cast lots upon the goats and the one the lot fell upon became the Scapegoat or "one to bear the sins of the people."

Our Scapegoat

Jesus became our scapegoat and they cast lots for His garments,
(2 Corinthians 5:21; Psalms 22:18; Matthew 27:35; Mark 15:24; Luke 23:33-34; John 19:23-24). The other goat upon which the Lord's lot fell was offered as a sin offer-

ing, as was the bullock. Both were killed and offered up as sin offerings; the bullock for the priest and his household; the goat for the sins of the people before the Lord. Their blood was sprinkled upon the Mercy Seat seven times. This was to atone for the uncleanness, and the transgressions of the Children of Israel.

After Aaron had made reconciliation with God and the people in the Holy of Holies, he then brought the scapegoat out of the tabernacle and laid his hands upon him confessing the sins, iniquities, and transgressions of the children of Israel and transferred them to his head. He was then sent away into the wilderness bearing the sins of the people, never to return again. The land where the scapegoat went was uninhabited so no one else could absorb the sins. They used a new goat each year, so God meant that those sins were to be totally abolished. This was what happened in the finished work of Calvary (Isaiah 53:1-12).

Analogy

There is an analogy to the scapegoat that should be noted and realized as a "revelation." He was known as "the goat that is allowed to escape;" and he came from a special species known as AZAZEL. The word AZAZEL was thought to be connected with the illicit worship of field-spirits or satyrs (or devils). Some theories say AZAZEL was the prince of the fallen angels. At any rate, the goat represented the culprit known as Satan and the Devil and the people's sins were cast back upon him and they were gone forever!

DAY OF ATONEMENT (YOM KIPPUR) INSTITUTED AS ANNUAL SERVICE: (Leviticus 16:29-34; Hebrews 9:7, 24).

Code of Laws For The Priests
(Leviticus 6:8-11)

LAW OF THE SIN BURNT OFFERING: Because it burned upon the altar all night until morning and was burned into ashes, it was not to be eaten. The ashes represented the "sin" burned up by fire. The fire was never allowed to go out on the altar.

In verse 11, the priest in charge put on his garments of the priesthood to take the ashes off the altar; he then changed his garments again and took the ashes (the burned-up sins) outside the camp unto a clean place (Romans 6:6; Ephesians 4:22-24; Romans 13:14).

Verse 14 stated the law of the meat offering required the sons of Aaron to offer a handful of the flour, a handful of oil, and all of the frankincense upon the meat offering all of which was to be burned unto the Lord. The remainder of the meat offering was to be eaten by Aaron and his sons in the Holy Place along with the unleavened bread. God had given to them His portion of the offering made by fire and it was very holy. We cannot outgive God; He still outgives His children.

All the males among the children of Aaron were to eat it. It was a statute made forever concerning the offerings of the Lord made by fire for all generations. Everyone that touched the offerings would be holy.

A statute is different from a law. A law could be changed or broken. A statute is irrevocable and could not and cannot be changed. It was decreed and permanent.

Ordination Of Aaron And Sons
(Leviticus 8-9; Exodus 29)

Preparation For The Ordination
(Leviticus 8:1-6)

Aaron and his sons were to take the priest's garments, the anointing oil and perfume, a bullock for the sin offering, two rams, and a basket of unleavened bread in preparation for their ordination.

After they had entered the tabernacle, and were washed by water by Moses, (Ephesians 5:26), they were clothed in the priestly garments. Then Moses took the anointing oil and anointed the whole tabernacle and all the furniture in it, thus sanctifying it. He sprinkled the oil upon the altar seven times, on all the vessels, the laver and his foot. He then poured the anointing oil upon the head of Aaron, to sanctify him (Psalms 133).

Standards For Priesthood And Sacrifices
(Leviticus 21-22)

Priest could not shave head or trim beard: Leviticus 21:5; Ezekiel 44:20.

Restricted in the choice of a wife: Leviticus 21:7, 13-14; Ezekiel 44:22; I Timothy 3:2-4; Titus 1:7-9.

Man with physical disability or blemish not qualified for Priesthood: Leviticus 21:18-21.

Types of the flesh:

(1) *blind man*—cannot see the truth; has no spiritual eyes for the Word of God.

(2) *lame man*—will not walk the straight narrow way, nor walk in the Spirit of the Lord.

(3) *flat nose*—cannot smell evil or discern between good and evil; will call good evil and evil good.

(4) *superfluous*—will add to or take from scriptures; will lead into wrong doctrines or heresies.

(5) *brokenfooted*—will not continue the ministry. Starts out, but stops when the walk gets too hard; usually goes into some other vocation.

(6) *brokenhanded*—handles the Word of God wrong; misrepresents the ministry by manipulation or underhanded procedures.

(7) *brokenback*—has no backbone to stand up for the true gospel; has cowardly ways when a crisis occurs.

(8) *dwarf*—retarded growth; especially spiritual growth; has no vision for the people; leans only on one doctrine and not on Christ as a whole.

(9) *blemished eye*—always blaming someone else for his lack of ministry; cannot see the trees for the forest; his eye has double-vision; is not single-eyed on Jesus Christ.

The Seven Feast Days

(1) *PASSOVER*—Leviticus 23:4-8. The fourteenth day of Nisan was the Passover when the Death Angel passed over Egypt and God spared the firstborn of the Hebrews that had the Blood on the doorpost; he killed the firstborn of every Egyptian household, including the beasts and cattle.

(2) *DAY OF UNLEAVENED BREAD*—The fifteenth day of Nisan was when they had to eat unleavened bread for seven days and do no work during those days. It was a

type of purity and devotion to the early church. (Leaven is a type of sin and hypocrisy).

(3) *FIRST FRUITS*—Leviticus 23:9-14. At harvesttime, the children of Israel were to bring a sheaf of their firstfruits unto the Lord as well as a male yearling lamb to be offered as a sacrifice. This had to be done including a meat offering before the household could eat bread, parched corn, or green-ears. This was to be a statute forever; that all first fruits of every harvest be offered to the Lord. Our ten per cent tithe has one of its beginnings here. It is also a type of our Spirit life because Jesus Christ became the first fruit for us, as He was raised from the dead and is seated in heavenly places on the right hand of the Father.

(4) *PENTECOST*—Seven weeks after the firstfruits of harvest (50 days) there were to be ingatherings and new offerings to be made of all the leavened bread this time. There were to be two loaves signifying a double portion of the firstfruits. The giving of the Holy Spirit in power on the day of Pentecost signified our power to go into all the world as a witness. In the age of the Holy Spirit, God's people are to enter into His rest and let Him do all the work (Hebrews 3:4).

(5) *TRUMPETS*—This was the feast of trumpets when the shofar was blown and the people rested from their labors. When the Bride of Christ shall cease from her labors and the Church is raptured out of the world to be with the Bridegroom, she shall hear a trumpet blown also (1 Thessalonians 4:16-17).

(6) *ATONEMENT*—This was the 10th day of Tisri when the High Priest entered into the Holy of Holies and

sprinkled the blood of a goat upon the Mercy Seat. The other goat offered was the Scapegoat who escaped into the wilderness bearing the people's sins. This will follow the Tribulation, the return of Christ to David's throne in Jerusalem and the acceptance of the Messiah. It is also the time of the White Throne Judgement of all who rejected Jesus and their punishment.

(7)   *TABERNACLES*—This was the 15th day of the seventh month. There was to be a feast unto the Lord for seven days, beginning with a sabbath and ending with a sabbath. There was no work to be done and a solemn assembly was held. They were to take branches of palm, willow and all kinds of trees to make booths to rejoice in seven days. They were to dwell in the booths seven days. This feast is a type of the Millennium, the New Jerusalem, and God's Eternity.

Miscellaneous Laws
(Leviticus 24)

Use of lamps in ritual: Leviticus 24:1-4.

Fate of a blasphemer: Leviticus 24:10-16; 23.

Legislation covering killing and personal injury of both man and beast: Leviticus 24:17-22.

Sabbatical Year And Year Of Jubilee
(Leviticus 25)

SABBATICAL YEAR—The children of Israel were to plant their fields six years and prune their vineyards six years; but in the seventh year, after the harvest, they were to let the fields and vineyards lay dormant. This was to give the land a rest. The crops and vineyards that came up voluntarily were to be left for the household, the servants, and all others that dwelt in that household to partake of that year. It still goes back to God's day of rest. Even the land needs a rest from tilling, cultivating and bringing forth crops.

YEAR OF JUBILEE—Every 50 years, the Trumpet of Jubilee was to sound. On the tenth day of the seventh month, the trumpet was to sound throughout all the land. Every man was to be returned to his possessions and if he was sold into slavery, he was to be returned to his family. That fiftieth year a person could not sow, reap or gather in the harvest. There was to be no oppression upon each other. *". . . but thou shall fear the Lord . . . and ye shall dwell in the land in safety. And the land shall yield her fruit, and ye shall eat your fill, and dwell in safety"* (verse 17).

When they asked how they were to eat in the seventh year, the Lord said He would command His blessing upon the land in the sixth year and it would bring forth fruit for three years. When they sowed the eighth year, they would still be eating of the old store in the ninth year.

All hired servants could be redeemed in the year of Jubilee or returned to their families; if he is sold to someone else, he can be redeemed by his kin or he may redeem himself. All people were to be set free of debts, and of all things that would encumber them to someone else. We are set free when we let the Holy Spirit come into our lives and do the Lord's work for us.

BLESSINGS ON THE OBEDIENT: Leviticus 26:3-13; Deuteronomy 28:1-14; 1 Peter 2:9

CURSES ON THE DISOBEDIENT: Leviticus 26:14-43; Deuteronomy 18:15-68

VOWS: Leviticus 27:1-29.

TITHES: Leviticus 27:30-33. The tenth part of every increase belonged to the Lord and was holy unto Him; even if it was seed of the field, fruit of the tree, flock, or herd.

SEVEN FEASTS OF THE TABERNACLE

(1) PASSOVER	(2) UNLEAVENED BREAD	(3) FRUITS	(4) PENTECOST	(5) TRUMPETS	(6) ATONEMENT	(7) TABERNACLE
ANCIENT ISRAEL						
Leviticus 23:5	Leviticus 23:6	Leviticus 23:10	Leviticus 23:16	Leviticus 23:32	Leviticus 23:27-29	Leviticus 23:34-37
Lamb Unleavened Bread Bitter Herbs 14th day of Nisan	15th day Nisan Eat unleavened bread seven days; no work	Wave of Sheaf Offering; male yearling lamb for burnt offering	Ingatherings Wheat Harvest Two loaves of leavened bread	Shofar blown	10th day of Tisri Two goats Mercy Seat Blood	Extensive sacrifice Water pouring Lights for 7 days Dwell in booths
MODERN JUDAISM						
Leaven Search Go to Synogogue Prayers Meal	Just eat unleavened bread	Nothing	Fast three days Read Torah all night Praise God	Soul searching during Holy days	Swinging of the Fowl Fasting Long Prayer (Yom Kippur)	Dwell in booths, Palms, citron, etc.
NEW TESTAMENT CHRISTIANITY						
Redemption I Corinthians 5:7-8 I Peter 1:19-23	Purity and devotion to the Early Church	Resurrection of Jesus Christ I Corin. 15:20	Giving of the Holy Spirit Acts 2:4	Sound of the Trumpet for Israel regathered; Rapture of the Bride of Christ I Thess. 4:16-17	Jesus sitting on David's Throne at Jerusalem— Acceptance of the Messiah Zech. 14:9	The Millennium— New Jerusalem and God's Eternity Zech. 14:16-21

NUMBERS

THE FOURTH BOOK OF MOSES

WILDERNESS WANDERINGS

— ELLIOTT

Chapter 13

FROM SINAI TO KADESH-BARNEA

Numbers Divided into Four Major Sections:

I.   Preparations for departure from Sinai: 1:1–10:10;

II. From Sinai to the Plains of Moab: 10:11–21:35;

III. Prophecies of Balaam: 22:1–25:18;

IV. Instructions and Preparations for Entering the Promised Land: 26:1–36:13 (Scofield)

Numbers derives its name from the record of the two different census taken in the wilderness. In this first chapter we read that the Lord spoke to Moses in the wilderness of Sinai, in the tabernacle of the congregation, on the first day of the second month, and in the second year after they were delivered by the Lord from Egyptian bondage. In chapter 26, we find another numbering of the people God has chosen to inherit the land flowing with milk and honey. (Suggested date of these records: 1450–1410 B.C.).

Numbers begins with "And," for the first part concludes the divine record of the experiences at Sinai, thus we are pointed back to Exodus. Most of Numbers is taken up with the 40 years of wanderings, from the time Israel departed from Sinai until they reached the Jordan River. This book is a record of the continued failings of Israel, and the continued mercy and grace of their God. These were a people who had been Redeemed from bondage; possessed the law; led by Moses, a most perfect type of Christ; erected the sacred tabernacle; and supernaturally guided by cloud and a pillar of fire. Thus, they should have walked triumphantly in the perfect will of the Lord; yet, they complained and walked in unbelief, disregarding the precious gospel that had been entrusted to them. We must keep in mind that this is a nation in its infant stages.

ISRAELITES DEPARTED FROM EGYPT: 15th day of the 1st month (Numbers 33:3; Exodus 12:2,5).

ISRAELITES REACHED WILDERNESS OF SINAI: 1st day (new moon) of the 3rd month (Exodus 19:1),

GOD REVEALED HIMSELF TO THE ISRAELITES: 3rd day (Exodus 19:16-17),

THE TABERNACLE WAS ERECTED: 1st day of the 1st month, of the 2nd year (Exodus 40:17),

CENSUS TO BE TAKEN: 1st day of the 2nd month of the second year (Numbers 1:1). On the 20th day of the

same month *". . . the cloud was taken up from over the tabernacle of the testimony, and the people of Israel set out by stages from the wilderness of Sinai."*
(Numbers 10:11).

In Deuteronomy we note reference is made to the 1st day of the 11th month of the 40th year, or about 38 years and nine months removed from the date of their deliverance from Egypt. May we note here that the journey from Sinai to Kadesh-Barnea by way of the Gulf of Aqaba was a distance of no more than 11 days (Deuteronomy 1:2). By way of Edom and Moab, this trip was hardly more than a couple of weeks.

"These are the generations of Aaron and Moses in the day that the Lord spake with Moses in Mount Sinai. And these are the names of the sons of Aaron: Nadab the firstborn, and Abihu, Eleazar, and Ithamar. These are the names of the sons of Aaron, the priests which were anointed, whom he consecrated to minister in the priest's office. And Nadab and Abihu died before the Lord, when they offered strange fire before the Lord, in the wilderness of Sinai, and they had no children: and Eleazar and Ithamar ministered in the priest's office in the sight of Aaron their father." *(Numbers 3:1-4)*

The two eldest sons of Aaron offered strange fire upon the altar, and they fell dead leaving no children. This example was set before the children of Israel as a warning of the quick punishment that would befall the disobedient in regard to the regulations of the ministry of the priesthood.

The Nazarite Vow

(or Nazarite: one separated) (Numbers 6)

Voluntary Laws of Separation for Man or Woman:

> HE SHALL SEPARATE HIMSELF FROM WINE AND STRONG DRINK
>
> HE SHALL NOT DRINK VINEGAR OF WINE
>
> OR VINEGAR OF STRONG DRINK
>
> OR LIQUOR OF GRAPES
>
> HE SHALL NOT EAT RIPE GRAPES OR DRIED GRAPES
>
> HE SHALL EAT NOTHING MADE OF THE VINE, FROM THE KERNELS TO THE HUSK,
>
> HE SHALL HAVE NO RAZOR COME UPON HIS HEAD DURING HIS NAZARITESHIP
>
> HE SHALL BE HOLY
>
> HE SHALL NOT BE DEFILED FROM THE DEAD, EVEN FOR FATHER, MOTHER, SISTER, OR BROTHER

Numbers 7 through 9

In these three chapters we have long and detailed accounts of offerings, anointings, names of the twelve princes of the congregation, and purification of the Levites. These three chapters are the longest in the entire book of Numbers. We do not lightly mention these twelve days due to lack of interest, but rather due to lack of space. *"And it came to pass on the day that Moses had fully set up the tabernacle, and had anointed it, and sanctified it, and all the instruments thereof, both the altar and all the vessels thereof, and had anointed them, and sanctified them; That the princes of Israel, heads of the house of their fathers, who were the princes of the tribes, and were over them that were numbered, of-*

fered: And they brought their offering before the Lord, six covered wagons, and twelve oxen; a wagon for two of the princes, and for each one an ox: and they brought them before the tabernacle."   *(Numbers 7:1-3)*

Moses was instructed by the Lord to take the offerings for they were for the service of the tabernacle. These things were given to the Levites. Each of the leaders brought dedicated gifts each on the day assigned to him, and this took 12 days. At this point may we quote from C. M. MacIntosh along these lines: "This is divine. And may we not say that this seventh chapter of Numbers is one of specimen-pages from the book of eternity, on which the finger of God has engraved the names of His servants, and the record of their work? We believe it is; and if the reader will turn to the twenty-third of the second Samuel, and the sixteenth of Romans, he will find two similar pages. In the former, we have the names and the deeds of David's worthies; in the latter, the names and the deeds of Paul's friends at Rome. In both, we have an illustration of what, we feel persuaded, is true of all the saints of God and the servants of Christ from first to last. Each one has his own special place on the roll, and each one his place in the Master's heart, and all will come out by and by . . ."

"And the Lord spake unto Moses, saying, Speak unto Aaron, and say unto him, When thou lightest the lamps, the seven lamps shall give light over against the candlestick. And Aaron did so; he lighted the lamps thereof over against the candlestick, as the Lord commanded Moses."   *(Numbers 8:1-3)*

God told Moses to tell Aaron that when he *"lights the seven lamps"* he is to set them so that they will throw their light forward and the light will shine upon the table of shewbread as well as the altar of incense over against the veil. In Matthew 5:16, we are reminded of the Word of Jesus: *"Let your light so shine before men, that they may see your good works, and glorify your Father which is in heaven."* Aaron, the high priest, was to light the lamps; and it was also his duty to trim the lamps.

Keeping the Passover

In chapter nine, the Lord gave instructions to Moses in the wilderness of Sinai, in the first month of the second year after they had come out of Egypt, saying, *"Let the children of Israel also keep the passover at his appointed season. In the fourteenth day of this month, at even, ye shall keep it in his appointed season: according to all the rites of it, and according to all the ceremonies thereof, shall ye keep it. And Moses spake unto the children of Israel, that they should keep the passover. And they kept the passover on the fourteenth day of the first month at even in the wilderness of Sinai: according to all that the Lord commanded Moses, so did the children of Israel"* (verses 2-5).

May we at this point pause and dwell for a moment upon the closing thoughts of chapter nine. In the middle of nowhere, a no-man's-land, we view two or three million Jews who have absolutely no clue as to where they are or really where they were going; they did not know the route they were to follow. What a picture of total dependence upon Jehovah for guidance and food. When they camped, they did not know when they would move again or halt again; but God had made a way.

These next verses are so beautiful, we must read them with our hearts lifted up towards the Lord our Provider:

"And on the day that the tabernacle was reared up the cloud covered the tabernacle, namely, the tent of the testimony: and at even there was upon the tabernacle as it were the appearance of fire, until the morning. So it was always: the could covered it by day, and the appearance of fire by night. And when the cloud was taken up from the tabernacle, then after that the children of Israel journeyed: and in the place where the cloud abode, there the children of Israel pitched their tents. At the commandment of the Lord the children of Israel journeyed, and at the commandment of the Lord they pitched: as long as the cloud abode upon the tabernacle they rested in their tents. And when the cloud tarried long upon the tabernacle many days, then the children of Israel kept the charge of the Lord, and journeyed not."

"And so it was, when the cloud was a few days upon the tabernacle; according to the commandment of the Lord they abode in their tents, and according to the commandment of the Lord they journeyed. And as it was, when the cloud abode from even unto the morning, and that the cloud was taken upon in the morning, then they journeyed: whether it was by day or by night that the cloud was taken up, they journeyed. Or whether it were two days, or a month, or a year, that the cloud tarried upon the tabernacle, remaining thereon, the children of Israel abode in their tents, and journeyed not: but when it was taken up, they journeyed. At the commandment of the Lord they rested in the tents, and at the commandment of the Lord they journeyed: they kept the charge of the Lord, at the commandment of the Lord by the hand of Moses." *(Numbers 9:15-23)*

Two Silver Trumpets

God instructed Moses to make two trumpets of beaten silver to be used for summoning the people to assemble, and for signaling them to break up camp to move on. When two trumpets were blown, they knew they were to gather at the entrance of the Tabernacle. If only one trumpet sounded, they knew the chiefs of the tribes of Israel were to gather to hear the Word of the Lord.

FIVE USES OF THE TRUMPETS:

(1)   To assemble

(2)   To move camp

(3)   War

(4)   Make camp

(5)   Memorial (Worship)

"And the sons of Aaron, the priests, shall blow with the trumpets; and they shall be to you for an ordinance for ever throughout your generations."

(Numbers 10:8)

God promised the children of Israel that when they entered the Promised Land, and war was at hand, if they would sound the trumpets, He would hear and save them from their enemies. Then on the twentieth day of the second month, in the second year, the cloud was taken up from off the tabernacle of the testimony, and the children of Israel began the first stage of their journey out of the wilderness of Sinai; and the cloud led them into the wilderness of Paran, and there it rested.

"And they departed from the mount of the Lord three days' journey: and the ark of the covenant of the Lord went before them in the three days' journey, to search out a resting place for them. And the cloud of the Lord

was upon them by day, when they went out of the camp. And it came to pass, when the Ark set forward, that Moses said, Rise up, Lord, and let thine enemies be scattered; and let them that hate thee flee before thee. And when it rested, he said, Return, O Lord, unto the many thousands of Israel.'' (Numbers 10:33-36)

In Psalms 68:1, we read a similiar passage, *''Let God arise, let his enemies be scattered: let them also that hate him flee before him.''* In Psalms 105:39, we read, *''He spread a cloud for a covering, and fire to give light in the night.''*

We cannot at this time cover the seven trumpets in Revelation.

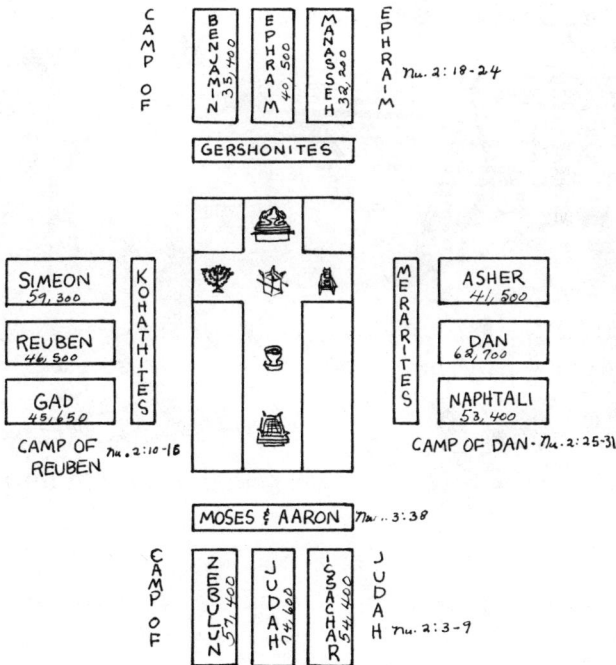

A Cross Within A Cross

Aaron's Rod That Budded

Chapter 14

DEPARTURE FROM SINAI

"And when the people complained, it displeased the Lord: and the Lord heard it; and his anger was kindled; and the fire of the Lord burnt among them, and consumed them that were in the uttermost parts of the camp. And the people cried unto Moses; and when Moses prayed unto the Lord, the fire was quenched. And he called the name of the place TABERAH: because the fire of the Lord burnt among them."

(Numbers 11:1-3)

The tabernacle was taken down, and the children of Israel left the wilderness of Sinai for the Land of Promise by way of the wilderness of Param. Along the way the people kindled the anger of the Lord by complaining. When God heard complaints, He was greatly displeased and sent fire among them at the far end of the camp. Moses prayed unto the Lord that He would stop the fire and it was quenched. The name of the place was called "Taberah," which means "burning."

Now we approach a most serious warning to all of us. It is no light matter for Christians to associate with the "mixed multitudes." It is ever the purpose of Satan to lead the Christian into some kind of "lukewarm" effort which will eventually lead either to false doctrines, or backsliding through complaining and murmuring.

"And the mixed multitude that was among them fell a-lusting: and the children of Israel also wept again, and said, Who shall give us flesh to eat? We remember the fish, which we did eat in Egypt freely; the cucumbers, and the melons, and the leeks, and the onions, and the garlic: But now our soul is dried away: there is nothing at all, beside this manna, before our eyes. And the manna was as coriander seed, and the colour thereof as the colour of bdellium. And the people went about, and gathered it, and ground it in mills, or beat it in a mortar, and baked it in pans, and made cakes of it: and the taste of it was as the taste of fresh oil. And when the dew fell upon the camp in the night, the manna fell upon it. Then Moses heard the people weep throughout their families, every man in the door of his tent: and the anger of the Lord was kindled greatly; Moses also was displeased. And Moses said unto the Lord, Wherefore hast thou afflicted thy servant? and wherefore have I not found favour in thy sight, that thou layest the burden of all this people upon me? Have I conceived all these people? Have I begotten them, that thou shouldest say unto me, Carry them in thy bosom, as a nursing father beareth the sucking child, unto the land which thou swarest unto their fathers? Whence should I have

flesh to give unto all this people? for they weep unto me, saying, Give us flesh, that we may eat. I am not able to bear all this people alone, because it is too heavy for me. And if thou deal thus with me, kill me, I pray thee, out of hand, if I have found favour in thy sight; and let me not see my wretchedness."   *(Numbers 11:4-15)*

In this portion of our narrative we see the urgent need for total dependence upon the Lord who alone can keep us from grumbling, if we keep our eyes upon Him. It stated that the "mixed multitude" fell to lusting, and the children of Israel were drawn into their net. They were weary of Manna from heaven, and complained against Moses who in turn complained and wept before the Lord; we certainly learn from this outburst of emotions on the part of Moses and the children of God that at the place of "opportunity for trial" we show forth our faith in God. We are reminded here of another prophet named Elijah, who flung himself at the foot of the juniper tree and cried that he was the only one left who served the Lord. Moses cried to the Lord for deliverance; he asked the Lord, "Have I conceived all this people?" He was tired; tired of their constant complaining, and the weight of it had reached a peak with this illustrious servant of Jehovah. He pleaded for the Lord to take his life. One writer reminded us that these two men were seen together on the Mount of Transfiguration. The Lord of Glory instructs us not to fear; and when the way is tiring and seemingly endless, He gives us life and an abundance of encouragement to keep us going. Moses told the Lord that death would be better than the burden of these Hebrew people.

"And the lord said unto Moses, Gather unto me seventy men of the elders of Israel, whom thou knowest to

be the elders of the people, and officers over them; and bring them unto the tabernacle of the congregation, that they my stand there with thee. And I will come down and talk with thee there: and I will take of the spirit which is upon thee, and will put it upon them; and they shall bear the burden of the people with thee, and thou bear it not thyself alone."   (Numbers 11:16-17)

Here we have an example of Old Testament body ministry. Moses would no longer have the full measure of power that was upon him, but it would be divided among the 70 elders, the number of soles that went down into Egypt. In later times the Sanhedrin, or the great council of the Jews, consisted of 70 men. Now Moses would henceforth be a joint instrument instead of the sole one. We note that Moses undervalued the honor that the Lord had placed upon him by allowing him to be the prophet among them. Many times during their journey across the sands, they, too, misjudged the full intentions of God and sought to kill their leader. Often they forgot that God had ordained them to be a peculiar people unto Him.

Matthew Henry wrote, "If he could not bear the toil of government, which was but running with the footman, how would he bear the terrors of war, which was contending with horses?" Moses took too much upon himself at this time. He said, "I am not able to bear all this people alone, because it is too heavy for me." Was not this the Moses who previously cried out to the people, *". . . Fear ye not, stand still, and see the salvation of the Lord, which he will show to you today: for the Egyptians whom ye have seen today, ye shall see them again no*

*more forever. The Lord shall fight for you, and ye shall
hold your peace.''*

(Exodus 14:13-14)

Quail From Heaven

God told Moses to have the children of Israel sanctify
themselves for the next day they would get meat to eat.
The Lord said, "I heard your tears in my ears, and how
well it went with you in Egypt. I will send you meat to
eat—not one day—or two days—not even five days—but
you will eat it until it comes out your nostrils! I will do
this because you have complained against Me and asked
why I brought you out of Egypt."

Moses asked the Lord if He would slay all their animals to get this meat. He reminded the Lord that there
were six hundred thousand footmen, not counting all the
others. It would seem that at this point even Moses had
forgotton the parting of the Red Sea, and the water from
the rock in the middle of the desert.

*"And the Lord said unto Moses, Is the Lord's hand
waxed short? thou shalt see now whether my word shall
come to pass unto thee or not."*   *(Numbers 11:23)*

Any careful reader of the Word can see that Moses
doubted the Word of the Lord at that moment. In the gospels we read of a similiar occurrence when Jesus fed the
four thousand, *". . . In those days the Multitude being
very great, and having nothing to eat, Jesus called his
disciples unto him, and saith unto them, I have compassion of the multitude, because they have now been
with me three days, and have nothing to eat: And if I
send them away fasting to their own houses, they will
faint by the way: for divers of them came from far. And*

*his disciples answered him, From whence can a man
satisfy these men with bread here in the wilderness?"*
(Mark 8:1-4)

Kibroth-hattaavah

The Lord sent a wind that brought quail from the sea,
and caused them to fall in the camp and all around it.
While they gathered the birds by the bushels, and while
they were eating and before it was chewed, God smote
the people with a heavy plague, and the name of the place
was called "THE GRAVES OF LUST," OR "THE GRAVES
OF THE GREEDY." Make no mistake about it, the innocent was not plagued with the wicked. God know the
hearts of all men, and He makes no mistake when He
brings in judgment.

Hazeroth

*"And the people journeyed from Kibroth-hattaa-
vah unto Hazeroth; and abode at Hazeroth.*
(Numbers 11:35)

*"And they departed from Kibroth-hattaavah, and
encamped at Hazeroth."* *(Numbers 33:17)*

Leprosy in the Camp (Hazeroth)

*"And Miriam and Aaron spake against Moses be-
cause of the Ethiopian woman whom he had married:
for he had married an Ethiopian woman. And they said,
Hath the Lord indeed spoken only by Moses? Hath He
not spoken also by us? And the Lord heard it. (Now the
man Moses was very meek, above all the men which
were upon the face of the earth.) And the Lord spake
suddenly unto Moses, and unto Aaron, and unto Miriam, Come out ye three unto the tabernacle of the con-*

306

gregation. And they three came out. And the Lord came down the pillar of the cloud, and stood in the door of the tabernacle, and called Aaron and Miriam: and they both came forth.''

(Numbers 12-5)

We are informed that Moses had married a Cushite woman, and his own brother and sister spoke against him in rebellion not only about his private life, but also the ministry. The Word says, *"Moses was a meek man . . . and the Lord spoke suddenly.''* Some believe this was Zipporah; others believe Moses had married either a Cushite or Arabian after his wife's death.

The Lord came down in the pillar of the cloud, and stood in the door of the tabernacle to settle the argument. He called them forth and instructed them to listen to Him. The Lord said that He would speak to His prophets by dream or vision, but with His faithful servant, Moses, He would speak mouth to mouth, or face to face.

". . . wherefore then were ye not afraid to speak against my servant Moses?'' *(Numbers 12:8)*

Just as the cloud departed from the tabernacle, Miriam became leprous, white as snow. Aaron pleaded with Moses to forgive them and pray for their sister.

"And Moses cried unto the Lord, saying, Heal her now, O God, I beseech thee.'' *(Numbers 12:13)*

Miriam was shut out of the camp for seven days, and the people waited for her to return before they moved camp. (Throughout the Bible, leprosy is a type of sin.) After this, the people left Hazeroth, and pitched in the wilderness of Paran.

FROM EGYPT TO KADESH-BARNEA

Recorded by Moses at the command of God:

From Rameses to Succoth to

Etham to

Pihahiroth (before Baal-Zephon before Midgol)

From Piahiroth to

Marah to

Elim (twelve fountains-ten palms) to

an encampment by the Red Sea to

an encampment in the wilderness of sin to

Dophkah to

Alush to

Rephidim (no water to drink) to

Sinai to

Kibrothhattaavah to

Rithmah to

Rimmonparez to

Libnah to

Rissah to

Kehelathah to

Shapher to

Haradah to

Makheloth to

Tahath to

Tarah to

Mithcah to

Hashmonah to

Moserokth to

Benejaakan to

Horhagidgad to

Jotbathah to

Ebronah to

Eziongaber to

the wilderness of sin which is Kadesh, to Mount Hor in the edge of the Land of Edom (Aaron died in this mount in the fortieth year after the children of Israel were come out of the land of Egypt, in the first day of the fifth month).

From Mount Hor to

Zalmonah to

Punon to

Oboth to

Ijeabarim (in the border of Moab) to

Dibongad to

Almondiblathaim to

Abarim before Nebo to

Moab plains by Jordan near Jericho (Bethjesimoth)

Even unto Abelshittim in the plains of Moab.

Breakdown of Faith–12 Spies Sent Out

"And the Lord spake unto Moses, saying, Send thou men, that they may search the land of Canaan, which I give unto the children of Israel: of every tribe of their fathers shall ye send a man, every one a ruler among them. And Moses by the commandment of the Lord sent

them from the wilderness of Paran: all those men were heads of the children of Israel.'' *(Numbers 13:1-3)*

We read in the above scriptures that Moses, by commandment, sent spies over into the land of Canaan to check out the land, its people, and the living conditions. In order to better understand just what really happened, and why God sentenced the children of Israel to 40 years of wanderings, we need to read this along with the account given in Deuteronomy where Moses is retelling this story to the children of Israel, reminding them of their request for spies. This proves to us that the motion came originally from the people due to their unbelief. They refused to take God's Word that it was a good land, and He had provided it just for them:

''And when we departed from Horeb, we went through all that great and terrible wilderness, which ye saw by the way of the mountain of the Amorites, as the Lord our God commanded us; and we came to Kadesh-barnea. And I said unto you, Ye are come unto the mountain of the Amorites, which the Lord our God doth give unto us. Behold, the Lord thy God hath set the land before thee: go up and possess it, as the Lord God of thy fathers hath said unto thee; fear not, neither be discouraged. And ye came near unto me every one of you, and said, We will send men before us, and they shall search us out the land, the bring us word again by what way we must go up, and into what cities we shall come.''

''And the saying pleased me well: and I took twelve men of you, one of a tribe: And they turned and went up into the mountain, and came unto the valley of Esh-

col, and searched it out. And they took of the fruit of the land in their hands, and brought it down unto us, and brought us word again, and said, It is a good land which the Lord our God doth give us. Notwithstanding ye would not go up, but rebelled against the commandment of the Lord your God. And ye murmured in your tents, and said, Because the Lord hated us, he hath brought us forth out of the land of Egypt, to deliver us into the hand of the Amorites, to destroy us. Whither shall we go up? Our brethren have discouraged our heart, saying, The people is greater and taller than we; the cities are great and walled up to heaven; and moreover we have seen the sons of the Anakims there. Then I said unto you, dread not, neither be afraid of them. The Lord your God which goeth before you, he shall fight for you, according to all that he did for you in Egypt before your eyes; And in the wilderness, where thou hast seen how that the Lord thy God bare thee, as a man doth bear his son, in all the way that ye went, until ye came into this place."

"Yet in this thing ye did not believe the Lord your God, who went in the way before you, to search you out a place to pitch your tents in, in fire by night, to shew you by what way ye should go, and in a cloud by day. And the Lord heard the voice of your words, and was wroth, and sware, saying, Surely there shall not one of these men of this evil generation see that good land, which I sware to give unto your fathers, save Caleg the son of Jephunneh; he shall see it, and to him will I give the land that he hath trodden upon, and to his children, because he hath wholly followed the Lord. Also the Lord was angry with me for your sakes, saying, Thou also

311

shalt not go in thither. But Joshua the son of Nun, which standeth before thee, he shall go in thither: encourage him: for he shall cause Israel to inherit it."

"Moreover your little ones, which ye said should be a prey, and your children, which in that day had no knowledge between good and evil, they shall go in thither, and unto them will I give it, and they shall possess it. But as for you, turn you, and take your journey into the wilderness by the way of the Red sea. Then ye answered and said unto me, We have sinned against the Lord, we will go up and fight, according to all that the Lord our God commanded us. And when ye had girded on every man his weapons of war, ye were ready to go up into the hill. And the Lord said unto me, Say unto them, Go not up, neither fight; for I am not among you; lest ye be smitten before your enemies. So I spake unto you; and ye would not hear, but rebelled against the commandment of the Lord, and went presumptuously up into the hill. And the Amorites, which dwelt in that Mountain, came out against you, and chased you, as bees do, and destroyed you in Seir, even unto Hormah. And ye returned and wept before the Lord; but the Lord would not hearken to your voice, nor give ear unto you. So ye abode in Kadesh many days, according unto the days that ye abode there."   (Deuteronomy 7:19-46)

The Report of the Spies

And they returned from searching of the land after forty days. And they went and came to Moses, and to Aaron, and to all the congregation of the children of Israel, unto the wilderness of Paran, to Kadesh; and brought back work unto them, and unto all the con-

*gregation, and showed them the fruit of the land. And
they told him, and said, We came unto the land whither
thou sentest us, and surely it floweth with milk and
honey; and this is the fruit of it. Nevertheless the people
be strong that dwell in the land, and the cities are
walled, and very great; and moreover we saw the children of Anak there. The Amalekites dwell in the land of
the south: and the Hittites, and the Jebusites, and the
Amorites, dwell in the mountains: and the Canaanites
dwell by the sea, and by the coast of Jordan. And Caleb
stilled the people before Moses, and said, Let us go up
at once, and possess it; for we are well able to overcome
it. But the men that went up with him said, We be not
able to go up against the people; for they are stronger
than we. And they brought up an evil report of the land
which they had searched unto the children of Israel,
saying, the land, through which we have gone to search
it, is a land that eateth up the inhabitants thereof; and
all the people that we saw in it are men of a great stature. And there we saw the giants, the sons of Anak,
which come of the giants: and we were in our own sight
as grasshoppers, and so we were in their sight.*

(Numbers 13:25-33)

The spies were away from the camp for forty days.
They traveled all the way from the wilderness of Zin to
Rehob near Hamath, going northward, then passed
through the Negev, then arrived at Hebron. It was in the
valley of Eschol on their way back home that they gathered the grapes and the pomegranates. (Eschol means
"Cluster of Grapes." When they returned to report to
Moses and the people, only two of the twelve gave a good
report. Their report ran something like this: the people

313

are giants; the cities are walled; they are in constant war and consuming one another; listen not to Caleb and Joshua; we are not able to go against these people; we are as grasshoppers in their sight.

Results of an Evil Report

This evil report produced immediate terror in the hearts of the people, and Caleb was unable to allay their fears. All during the night the people wept and murmured against Moses and Aaron.

"And all the children of Israel murmured against Moses and against Aaron: and the whole congregation said unto them, Would God that we had died in the land of Egypt! Or would God we had died in this wilderness. And wherefore hath the Lord brought us into this land, to fall by the sword, that our wives and our children should be a prey? Were it not better for us to return into Egypt? And they said one to another, let us make a captain, and let us return into Egypt. Then Moses and Aaron fell on their faces before all the assembly of the congregation of the children of Israel."

(Numbers 14:2-5)

When unbelief is at work in the hearts of men, there will be always be "nevertheless," or a "but" we cannot conquer. Once again the whole assembly took their eyes off the Lord and fell into the sin of murmuring and complaining. All night long they cried because they were like "grasshoppers" compared to the men in Canaan; they wept because they wanted to return to Egypt where it was safe and peaceful! The language of God is, "We are well able to conquer," but the language of the devil is, "We cannot take the land." These people had at this point shut out God. Nowhere in all the camp do we hear the cry, "What shall we do, Lord?" They have come a long way from the SONG OF THE REDEEMED in Exodus 15. In 1 Corinthians 10:1-5, Paul warns against this unbelief by telling the Corinthians not to forget what happened in the wilderness when these people did not obey God, and they desired evil things. In Hebrews 3 and 4 this evil is spoken against.

While Moses and Aaron were on their faces before the Lord, Caleb and Joshua rent their clothes, and tried to still the anger of the people.

"If the Lord delight in us, then he will bring us into this land, and give it us; a land which floweth with milk and honey. Only REBEL NOT ye against the Lord, neither fear ye the people of the land; for they are bread for us: their defence is departed from them, and the Lord is with us: fear them not." (Numbers 14:8-9)

The only response they received from the people was talk of stoning them to death. It was at that moment that the Glory of the Lord appeared in the tabernacle of the congregation before all of the children of Israel.

"And the Lord said unto Moses, How long will these people provoke me? And how long will it be ere they believe me, for all the signs which I have shown among them? I will smite them with the pestilence, and disinherit them, and will make of thee a greater nation and mightier than they." (Numbers 14:11-12)

This is the second time we have encountered this statement from the Lord; and the second time Moses interceded in behalf of the children of Israel.

Moses Intercedes for Israel

"And Moses said unto the Lord, then the Egyptians shall hear it, (for thou broughtest up this people in thy might from among them;) And they will tell it to the inhabitants of this land: for they have heard that thou Lord art among this people, that thou Lord art seen face to face, and that thy cloud standeth over them, and that thou goest before them, by day time in a pillar of a cloud, and in a pillar of fire by night. Now if thou shalt kill all this people as one man, then the nations which have heard the fame of the thee will speak, saying, Because the Lord was not able to bring this people into the land which he sware unto them, therefore he hath slain them in the wilderness. And now, I beseech thee, let the power of my Lord be great, according as thou hast spoken, saying, the Lord is long suffering, and of great mercy, forgiving iniquity and transgression, and by no means clearing the guilty, visiting the iniquity of the fathers upon the children unto the third and fourth generation. Pardon, I beseech thee, the iniquity of this people according unto the greatness of thy mercy, and as thou hast forgiven this people, from Egypt even until now." (Numbers 14:13-19)

Pardoned According To Thy Word

"And the Lord said, I have pardoned according to thy word." (Numbers 14:20)

Moses interceded for the people on the grounds of God's Mercy and Longsuffering; he reminded the Lord that the Egyptians were watching their every move, and if He destroyed His people, surely the enemy would laugh at their calamity and declare God could not finish His work. We must note that while the people were intent upon doing harm to their leaders, God appeared and honored them by His Presence. God never made a move for or against His people without first talking it over with His servant Moses. God had put Himself in a place where He had to go through Moses to get to His own people. Here Moses is seen as a type of Christ who interceded for those who persecuted Him and despitefully used Him, leaving us His example of mercy and grace. Moses prayed for their pardon; he prayed that the Lord would not bring justice upon them; His several pleas for the nation were strong and most urgent. We should note that Moses made mention of the fact that the Lord had forgiven them all the way from Egypt up to now.

"But as truly as I live, all the earth shall be filled with the glory of the Lord. Because all those men which have seen my glory, and my miracles, which I did in Egypt and in the wilderness, and have tempted me now these ten times, and have not hearkened to my voice; Surely they shall not see the land which I sware unto their fathers, neither shall any of them that provoked me see it: But my servant, Caleb, because he had another spirit with him, and hath followed me fully, him will I bring into the land whereinto he went; and his seed shall possess it. (Now the Amalekites and the Canaanites dwelt in the valley.) Tomorrow turn you, and get you into the wilderness by the way of the Red sea."
(Numbers 14:21-25)

We may rest assured that God has a good set of books. In verse 22, He said they had tempted Him in the wilderness ten times, and they had not listened to His voice or obeyed His commandments; therefore, they would never enter the land He had promised their forefathers.

317

Sentence Is Passed

"*And the Lord spake unto Moses and unto Aaron, saying, How long shall I bear with this evil congregation, which murmur against me? I have heard the murmurings of the children of Israel, which they murmur against me. Say unto them, As truly as I live, saith the Lord, as ye have spoken in mine ears, so will I do to you: Your carcases shall fall in this wilderness; and all that were numbered of you, according to your whole number, from twenty years old and upward, which have murmured against me, Doubtless ye shall not come into the land, concerning which I sware to make you dwell therein, save Caleb the son of Jephunneh, and Joshua the son of Nun. But your little ones, which ye said should be a prey, them will I bring in, and they shall know the land which ye have despised. But as for you, your carcases, they shall fall in this wilderness. And your children shall wander in the wilderness forty years, and bear your whoredoms, until your carcases be wasted in the wilderness.*"

"*After the number of the days in which ye searched the land, even forty days, each day for a year, shall ye bear your iniquities, even forty years, and ye shall know my breach of promise. I the Lord have said, I will surely do it unto all this evil congregation, that are gathered together against me: in this wilderness they shall be consumed, as there they shall die. And the men, which Moses sent to search the land, who returned, and made all the congregation to murmur against him, by bringing up a slander upon the land, Even those men that did bring up the evil report upon the land, died by the plague before the Lord. But Joshua the son of Nun, and Caleb the son of Jephunneh, which were of the men that went to search the land, lived still. And Moses told these sayings unto all the children of Israel: and the people mourned greatly.*

And they rose up early in the morning, and gat them up into the top of the mountain, saying, Lo, we be here, and will go up unto the place which the Lord hath promised: for we have sinned. And Moses said, Wherefore now do ye transgress the commandment of the Lord? But it shall not prosper. Go not up, for the Lord is not among you; that ye be not smitten before your enemies. For the Amalekites and the Canaanites are there before you, and ye shall fall by the sword: because ye are turned away from the Lord, therefore the Lord will not be with you. But they presumed to go up unto the hill top: nevertheless the ark of the covenant of the Lord, and Moses, departed not out of the camp. Then the Amalekites came down, and the Canaanites which dwelt in that hill, and smote them, and discomfited them, even unto Hormah."   *(Numbers 14:26-45)*

God agreed to forgive and pardon the sinning people as Moses had requested; but His Glory would yet fill the entire earth. All of those who had seen the Glory of the Lord in His miracles in both Egypt and the wilderness would never enter the LAND OF PROMISE because of their unbelief. Instead, their bones would bleach in the wilderness; except for Caleb who had brought back a good report from the land of the Amalekites and the Canaanites. Since the spies were in the land for 40 days, the Lord gave them a sentence of 40 years of wandering just outside their final destination. And even while the Lord was still speaking to His servant Moses, the ten men who had brought back an evil report and led the rebellion, fell dead of a plague before the Lord. God had held these men responsible for the sins of Israel. In spite of this sentence, some of the people attempted to enter the land, although God had told them He would not be with them. Moses said, "No, it is too late. God will not be with us! No! You will be crushed by the enemy! You disobeyed the Lord, and He is not with you in this matter."

They would not listen to Moses. They presumed upon the Lord, though neither the Ark nor Moses left the camp to join them. The Canaanites and the Amalekites who lived in the hills came down and attacked them and chased them into Hormah.

Fringes On Their Garments

"And the Lord spake unto Moses, saying, Speak unto the children of Israel, and bid them that they make them fringes in the borders of their garments throughout their generations, and that they put upon the fringe of the borders a ribband of blue: And it shall be unto you for a fringe, that ye may look upon it, and remember all the commandments of the Lord, and do them; and that ye seek not after your own heart and your own eyes, after which ye use to go a-whoring: That ye may remember, and do all my commandments, and be holy unto your God. I am the Lord your God, which brought you out of the land of Egypt, to be your God: I am the Lord your God." (Numbers 15:37-41)

In the first part of Numbers 15, the children of Israel were given further instructions they were to follow upon entering the Land of Promise. We have covered sacrifices and offerings in other places.

The fringes in the borders of their garments speak to us of the Lord Jesus and the woman who had the issue of blood, and drew near to Him and wanted to touch, as it were, even the hem of His garment. She had said in her heart that just to touch the fringe would cause her to be healed (Mark 5:25-28). That unnamed woman had the faith to reach out to Jesus and be made totally whole from all her infirmities. In Matthew 23:5, we hear the condemning words of the Lord as He spoke to the scribes and the Pharisees: *"But all their works they do for to be seen of men: they make broad their phylacteries, and enlarge the borders of their garments."*

Korah's Rebellion

The date of the history of this part of our story in Numbers 16 is uncertain. Many scholars believe it happened earlier in their journey; however, new laws often bring new rebellions. Korah, son of Ishar, and descendant of Levi, along with Dathan, Abiram, and On, from the tribe of Reuben, conspired to incite a riot against Moses claiming he took too much responsibility upon himself. Their words were hot and hard against Moses who talked with the Lord face to face, and was said by the Lord to be a meek man—the meekest man upon the earth.

And when Moses heard it, he fell upon his face. Moses told the men that the Lord would show them who belonged to Him. He would prove to them on the morrow who was holy, and who had been chosen by Him. Moses spoke to Korah and all his followers to take censers, put fire therein, and put incense in them before the Lord the next day.

321

Sons of Levi Rebuked

"Seemeth it but a small thing unto you, that the God of Israel hath separated you from the congregation of Israel, to bring you near to himself to do the service of the tabernacle of the Lord, and to stand before the congregation to minister unto them? And he hath brought thee near to him, and all thy brethren the sons of Levi with thee: and seek ye the priesthood also?"

(Numbers 16:9-10)

The Gainsaying Of Core

"Woke unto them! for they have gone in the way of Cain, and ran greedily after the error of Balaam for reward, and perished in the gainsaying of Core."

(Jude 1:11)

Moses called for Dathan and Abiram, the sons of Eliab, to come before him and they refused to come, sending word that Moses had lied to them and led them astray.

"Is it a small thing that thou hast brought us up out of the land that floweth with milk and honey, to kill us in the wilderness, except thou make thyself altogether a prince over us? Moreover thou hast not brought us into a land that floweth with milk and honey, or given us inheritance of fields and vineyards: wilt thou put out the eyes of these men? we will not come up." *(Numbers 16:13-14)*

Moses became very angry at that point and told the Lord not to accept their sacrifices. He laid out his own merits before the Lord: "I have not stolen so much as one donkey from these people. I have not hurt a one of them." Next, he told Korah to meet with him on the morrow and Aaron would be with him. Each man was to bring his censers with incense on them. It was a censer for each man, a total of 250. They came with their censers and lit them and placed the incense on them at the entrance of the Tabernacle before Moses and Aaron. Meanwhile, Korah continued to talk around the camp and stir up the people to take sides against their leaders. Many of the people were onlookers; they were not sure just what they believed. Then the glory of the Lord appeared at the tabernacle door for all to see.

More Intercession

"And the Lord spake unto Moses and unto Aaron, saying, Separate yourselves from among this congregation, that I may consume them in a moment. And they fell upon their faces, and said, O God, the God of the spirits of all flesh, shall one man sin, and wilt thou be wroth with all the congregation? And the Lord spake unto Moses, saying, Speak unto the congregation, saying, Get you up from about the tabernacle of Korah, Dathan, and Abiram."   *(Numbers 16:20-24)*

The Lord instructed Moses to tell all the people to get away from the tents of Korah, Dathan, and Abiram, or they would be destroyed with the wicked. Moses quickly followed the orders of the Lord so the entire camp would not perish with these wicked men. He had hardly finished speaking when the ground suddenly split open and Korah, Dathan, Abiram, and all their wives and little ones, fell into Sheol; then the earth closed over them. People ran in every direction screaming and crying from fear. Fire came forth from God and burned up the 250 men who were offering incense.

"And the Lord spake unto Moses, saying, Speak unto Eleazar the son of Aaron the priest, that he take

up the censers out of the burning, and scatter thou the fire yonder; for they are hallowed. The censers of these sinners against their own souls, let them make them broad plates for a covering of the altar: for they offered them before the Lord, therefore they are hallowed: and they shall be a sign unto the children of Israel. And Eleazar the priest took the brasen censers, wherewith they that were burnt had offered; and they were made broad plates for a covering of the altar: To be a memorial unto the children of Israel, that no stranger, which is not of the seed of Aaron, come near to offer incense before the Lord; that he be not as Korah, and as his company: as the Lord said to him by the hand of Moses."

(Numbers 16:36-40)

Again the congregation was saved through the intercession of Moses. God and Moses were seen working together in this matter. No sooner had Moses spoken judgment to the rebels, than God had carried it out.

Moses Makes Atonement

"But on the morrow all the congregation of the children of Israel murmured against Moses and against Aaron, saying, Ye have killed the people of the Lord. And it came to pass, when the congregation was gathered against Moses and against Aaron, that they looked toward the tabernacle of the congregation: and behold, the cloud covered it, and the glory of the Lord appeared." *(Numbers 16:41-41)*

When Moses and Aaron came before the tabernacle of the congregation, he Lord told them to get out of the way for He was going to consume the people in one split second. Moses and Aaron fell upon their faces to intercede, but what could they say? The plague had already begun.

"And Moses said unto Aaron, Take a censer, and put fire therein from off the altar, and put on incense, and go quickly unto the congregation, and make an atonement for them: for there is wrath gone out from the Lord; the plague is begun. And Aaron took as Moses commanded, and ran into the midst of the congregation; and, behold, the plague was begun among the people: and he put on incense, and made an atonement for the people. And he stood between the dead and the living; and the plague was stayed. Now they that died in the plague were fourteen thousand and seven hundred, beside them that died about the matter of Korah. And Aaron returned unto Moses unto the door of the tabernacle of the congregation: and the plague was stayed." *(Numbers 16:46-50)*

The incense kindling on the coals taken from the altar of burnt-offering where the sacrifices had been brought, typified the accepted mediatorial intercession of our great High-priest, the Lord Jesus Christ. Just when man had not a plea left upon this earth, the Lord interceded and His great intercession prevailed with God.

Aaron's Rod Budded

In Numbers 17, God informed Moses to have each of the tribal chiefs bring a wooden rod with his own name inscribed upon it. Aaron's name was to appear on the rod of the tribe of Levi. The Lord instructed Moses to place the rods in the tabernacle of the congregation before the testimony, and He would meet him there.

"And it shall come to pass, that the man's rod, whom I shall choose, shall blossom: and I will make to cease from me the murmurings of the children of Israel, whereby they murmur against you. And Moses spake unto the children of Israel, and every one of their princes gave him a rod apiece, from each prince one, according to their fathers' house, even twelve rods: and the rod of Aaron was among their rods. And Moses laid up the rods before the Lord in the tabernacle of witness. And it came to pass, that on the morrow Moses went into the tabernacle of witness; and, behold the rod of Aaron for the house of Levi was budded, and brought forth buds, and bloomed blossoms, and yielded almonds. And Moses brought out all the rods from before the Lord unto all the children of Israel: and they looked, and took every man his rod. And the Lord said unto Moses, Bring Aaron's rod again before the testimony, to be kept for a token against the rebels; and thou shalt quite take away their murmurings from me, that they die not. And Moses did so: as the Lord commanded him, so did he. And the children of Israel spake unto Moses, saying, Behold, we die, we perish, we all perish. Whosoever cometh any thing near unto the tabernacle of the Lord shall die: shall we be consumed with dying?"

(Numbers 17:5-13)

Aaron's rod became a living branch; it budded and blossomed, and yielded almonds. In some places there were buds, while in other places there were blossoms and fruit—all on the same rod. No nation upon the face of this earth was ever blessed with such miracles, one after the other, as was the nation of Israel while being led by Moses through the howling wilderness towards the land of

Promise. The budding of Aaron's rod was plain indication to the people that God had chosen Aaron for the priesthood, and not any other of the princes of the tribes. Matthew Henry here observed that Aaron was distinguished from them, and manifested to be under the special blessing of heaven, which sometimes yields increase where there is neither planting nor watering by the hand of man. Bishop Hall noted that fruitfulness is the best evidence of a divine call, and that the plants of God's setting, and the boughs cut off from them, will flourish. The trees of the Lord, though they seem dry trees, are full of sap. The priesthood was designed not only to honor Aaron, but to bless the children of Israel. This typifies Christ, who ordained his apostles and ministers that they should go and bring forth fruit, and that their fruit should remain (John 15). On and on we could go with this as the perfect type of our Lord Jesus as our High Priest.

One writer said the question was divinely settled. Priesthood is founded upon that precious grace of God which brings life out of death. This is the source of priesthood. All the human authority and effort could never infuse life into a dead stick or cause that stick to become the channel of blessing to souls. It is the quickening power of God that makes all things possible. Aaron's rod that budded speaks to us of Jesus as the Resurrection and the Life.

Death of Miriam

"Then came the children of Israel, even the whole congregation, into the desert of Zin in the first month: and the people abode in Kadesh; and Miriam died there, and was buried there."   (Numbers 20:1)

327

This 20th chapter begins the history of the last year of the wanderings of the children of Israel, and the death of Miriam. She was the beloved sister who had stood watch as Moses was drawn from the river by the daughter of Pharaoh; we view her again after the crossing of the Red Sea, timbrel in hand, praising God for all His wondrous works in their behalf. But Aaron and Miriam murmured, and would not enter Canaan.

Moses Strikes The Rock

At Kadesh there was not enough water to drink, and the children of Israel once again rebelled against Moses and Aaron, declaring that death along with their dear brothers whom the Lord killed would be far better than dying of thirst in the wilderness. In this chapter we see Moses, the servant of God, going through some of the hardest trials of his colorful life. Miriam is gone, and the people are threatening rebellion again.

"And why have ye brought up the congregation of the Lord into this wilderness, that we and our cattle should die there? And wherefore have ye made us to come up out of Egypt, to bring us in unto this evil place? It is no place of seed, or of figs, or of vines, or of pomegranates; neither is there any water to drink. And Moses and Aaron went from the presence of the assembly unto the door of the tabernacle of the congregation, and they fell upon their faces: and the glory of the Lord appeared unto them. And the Lord spake unto Moses, saying, Take thy rod, and gather thou the assembly together, thou, and Aaron thy brother, and speak ye unto the rock before their eyes; and it shall give forth his water, and thou shalt bring forth to them water out of the rock:

so thou shalt give the congregation and their beasts drink. And Moses took the rod from before the Lord, as he commanded him. And Moses and Aaron gathered the congregation together before the rock, and he said unto them, Hear now, ye rebels: must we fetch you water out of this rock? And Moses lifted up his hand, and with his rod he smote the rock twice: and the water came out abundantly, and the congregation drank, and their beasts also."   *(Numbers 20:4-11)*

It is deeply touching for us to see Moses again and again on his face before the Lord in behalf of this rebellious and stiff-necked people. It is a bit amusing to remember that at one point in their journey God claimed they belonged to Moses, and Moses in turn would have no part of that, and handed them back to the Lord as His people. We note here that Aaron and Moses apparently made no reply to the people, but took the matter straight to the Lord. We are to note here two objects of special interest in the above scriptures, the "rock" and the "rod." Moses and Aaron sought counsel of the Lord, and counsel was given, but not obeyed. Moses was commanded to take the rod, but was told to speak to the Rock, not strike it. *"SPEAK, AND THE ROCK WILL GIVE FORTH HIS WATER."*

In 1 Corinthians 10:4, we read, *"They drank of that spiritual rock that followed them: and that Rock was Christ."* It is plain and clear that the Rock was Christ-smitten for us. We have already studied in Exodus 17 that the rock was smitten and water issued forth to satisfy the thirst of the people and their cattle; smitten by the same rod that had turned the water of the Nile River into blood, and the same rod that had parted the Red Sea, for this was

329

the rod of authority in the hands of Moses. That was indeed in type Christ-smitten for us by the Lord of Righteousness. Now this smitting could take place only once; it could never be repeated. *"Knowing that Christ being raised from the dead dieth no more; death hath no more dominion over Him. For in that He died, He died unto sin once; but in that He liveth, He liveth unto God"* (Romans 6:9-10). In Hebrews 9:26 and 28, we read, *"But now once in the end of the world hath He appeared to put away sin by the sacrifice of Himself . . . so Christ was once offered to bear the sins of many."*

Moses had been commanded to take Aaron's rod and stand by the Rock and speak; God said, *". . . and it shall give forth His water . . ."* He was to take with him the "priestly rod—and speak with authority to the Rock." The atoning work is done, and now our great High Priest is in heaven at the right hand of the Father making intercession for the saints. Thus, we see it was a grave mistake for Moses to strike the Rock twice. He held in his hand the Rod of Grace, and a word would have sufficed to bring forth the water of life. We borrow a thought from MacIntosh at this point: "But Jehovah took care of His own glory. He sanctified Himself before the people, and notwithstanding their rebellious murmurings, and Moses' sad mistake and failure, the congregation of the Lord received a gushing stream from the smitten rock." This act of disobedience kept Moses from entering the Promised Land with the children of Israel. Moses at this point was not only guilty of unbelief, but also spoke as if he were the one who had furnished the power for their deliverance.

"And the Lord spake unto Moses and Aaron, Because ye believed me not, to sanctify me in the eyes of

the children of Israel, therefore ye shall not bring this congregation into the land which I have given them. This is the water of Meribah; because the children of Israel strove with the Lord, and he was sanctified in them."   *(Numbers 20:12-14)*

Because Edom refused to allow the children of Israel to pass over the land, they journeyed from Kadesh to Mount Hor. (These Edomites were the descendants of Esau.) The same God who refused years ago to allow Esau to kill Jacob now will not allow Israel to touch Edom.

Death of Aaron

These last few verses in chapter 20 deal with the death of Aaron, and are deeply touching to those who have followed God's children from Egypt to their present campsite.

"And the Lord spake unto Moses and Aaron in Mount Hor, by the coast of the land of Edom, saying Aaron shall be gathered unto his people: for he shall not enter into the land which I have given unto the children of Israel, because ye rebelled against my word at the water of Meribah. Take Aaron and Eleazar his son, and bring them up unto Mount Hor: And strip Aaron of his garments, and put them upon Eleazar his son: and Aaron shall be gathered unto his people, and shall die there. And Moses did as the Lord commanded: and they went up into Mount Hor in the sight of all the congregation. And Moses stripped Aaron of his garments, and put them upon Eleazar his son; and Aaron died there in the top of the mount: and Moses and Eleazar came down from the mount. And when all the congregation

saw that Aaron was dead, they mourned for Aaron thirty days, even all the hosue of Israel."

(Numbers 20:23-29)

Moses, who had once dressed Aaron in the priestly garments, was commanded by God to strip him of them. This chapter begins with the death of Miriam, and it ends with the death of Aaron. His earthly work was finished, and he laid down to die there in the mount as God had commanded.

The Serpent of Bronze

We note that between Numbers 14:45 and 20:14 there is a period of about 38 years according to Deuteronomy 2:14: *"And the space in which we came from Kadesh-barnea, until we were come over the brook Zered, was thirty and eight years; until all the generation of the men of war were wasted out from among the host, as the Lord sware unto them."* The death of Aaron marked the end of the wanderings. From that point on, Israel moved steadily towards their homeland, but their complaining never ended.

When the King of Arad learned that the children of Israel were approaching, he attacked, and took some of them prisoners. Then the Israelites turned to God and vowed if He would help them conquer the king and his people, they would completely wipe out the cities of that area. The Lord heard their vow, defeated the Cannaanites, and they destroyed the cities. Hormah ("Utterly Destroyed") was the name of the region. They returned to Mount Hor and continued their route southward along the Red Sea so they could pass the land of Edom. Along the way, the people were discouraged, and they began to murmur against God. They whined, and longed once again for the "flesh-pots" of Egypt; they complained about the water and the manna.

"And the Lord sent fiery serpents among the people, and they bit the people; and much people of Israel died. Therefore the people came to Moses, and said, we have sinned, for we have spoken against the Lord, and against thee; pray unto the Lord, that he take away the serpents from us. And Moses prayed for the people. And the Lord said unto Moses, Make thee a fiery serpent, and set it upon a pole: and it shall come to pass, that every one that is bitten, when he looketh upon it, shall live. and Moses made a serpent of brass, and put it upon a pole, and it came to pass, that if a serpent had bitten any man, when he beheld the serpent of brass, he lived."
(Numbers 21:6-9)

This seemed to be the epitome of unbelief. Over and over again these people forgot the miracles and the food from heaven, and groaned and complained to return to the land of darkness and bondage. God hardly discussed the matter; judgment was quick. The people were bitten by hideous poisonous snakes, and death was just as quick as His wrath against them. The fiery serpents speak to us of the devil among God's people; if they will not walk with Him, they will know the power of His sting and the agony of sudden death. The wilderness through which they passed was infested all along with these serpents. Out from under the cloud and protection of God, they became prey to them.

The serpent is a symbol of sin judged, for bronze speaks of divine judgment as we studied in the brazen altar; and the laver of bronze speaks to us of self judgment. In Ephesians 6:16, Satan's temptations are called his "fiery darts." The bronze serpent is a type of Christ who was made to be sin for us. In John 3:14-15, we read, *"And as Moses lifted up the serpent in the wilderness, even so must the Son of man be lifted up: That whosoever believeth in him should not perish, but have eternal life."*

Israel repented and confessed, and God's grace was sufficient. All they had to do was look up and "live." We might wonder about the history of the brazen serpent. In 2 Kings 18:4, we learn that Hezekiah did what was right in the sight of the Lord, according to all David his father did, and *"He removed the high places, and brake the images, and cut down the groves, and brake in pieces the brazen serpent that Moses had made: for unto those days the children of Israel did burn incense to it: and he called it Nehushtan."*

Then all of Israel traveled to Beer ("A Well"), where the Lord told Moses to summon the people, and He would give them water. Then Israel sang this song:

Spring Up,
O well;
sing ye unto it
The princes digged the well,
the nobles of the people digged it,
by the direction of the lawgiven,
with their staves.

They moved out of the wilderness into the valley in the plateau of Moab; from there they could see Mount Pisgah in the distance. They sent word to King Sihon for permission to pass through his land, but he refused and attacked them at Jahaz. Israel slaughtered them and occupied their land from the Aaron River to the Jabbok River, as far as the borders of the Ammonites. They dwelt in the cities that they had captured, including Heshbon, King Sihon's capital. Next, King Og of Bashan met them with his army at Edre-i, but the Lord told Moses not to fear, for the army was already conquered. The Lord was marching ahead of the children of Israel to bring them into the land He had promised so many centuries ago to Abraham, Isaac, and Jacob.

Balaam, The Covetous Prophet

Numbers 22 through 24 are a most important part of the history of the children of Israel. There will ever remain some mysteries about Balaam, which God has not chosen to reveal to us in His Word. This is a story rich and varied in instructions for us today, as well as conclusive proof that what God has blessed, man cannot curse or hinder. Balak's offer of gold and silver proved to be Balaam's downfall. When a man's heart is right with God, he will cast down the Balaam's of this world and look to God as his source of supply.

"And the children of Israel set forward, and pitched in the plains of Moab on this side of Jordan by Jericho. And Balak the son of Zippor saw all that Israel had done to the Amorites. And Moab was sore afraid of the people, because they were many: and Moab said unto the elders of Midian, Now shall this company lick up all that are round about us, as the ox licketh up the grass of the field. And Balak the son of Zippor was king of the Moabites at that time. He sent messengers therefore unto Ba-

laam the son of Beor to Pethor, which is by the river of the land of the children of his people, to call him, saying, Behold, there is a people come out from Egypt: behold, they cover the face of the earth, and they abide over against me: Come now therefore, I pray thee, curse me this people; for they are too mighty for me: peradventure I shall prevail, that we may smite them, and that I may drive them out of the land: for I wot that he whom thou blessest is blessed, and he whom thou cursest is cursed." (Numbers 22:1-6)

Thus we read that Balak was terrified when he looked up one day and saw the dust of those Israelites who had been held in tack by God for forty years coming at him. He declared to his diviners that they covered the face of the earth. He sent some of his most important men to Balaam, for he had heard of his reputation with God.

Balaam wanted their money; he invited the men to stay the night while he spoke with God. God came to Balaam and instructed him not to go back with them. Balaam sent them back without him; but Balak refused to be denied. He sent princes even greater than his first group, and begged Balaam to come to him and curse the people. He promised Balaam great honor and promotion if he would but come and curse God's people.

"And Balaam answered and said unto the servants of Balak, If Balak would give me his house full of silver and gold, I cannot go beyond the word of the Lord my god, to do less or more. Now therefore, I pray you, tarry ye also here this night, that I may know what the Lord will say unto me more. And God came unto Balaam a

night, and said unto him, If the men come to call thee, rise up, and go with them; but yet the word which I shall say unto thee, that shalt thou do.''

(Numbers 22:18-21)

In the words of MacIntosh: ''Miserable man!—most miserable! His name stands on the page of inspiration as the expression of one very dark and awful stage of man's downward history.'' In the epistle of Jude, verse 11, we read, *''Woe unto them! for they went in the way of Cain, and ran riotously in the error of Balaam for hire and perished in the gainsaying of Korah.''* The book of Jude is the declaration of woe unto the apostates. Cain was a tiller of the soil; Balaam was a prophet; Korah (Core) was a prince in Israel, which sets forth three different classes of people for us. This evil is not peculiar to any particular class or group of people. Jude tells us that the apostate first enters upon a wrong path, then he runs riotously down that path; finally he perishes at its end.

''Which have forsaken the right way, and are gone astray, following the way of Balaam the son of Bosor, who loved the wages of unrighteousness; but was rebuked for his iniquity: the dumb ass speaking with man's voice forbad the madness of the prophet.''

(2 Peter 2:15-16)

Balaam rose the next morning, saddled his ass, and went with the princes of Moab. But God was angry with him because he went, and the angel of the Lord stood against him as his adversary. If we do not note carefully the ''IF'' in verse 20, we will either excuse God for His actions against Balaam, or simply skip over the thought that comes to our mind. Did not God tell Balaam to go on with the men? The Word said, *". . . If the men come to call thee . . . And Balaam rose up in the morning . . ."* He most certainly got ahead of God in his excitement to curse that which God had blessed.

"And the ass saw the angel of the Lord standing in the way, and his sword drawn in his hand: and the ass turned aside out of the way, and went into the field: and Balaam smote the ass, to turn her into the way. But the angel of the Lord stood in a path of the vineyards, a wall being on this side, and a wall on that side. And when the ass saw the angel of the Lord, she thrust herself unto the wall, and crushed Balaam's foot againt the wall: and he smote her again. And the angel of the Lord went further, and stood in a narrow place, where was no way to turn either to the right hand or to the left. And when the ass saw the angel of the Lord, she fell down under Balaam: and Balaam's anger was kindled, and he smote the ass with a staff. And the Lord opened the mouth of the ass, and she said unto Balaam, What have I done unto thee, that thou hast smitten me these three times? And Balaam said unto the ass, Because thou hast mocked me: I would there were a sword in mine hand, for now would I kill thee. And the ass said unto Balaam, am not I thine ass, upon which thou hast ridden ever since I was thine unto this day? Was I ever wont to do so unto thee? And he said, Nay. Then the Lord opened the eyes of Balaam, and he saw the angel of the Lord standing in the way, and fell flat on his face. And the angel of the Lord said unto him, Wherefore hast thou smitten thine ass these three times? Behold I went out to withstand thee, because thy way is perverse before me: and the ass saw me, and turned from me, surely

338

now also I had slain thee, and saved her alive. And Balaam said unto the angel of the Lord, I have sinned; for I knew not that thou stoodest in the way against me: now therefore, if it displease thee, I will get me back again." (Numbers 22:23-35)

The Holy angels are adversaries to sin, and more times than we can ever know in this life we are sheltered and protected from the onslaughts of the devil by their drawn sword. God had promised Israel He would be an enemy to their enemies, and in this story we see the fulfillment of that prophecy. A point well taken by one writer is that the great question is not so much what the enemy may think of God's people, or what they may think about themselves, or of one another, but what does God think about them? The Lord declared that we are complete in Him. We are His workmanship; the apple of His eye. Therefore, the enemy is forever silenced, and all our filthy rags are as "pure white linen."

The angel told Balaam to go to Balak, but that he would speak only what he was told to speak. Upon his arrival, Balak met him offering again to promote him to great honor if he would curse the people of God.

"And Balaam said unto Balak, Lo, I am come unto thee: have I now any power at all to say any thing? the word that God putteth in my mouth, that shall I speak."
(Numbers 22:38)

Balaam went with the king to Kiriathhuzoth, and there King Balak sacrificed oxen and sheep, and gave animals to Balaam and the other men for their sacrifices. The next morning he took Balaam to the top of Mount Bamothbaal, so he could see the people of Israel spread out for miles around.

Balaam's Prophecy

At the request of Balaam, Balak built seven altars upon which they were to offer seven oxen and seven rams unto the Lord. On each altar they placed a bullock and a ram. Balaam went apart from the men and sought the Lord for His Word to the king. And the Lord put His Word in the mouth of Balaam:

"And he took up his parable, and said, Balak the king of Moab, hath brought me from Aram, out of the mountains of the east, saying, Come, curse me Jacob, and come, defy Israel. How shall I curse, whom God hath not cursed? or how shall I defy, whom the Lord hath not defied? for from the top of the rocks I see him, and from the hills I behold him: lo, the people shall dwell alone, and shall not be reckoned among the nations. Who can count the dust of Jacob, and the number of the fourth part of Israel? Let me die the death of the righteous, and let my last end be like his!"

(Numbers 23:7-10)

Balak Objected

"And Balak said unto Balaam, What hast thou done unto me? I took thee to curse mine enemies, and behold, thou hast blessed them altogether."

(Numbers 23:11)

The Balak's and the Balaam's of the world may join their forces, sacrifice their bullocks and their rams on seven altars every day of the week, and offer up their silver and gold, but all of this glitter combined could never evoke a single breath of curse or accusation from the mouth of God against His chosen people.

Yet Balak was a desperate man. He took Balaam to another vantage point where he could see the camps below. On top of Mount Pisgah, they built another seven altars, and offered up a young ram and a young bullock on each one. Balaam left the king and the princes of Moab standing beside the altars while he went out to seek the Word of the Lord. The Lord put more Words into the mouth of the prophet.

"And he took up his parable, and said, Rise up, Balak, and hear; hearken unto me, thou son of Zippor: God is not a man, that he should lie; neither the son of man, that he should repent: hath he said, and shall he not do it? or hath he spoken, and shall he not make it good? Behold, I have received commandment to bless: and he hath blessed; and I cannot reverse it. He hath not beheld iniquity in Jacob, neither hath he seen perverseness in Israel: the Lord his God is with him, and the shout of a king is among them. God brought them out of Egypt; he hath as it were the strength of an unicorn. Surely there is no enchantment against Jacob, neither is there any divination against Israel: according to this time it shall be said of Jacob and of Israel, What hath God wrought! Behold, the people shall rise up as a great lion, and lift up himself as a young lion: he shall not lie down until he eat of the prey, and drink the blood of the slain." (Numbers 23:18-24)

At this point Balak told Balaam if he could not curse the people, to just shut up about it. Balaam reminded the king that he could only say what the Lord told him to say; his mouth would not move in any other direction. But the king wanted to build a third set of altars, to try just once more to change God's mind about His people. By now Balaam had realized that Jehovah planned to bless Israel, and there was nothing he could do about it. He looked down from Mount Peor, where the king had taken him, and he opened his mouth as the Spirit of the Lord came upon him, and he spoke this prophecy concerning them:

"And he took up his parable, and said, Balaam the son of Beor hath said, and the man whose eyes are open hath said: He hath said, which heard the words of God, which saw the vision of the Almighty, falling into a trance, but having his eyes open: How goodly are thy tents, O Jacob, and thy tabernacles, O Israel. As the valleys are they spread forth, as gardens by the river's side, as the trees of lign aloes which the Lord hath planted, and as cedar trees beside the waters. He shall pour the water out of his buckets, and his seed shall be in many waters, and his king shall be higher than Agag, and his kingdom shall be exalted. God brought him forth out of Egypt; he hath as it were the strength of an unicorn: he shall eat up the nations his enemies, and shall break their bones, and pierce them through with his arrows. He couched, he lay down as a lion, and as a great lion: who shall stir him up? Blessed is he that blesseth thee, and cursed is he that curseth thee."

(Numbers 24:3-9)

With the natural eyes, those tents and tabernacle below might have appeared as "black as the tents of Kedar;" but viewed in a vision by the Lord, they were "goodly" and most precious in the eyes of the Lord. To the Lord they were as beautiful as green valleys and fruitful gardens by the sides of the rivers where their roots run deep. EXALTED! EXALTED! are the children of God. We should ever view them from the mountain tops not the valleys below.

342

By now the king was in a rage. He struck his hands together and said, "I called you here to curse these people; they are my enemies coming to consume me, and you have these three times blessed them. I thought to promote you, but now I want you to flee from my presence. Get out of my sight! God has kept you from sinning with your mouth." Balaam told the king he would not return to his own people, but first he would tell him what God's people were going to do to him and his people.

The Messianic Kingdom Prophesied

"And he took up his parable, and said, Balaam the son of Beor hath said, and the man whose eyes are open hath said: He hath said, which heard the words of God, and knew the knowledge of the most High, which saw the vision of the Almighty, falling into a trance, but having his eyes open: I shall see him, but not now: I shall behold him, but not nigh: there shall come a Star out of Jacob, and a Sceptre shall rise out of Israel, and shall smite the corners of Moab, and destroy all the children of Sheth. And Edom shall be a possession, Seir also shall be a possession for his enemies; and Israel shall do valiantly. Out of Jacob shall come he that shall have dominion, and shall destroy him that remaineth of the city. And when he looked on Amalek, he took up his parable, and said, Amalek was the first of the nations; but his latter end shall be that he perish for ever. And he looked on the Kenites, and took up his parable, and said, Strong is thy dwellingplace, and thou puttest thy nest in a rock. Nevertheless the Kenite shall be wasted, until Asshur shall carry thee away captive. And he took up his parable, and said, Alas, who shall live when God

doeth this! And ships shall come from the coast of Chittim, and shall afflict Asshur, and shall afflict Eber, and he also shall perish for ever. And Balaam rose up, and went and returned to his place: and Balak also went his way."   *(Numbers 24:15-25)*

The Doctrine Of Balaam

The doctrine of Balaam is mentioned in Revelation 2:24: *"The doctirne of Balaam, who taught Balak to cast a stumbling block before the children of Israel, to eat things sacrificed to idols, and to commit fornication."* Balaam took the way of Cain, and no doubt lived riotously afterward, but he perished miserably with the enemies of Israel. In Joshua 13:22, we read, *"Balaam also the son of Beor, the soothsayer, did the children of Israel slay with the sword among them that were slain by them."*

While Israel was camped at Acacia, the people began to "party" with the Moabites, and soon they bowed down and worshipped their gods. From the tops of the mountains all was fair, but in the plains of Moab the scene changed. We know that God will never reverse His decision; He is not a man that He should lie, neither the Son of Man that He should repent. He has spoken and all He has said will come to pass. Balaam, having failed in his attempt to curse God's people, had now succeeded in seducing them into sins so gross that God commanded the leaders of each tribe to be executed.

"And the Lord said unto Moses, Take all the heads of the people, and hang them up before the Lord against the sun, that the fierce anger of the Lord may be turned away from Israel. And Moses said unto the judges of

*Israel, Slay ye every one of his men that were joined
unto Baal-peor.''*   *(Numbers 25:4-5)*

One of the Israeli men insolently brought a Midianite
woman into the camp where the people were weeping
before the Lord; Phinehas (son of Eleazar and grandson of
Aaron the priest) saw it, grabbed a spear, ran into the tent
where the man had taken the woman, and killed both of
them. Then the plague was stayed because of the zeal of
Phinehas. Twenty-four thousand people died as a result
of Israel's sin. God gave Moses the command to destroy
the Midianites before they destroyed Israel. The rest of the
book of Numbers contains more instructions and
preparations for their entrance into Canaan.

Notes:

THE WATERS OF SEPARATION—purified a person
who had touched a dead body or human bone, or by entering a tent within seven days after a death had occurred.
The cathartic agent was applied on the third and seventh
day after contact with a dead body, human bone, or a
grave. It was applied by sprinkling a bunch of hyssop on
the person being cleansed.

It was also used to purify open vessels of gold, silver,
bronze and iron booty taken in battle (Numbers 31:21-
23).

The elements used in making the Waters of Separation were ashes of a red heifer, cedarwood, hyssop, and
scarlet thread mixed in Spring water.

RED HEIFER—The Hebrew word is *para adumah*
meaning ''red cow.'' It had to be unblemished by lame-
ness or blindness and could never have been under a

yoke. She was burned upon an altar with her own dung as fuel. Her ashes were mixed with other ingredients in spring water to make the Waters of Separation.

The blood of Jesus Christ is contrasted with the ashes of an heifer in Hebrews 9:13-14; and 1 John 1:7. Israel was referred to many times as a rebellious heifer in Jeremiah 48:34; Egypt's conquest in Jeremiah 46:20; Ephraim was compared to a heifer that treaded out the corn in Hosea 10:11; Israel as a backsliding heifer in Hosea 4:16.

CEDARWOOD—A tough, reddish wood that gave off a sweet, fresh odor; most likely came from the Cedars of Lebanon.

HYSSOP—A mint shrub that has a strong odor and taste; once used as an herb to season food and as a medicine.

SCARLET THREAD—Denotes the royal bloodline from Rahab, the harlot in Jericho, through King David and on through Jesus Christ.

DEUTERONOMY

THE FIFTH BOOK
OF MOSES

FINAL INSTRUCTIONS
TO ENTER THE LAND

Chapter 15

THE LAW RESTATED

"Deuteronomy" is derived from the Greek word meaning "second lawgiving," the name given to this book by the Septuagint translators. In these discourses, Moses reviewed in the ears of the Hebrew people their history and the many lessons they had learned from Egypt to their 40 years of wanderings in the wilderness.

"Behold, I have set the land before you go in and possess the land which the Lord sware unto your fathers, Abraham, Isaac, and Jacob, to give unto them and to their seed after them . . . Behold, the Lord thy God hath set the land before thee: go up and possess it, as the Lord God of thy fathers hath said unto thee; fear not, neither be discouraged." (Deuteronomy 1:8, 21)

"For the Lord thy God hath blessed thee in all the works of thy hand: he knoweth thy walking through this great wilderness: these forty years the Lord thy God hath been with thee; thou hast lacked nothing."

(*Deuteronomy 2:7*)

"*And the Lord spake unto you out of the midst of the fire: ye heard the voice of the words, but saw no similitude; only ye heard a voice. And he declared unto you his covenant, which he commanded you to perform, even ten commandments; and he wrote them upon two tables of stone.*"   (*Deuteronomy 4:12-13*)

"*But the Lord hath taken you, and brought you forth out of the iron furnace, even out of Egypt, to be unto him a people of inheritance, as ye are this day. Furthermore the Lord was angry with me for your sakes, and sware that I should not go over Jordan, and that I should not go in unto that good land, which the Lord thy God giveth thee for an inheritance: But I must die in this land, I must not go over Jordan: but ye shall go over, and possess that good land. Take heed unto yourselves, lest ye forget the covenant of the Lord your God, which he made with you, and make you a graven image, or the likeness of any thing, which the Lord thy God hath forbidden thee. For the Lord thy God is a consuming fire, even a jealous God.*"

(*Deuteronomy 4:20-24*)

"*When the Lord thy God shall bring thee into the land whither thou goest to possess it, and hath cast out many nations before thee, the Hittites, and the Girgashites, and the Amorites, and the Canaanites, and the Perizzites, and the Hivites, and the Jebusites, seven nations greater and mightier than thou; And the Lord thy God shall deliver them before thee; thou shalt smite them, and utterly destroy them; thou shalt make no covenant with them: Neither shalt thou make marriages*

350

*with them; thy daughter thou shalt not give unto his
son, nor his daughter shalt thou take unto thy son."*
(Deuteronomy 7:1-3)

Moses felt the urgency to restate all the instructions
the Lord God had given to them all along their way to the
land of Canaan. In this context, he has given them a very
strict caution against any kind of association with those
who worship idols lest they be led astray.

Smite The "Ites" In The Land

Although there were many more nations than mentioned in Deuteronomy 7, we find these seven nations are
the main ones stemming from the seedline of Ham. We
must remember that Ham saw the miracle-working power
of God during the flood, and even prior to it; his father,
Noah, had preached salvation to the Antediluvians, and
he knew the right way to God. But in his rejected state,
because of his sin against his father, he perverted the gospel, and his seedline went off into idolatry. As we search
the scriptures of the Old Testament for the types and shadows of things promised in the New Testament we often
see ourselves in many of these Canaanite nations; but God
had made a way of escape through our Advocate, the Lord
Jesus Christ. "Ites" in the land are the results of past failures; they are used to test your trust in God, not to trip or
trap you. The children of Israel were told seven things to
do with those seven nations stronger than they. Their failure to completely wipe them out caused them to become
"thorns in their flesh."

We have been given weapons by the Lord to use
against the enemies of our soul. In 2 Corinthians 10:3-5,
we read, *"For though we walk in the flesh, we do not*

war after the flesh: (For the weapons of our warfare are not carnal, but mighty through God to the pulling down of strong holds;) Casting down imaginations, and every high thing that exalteth itself against the knowledge of God, and bringing into captivity every thought to the obedience of Christ;"

God has given us the authority to drive the "Ites" out of our life. In Deuteronomy 7, we note what the children of God were to do to the seven nations living in Canaan, though they were seven times stronger than they: (1) smite them; (2) utterly destroy them; (3) make no covenant with them; (4) show them no mercy; (5) do not marry them; (6) destroy their altars; and (7) break down their images, and burn them with fire. These same rules apply to us if we would live the victorious life in Him. We must smite all thoughts that are contrary to the Word of God; wrong thinking will lead to wrong doing. The children of Israel had to fight in the natural, but God had already told them He would go before them. We do not wrestle flesh and blood; we use the Word against unclean thoughts, and thoughts that do not line up with the Word in our healing and prosperity. When we use the Word of God against the enemy, we utterly destroy his power over us. To agree with his suggestions is to make covenant with him, and the Lord said to make no covenant with the unclean thing. In Amos 3:3, we read, *"Can two walk together, except they be agreed?"* God's Word to us is the same as it was to the children of Israel about marrying one of the "Ites."

Just as they were chosen of God, so are we. In our text, verses 6-7, we have the Lord's reason for His call: they are a Holy people because He chose them to be Holy;

they are a special people to Him because He chose them to be special. His promise of faithfulness went as far back as Abraham, and it reaches forward in time to us today. He will never fail His Own.

Chosen of God

"For thou art an holy people unto the Lord thy God: the Lord thy God hath chosen thee to be a special people unto himself, above all people that are upon the face of the earth. The Lord did not set his love upon you, nor choose you, because ye were more in number than any people; for ye were the fewest of all people: But because the Lord loved you, and because he would keep the oath which he had sworn unto your fathers, hath the Lord brought you out with a mighty hand, and redeemed you out of the house of bondmen, from the hand of Pharaoh king of Egypt. Know therefore that the Lord thy God, he is God, the faithful God, which keepeth covenant and mercy with them that love him and keep his commandments to a thousand generations; And repayeth them that hate him to their face, to destroy them: he will not be slack to him that hateth him, he will repay him to his face. Thou shalt therefore keep the commandments, and the statutes, and the judgments, which I command thee this day, to do them."

(Deuteronomy 7:6-11)

Conditions To Be Met

"Wherefore it shall come to pass, if ye hearken to these judgments, and keep, and do them, that the lord thy God shall keep unto thee the covenant and the mercy which he sware unto thy fathers: And he will love thee, and bless thee, and multiply thee: he will also bless

the fruit of thy womb, and the fruit of thy land, thy corn, and thy wine, and thine oil, the increase of thy kine, and the flocks of thy sheep, in the land which he sware unto thy fathers to give thee. Thou shalt be blessed above all people: there shall not be male or female barren among you, or among your cattle."

(Deuteronomy 7:12-14)

Healing In The Covenant

"And the Lord will take away from thee all sickness, and will put none of the evil diseases of Egypt, which thou knowest, upon thee; but will lay them upon all them that hate thee." *(Deuteronomy 7:15)*

History Of The Seven "Ites"

I. *HITTITES:*

Means "Cheth" or Heth (great-grandson of Noah: Genesis 10:15); in Hebrew it became Chathath, one of the original aboriginal Canaanite nations that brought terror to all those around them.

ROOT SIN OR SINS: to break down by violence or by confusion and fear; abolish; be afraid; amaze; beat down; discourage; dismay; scare; terrify; dread.

LOCATION: They were Indo-European invaders that once occupied Asia Minor or modern-day Turkey. They built a powerful kingdom from 1600 B.C. to 1200 B.C. They conquered an Asiatic people called the Hatti, who inhabited Hattusas on the Halys River. Today it is known as Kizil Irmak.

EARLY CULTURE: The Hittites were not considered an important people by most scholars. Although their culture thrived, they were not artistically inclined.

354

Their arts were crude and unoriginal. They did develop a hieroglyphic script and were great builders. Hittite ruins have been found near Ankara, Turkey.

RELIGION: The Hittites and Egyptians consorted together and participated in great wars. It is believed that they worshipped the Eygptian gods and goddesses. They were a warring people, trying to conquer even their allies, the Egyptians. They finally settled around Kadash. They were powerful invaders with large armies consisting of a huge number of horses and chariots. (2 Kings 7:6; Numbers 13:29; Joshua 3:10; Jeremiah 20: 7-12; 1 Corinthians 14:33).

Abraham was first to get involved with them. He purchased the Cave of Machpelah from them to bury Sarah and all his kin in the land of Canaan (Genesis 23:3-4).

TYPE OF MODERN-DAY CHRISTIAN: This person is always undecided; he cannot make up his mind to total commitment. He wants to be involved in world politics; he wants to annihilate his enemies instead of praying for them; he keeps one foot in the world in the name of Christianity. He will herald his signs and march in the name of Peace; No Nukes demonstrators, etc. He is rebellious about authority, always suspecting others to be deceitful and crafty because his nature is also like that. He is always causing confusion by gossip or vain imaginations. He is always eager to join sides against sides if derision is caused in the Body of Christ (Acts 19:24-32; James 3:16).

WORD TO CLAIM CONFIDENCE IN THE SPIRIT: (Psalms 71:1-5; Psalms 31:1-3; Psalms 25:1-5; 1 John 5:14-15; 1 John 3:21-22; 2:27-29).

OPPOSITE OF CONFUSION:

    (1)   Confidence

    (2)   Serenity

    (3)   Peace

    (4)   Assurance

    (5)   Joy

    (6)   Trust

    (7)   Reliance

    (8)   Quietness

    (9)   Tranquility

II. JEBUSITE:

"Yebuwe" in Hebrew and means trodden down; thrashing place; re-hasher.

ROOT SIN OR SINS: restlessness; unforgiveness for some sin in their life; unbelief.

LOCATION: Jebus was a city by which Jerusalem and its inhabitants were known before the conquest of King David (1011–971 B.C.) It was very small and located in the southeast portion of what is now modern-day Jersualem. It was north of Hinnam and sat on a hill.

In 1400 B.C. it was known as Ursalim which is Semitic for "city of peace." It later became known in Hebrew as Yerushalem which has that meaning today.

ORIGIN: *"Thy birth and thy nativity is of the land of Canaan; thy father was an Amorite, and thy mother, a Hittite"* (Ezekiel 16:3). They descended from Canaan (Genesis 10:16). They were related to the Amorites through Adoni-Zedek, king of Jerusalem (Joshua 10:1-27). The Jebusites could not be driven out of the land, but they dwell with the children of Judah in Jerusalem even today (Joshua 15:63). David took the Castle of Zion from them and named it City of David (1 Chronicles 11:4-9).

TYPE OF MODERN-DAY CHRISTIAN: A Jebusite has a restless spirit; an unteachable and contrary spirit. They are always learning, never growing. Grass always seems greener somewhere else. They are not rooted and grounded in the Word; never planted in the Body of Christ by the Holy Spirit. They have no commitment. They cannot be counted on or depended on for spiritual faithfulness. They waver with every wind of doctrine. They never forgive or forget their old life. They are always re-hashing past sins of others to justify their own self-esteem. Hebrews 3:7-15; Hebrews 4:11; Romans 7:11; Psalms 95:6-11 are scriptures warning against a restless spirit.

WORD TO CLAIM REST IN THE SPIRIT: (Exodus 23:12; 33:14; Joshua 1:13-14; Judges 3:11; 1 Kings 5:4-5; Psalms 16:9; Psalms 37:7; Proverbs 13:13-14; Isaiah 28:9-13).

OPPOSITE OF RESTLESSNESS: Peace. Psalms 4-8; John 14:27; Proverbs 3:17; James 3:17; Ephesians 2:14-17; Psalms 107:29. Other synonyms are:

- (1) calmness
- (2) tranquility
- (3) quietness
- (4) stillness
- (5) immobile
- (6) dead

III. CANAANITES:

"Knaaniy" in the Hebrew meaning "the land of Purple."

ROOT SINS OR SIN: Materialism, traders, earthy, false humiliation; accumulating things; making idols of their possessions.

LOCATION: They lived in the land between the Jordan River and the Mediterranean Sea. They were early Phoenicia, then later became Palestine. They stood in for their neighbors, the Ishmaelites, who conducted mercantile caravans.

EARLY CULTURE: They were highly cultural, having many scholars. They dwelt in fortified cities with very modern homes and elite people. They were great traders and prosperous businessmen. They dealt in dying cloth purple and had great textile industries and lots of timber. They developed the linear alphabet that later came to Greece and was the ancestor of our Greek alphabet of today.

RELIGION: They worshipped Baal and el, a fertility God. Their female goddesses were:

(1) Asherah—pregnant woman

(2) Astarte—harbored sacred prostitutes in the temple

(3) Anat—warrior goddesses

The Canaanites practiced sacred prostitution, homosexuality and orgiastic rites.

WORD WARNING AGAINST MATERIALISM AND RICHES AND ACTS OF PERVERSION: Proverbs 28:20-22; Matthew 13:22; Mark 4:19; Luke 8:14; Mark 10:17-25; 1 Timothy 6:3-10; Matthew 19:24; Luke 16:1-13; James 5:1-6; Romans 1:18-32; Leviticus 18:22-25; 20:13.

TYPE OF MODERN-DAY CHRISTIAN: They are the intellectuals and perfectionists who judge Christian character and success by outward appearances. They cannot stoop to minister to the drunk in the gutter, to the poor, depraved, down-and-outer, but prefer to testify to the up-and-outer. They thrive on getting and giving money and being recognized for it in the congregation, especially to the grand, impressive cathedrals and temples "they" helped to build. They delight to make a show of their religion through their false humiliation.

When human need is to be met, they would rather Sister Susie or Brother Johnnie do the ministering. They will pray for them though. They have a form of godliness, but deny the power thereof. They may even approve of homosexuality, proclaiming that it is a way of life to be tolerated rather than recognize it as sin and separation from God. They would rather not get involved with having to "oust" such characters from the congregation of the righteous, but let every man worship as he pleases. They never seem to have a real, broken, contrite heart before God nor do they come into covenant relationship with Him, separated from the world and its temptations.

RICHES OF GOD IS GREATER THAN RICHES OF THE WORLD: Genesis 13:2; Romans 10:12; Romans 9:23-24; Matthew 6:19; John 6:27; Ephesians 1:18; 3:16; Jeremiah 9:23-24; Matthew 27:57-60; Philippians 4:19.

IV. AMORITES:

"Emoriy" in Hebrew means mountaineer, westerner, or ruler.

ROOT SIN OR SINS: Self-exaltation, pride, lust, high minded, boastful.

LOCATION: They inhabited the fertile Crescent in Mesopotamia and hill country of Palestine; descended from Canaan, grandson of Noah (Genesis 10:16).

EARLY HISTORY: They were the early foes of the Israelites. Two Amorite kings, SIHON and OG were defeated at the Battle of Jahaz with Israel being victorious (Judges 11:19-23; Numbers 21:21-35). They were actually giants (Amos 2:9). They later became the Babylonian Empire under King Hammurabi who wrote the earliest known code of law. This law was parallel to "an eye for an eye, a tooth for a tooth." Following their fall to the Israelites, the tribe later became the Samaritans, the most hated people of the Jews.

EARLY CULTURE: They built and maintained magnificent palaces, temples, dwellings, statues, and cemeteries. They also left thousands of cuneiform tablets containing literary works, laws and royal decrees.

RELIGION: They were idol-worshippers. Idols they worshipped were:

(1) *SUCCOTH-BENOTH:* booths of daughters, worshipped by the Babylonians. This was a shrine where female deities were kept and ritual prostitutions were practiced.

(2) *ASHIMA:* god of offense, a pagan deity known as Ishum-bethel was transplanted to Palestine by the people of Hamath.

(3) *NERGAL:* known as "great warrior" was a city god of war, pestilence, hunting; he was associated with the planet Mars (derived from Roman god of war) in Samaria.

(4) *NIBHAZ:* a god idol in the form of a dog-headed man brought by the Avites to Samaria.

360

(5) *TARTAK:* an idol in the form of an ass or donkey.

(6) *ADRAMMELECH:* "fire king" idol was a historical idol descended from Assyria. Human sacrifices were made to him.

(7) *ANAMMELECH:* "kingly image," a pagan god that included child sacrifice; they practiced immolation of their own children.

WORD WARNING AGAINST IDOLATRY: 1 John 5:21; Psalms 96:1-13; Psalms 106:34-41; Isaiah 2:17-22; Ezekiel 2:1-32; Zechariah 10:1-12; 1 Corinthians 10:1-15.

TYPE OF MODERN-DAY CHRISTIAN: They will not obey the law of the land and will not submit to the authority of the brethren. They must always be the "chief" and all others be the "Indians or peons" under them. They always boast "This is *MY* ministry; *YOU* support or send *ME* out to preach." They will not take the lowly position preferring the brethren but will always claim the best for himself. He is always alone, and a braggert; he has to have the largest crowd, the most miracles, largest house, largest car, most money and the largest ministry. He always takes offense at the slightest rebuttal or admonition. He is always ready to fight his own rights in the name of the Lord.

GODLY AUTHORITY OPPOSITE OF SELF-EXALTATION AND HIGH-MINDEDNESS: Philippians 2:1-16; 1 Corinthians 15:21-28; Proverbs 29:1-2; Titus 2:1-15; 1 Peter 3:8-22; Mark 13:34-37; Colossians 3:1-25.

V. GIRGASHITE:

"Girgashiy" in Hebrew means "uncertain."

ROOT SIN OR SINS: "Contention, strife, hatred, discord, conflict, root of bitterness, critical spirit, oppressed, distressed.

LOCATION: They lived on the west side of the Jordan River. They were descended from Ham. Following their conflict with Joshua they went into Africa and disappeared into history.

TYPE OF MODERN-DAY CHRISTIAN: The Girgashite is aptly described in Romans 3:10-18 (Legalistic flesh under law):

(1) He does not seek God

(2) He is unprofitable

(3) He is full of cursing and bitterness

(4) He is swift to shed blood

(5) He is destructive and miserable

(6) He does not know peace

(7) He has no reverance nor fear of God

WORD WARNING AGAINST BITTERNESS AND CONTENTION: Hebrews 12:15; Proverbs 14:10; Isaiah 38:14-20; Acts 8:21-23; Deuteronony 29:18; Ephesians 4:31-32; Colossians 3:19.

OPPOSITE OF CONTENTION IS CONTENTMENT: 1 Timothy 6:6-8; Luke 3:10-14; Philippians 4:11; Hebrews 13:5-8;.

PATIENCE: James 1:2-4; Luke 8:15; Luke 21:19; Hebrews 10-36; James 5:7; Romans 5:1-5; Romans 15:1-7; Romans 2:5-11; Romans 12:9-21.

IV. HIVITES:

Means "Chivvy," cave dweller, a villager of an aborginal tribe in Palestine. They were synonymous with the Horites of that era.

ROOT SIN OR SINS: Apathy, or "don't care" attitude; quit too soon; full of guile; liars; crafty.

LOCATION: The Hivites lived in the valley of Lebanon near Gibeon and east of the seaport city of Tyre. They were a part of the Mesopotamian kingdom of Mitanni approximately 2000 B.C. They were driven south by the Hyksos where they settled.

EARLY CULTURE: They were the only Canaanite nation Joshua did not smite (Joshua, 10:4). They were the only tribe to make peace with Israel (Joshua, 11:14-19; 9:3-27). They became slaves to the Israelites, hewers of wood and drawers of water for the congregation and for the altar of God.

RELIGION: The Hivites were responsible for institutionalizing the Levirate Marriage ceremony among the Israelites. When a man dies, his brother or next of kin is obliged to marry his childless widow (Deuteronomy 25:5-10). If the brother-in-law refuses to oblige, he must undergo a ceremony of public shaming in which HALITZAH (the loosing of the shoe from the levir's foot, and widow spitting in his face) is a part. Biblical examples are Tamar and her father-in-law, Judah; and Ruth, who became the wife of Boaz after being loosed by such a ceremony. Later in the Talmudic Law, the Levirate marriage was discouraged and forbidden.

Josephus states there were three puposes for the Levirate marriage:

(1) To retain the family name

(2) To keep the family property intact

(3) To make provision for the widow

The Sadducess tried to trap Jesus in a question concerning the resurrection involving this custom in Matthew 22:23-30.

TYPE OF MODERN-DAY CHRISTIAN: They become afraid when they saw the power of God at work. Flesh will compromise so it will not have to die. This person will always stay in one place doing the same thing; they never launch out in their own ministry. They become slaves to one ideal, one tradition, and one body of believers. They quit learning, and are satisfied living in past experiences, past knowledge, past healings, and past revelations. They never enlarge their experiences with God.

They are always down; have to be prayed up. They have lost the joy of their salvation and always have a "Woe is ME" attitude. They walk and talk and live in Romans 7 continually.

WORD TO CLAIM PERSEVERANCE IN THE SPIRIT: Matthew 16:24-26; Mark 8:34; Luke 9:23; Luke 9:59-62; Luke 14:16-24.

OPPOSITE OF APATHY/OR QUITTING:

(1)   Preseverance: Luke 14:26-35

(2)   Spirtual commitments: Galatians 2:20; Ephesians 6:10-18; 1 Timothy 2:1-5

(3)   Willing to pay the price. Job 28:12-28; Psalms 50:15-16; Philippians 5:13; Romans 12:9-21; John 15:12-13.

(4)   Press Onward: Phillippians 3:9-14; Hebrews 3:1; 1 Timothy 6:11-16.

VII. PERIZZITES:

"Perizziy" in Hebrew means lonely dweller in unwalled village or open country.

ROOT SIN OR SINS: Independence; wilderness wanderers, squatters, temporary homesteaders, loners; lived off the fleshly attributes of all the other nations around them.

LOCATION: Abram first had authority over them. (Genesis 15:18-21). Jacob was afraid of them. They later became merged with the Canaanites, (Genesis 34:1-31). King Solomon forced them into slavery (1 Kings (9:20). When they returned from captivity in Babylon they had no lineage (Ezra 2:55-58). Most villages and cities of the nations were surrounded by high walls and ramparts, defended by high towers and heavily fortified gates. The Perizzite villages were unwalled but they had a tower or castle where inhabitants fled in time of danger.

TYPE OF MODERN-DAY CHRISTIAN: The Perizzite became one and mingled with all other tribes. He never tries to ward off enemies. He is always open to attack. He becomes an easy prey for invaders because of his lonely nature. He is always willing to compromise.

He wanders alone and is restless, never abiding in one place; He is nomadic. When he becomes confused, he quits or becomes apathetic and does not try anymore. His material belongings are accumulated as he passes through the land. He always gets something for nothing. He brags about how his needs are met or supplied even though he did not work to earn it.

When contention or strife arises, he is always ready to cut down and criticize others, yet he never takes a side.

He is always "neutral," in the middle of the road, while agitating others on both sides.

He is very self-exalted and self-sufficient in everything he does. He does not need a Body of Believers with whom to worship; he does not need a covering; he does not need to sit and learn under annoited teachers; he does not need to study the Word.

He is always saying, "Bless God, I am filled with the Holy Ghost. I don't need Bible School or Bible study. The Spirit tells me what to do. No man is going to tell me what to do in a church. Bless God, I am free."

"Pride and lust creeps in and opens doors for demonic oppression and heresay and wrong teaching. Lonely spirits gravitate to other lonely spirits and are easily deceived. There is no armour of God to fight the fight of faith. He soon follows false teachers or even cults; even there, he has no respect of authority or law of submission.

TO DISCERN FLESHLY ATTRIBUTES BY THE WORD OF GOD: 1 Corinthians 5:9-13; Matthew 18:15-22; Galatians 1:6-12; Galatians 5:19-21; Ephesians 4:28-32; Philippians 3:2-3; 2 Thessalonians 2:1-12; 1 Timothy 4:1-16; 2 Timothy 3:1-17; 4:2-5; Titus 1:10-16; 2 Peter 2:1-22; I John 2:15-29; 1 John 4:1-21; 2 John 7-11; Jude 4-19.

TO OVERCOME THESE FLESH DESIRES BY THE WORD: 1 Corinthians 6:1-11; Galatians 2:20; Galatians 5:22-26; 6:12-18; Ephesians 6:10-18; Philippians 4:8-9; 1 Thessalonians 2:10-13; 1 Thessalonians 1:1-24; 2 Thessalonians 2:13-17; Titus 2:1-15; 1 John 5:1-15; Jude 20-25; Revelation 21:6-8; Revelation 22:11-21.

Warnings to the People

Over and over again Moses sounded out warnings to the children of Israel against backsliding and forgetting the Lord who brought them out of bondage to make them a special people of the covenant. He warned that they must never take the praise for wealth unto themselves. These people (like all of us) must realize that it was God who had given them the power to get wealth, and it had not come through any goodness of their own.

"Therefore thou shalt keep the commandments of the Lord thy God, to walk in his ways, and to fear him. For the Lord thy God bringeth thee into a good land, a land of brooks of water, of fountains and depths that spring out of valleys and hills; A land of wheat, and barley, and vines, and fig trees, and pomegranates; a land of oil olive, and honey; A land wherein thou shalt eat bread without scarceness, thou shalt not lack anythin in it; a land whose stones are iron, and out of whose hills thou mayest dig brass. When thou hast eaten and art full, then thou shalt bless the Lord thy God for the good land which He hath given thee."

(Deuteronomy 8:6-10)

Warning

"Beware that thou forget not the Lord thy God, in not keeping his commandments, and his judgements, and his statutes, which I command thee this day. Lest when thou hast eaten and art full, and hast built goodly houses, and dwelt therein; And when thy herds and thy flocks multiply, and thy silver and thy gold is multiplied, and all that thou hast is multiplied; Then thine heart be lifted up, and thou forget the Lord thy God, which brought thee forth out of the land of Egypt, from

the house of bondage; Who led thee through that great and terrible wilderness, wherein were fiery serpents, and scorpions, and drought, where there was no water; who brought thee forth water out of the rock of flint; Who fed thee in the wilderness with manna, which thy fathers knew not, that he might humble thee, and that he might prove thee, to do thee good at thy latter end; And thou say in thine heart, MY POWER AND THE MIGHT OF MINE HAND HA TH GOTTEN ME THIS WEALTH. But thou shalt remember the Lord thy God: FOR IT IS HE THA T GIVETH THEE POWER TO GET WEALTH, THAT HE MAY ESTABLISH HIS COVENANT WHICH HE SWARE UNTO THY FATHERS, AS IT IS THIS DAY. And it shall be, if thou do at all forget the Lord thy God, and walk after other gods, and serve them, and worship them, I testify against you this day that ye shall surerly perish. As the nations which the Lord destroyeth before your face, so shall ye perish; because ye would not be obedient unto the voice of the Lord your God."

By the time Moses finished retelling their history, it was evident to the children of Israel that they did not have much to brag about in their own strength. He recorded over and over that they were stiffnecked and rebellious against the Lord who had brought them out of Egypt, and had led them those forty years in spite of their complaining.

"And now Israel, what doth the Lord thy God require of thee, but to fear the Lord thy God, to walk in all His ways, and to love Him, and to serve the Lord thy God with all thy heart an all thy heart and with all thy soul, To keep the commandments of the Lord, and his statutes, which I command thee this day for thy good."

(Deuteronomy 10:12-13)

A Blessing and a Curse

It is interesting to note how many times long life on this earth is associated with "love the Lord your God, and obey His commandments." The following list is by no means a complete one; we will list some of the conditional promises:

Exodus 23:25: God will bless your bread and your water and will take away your sickness.

Deuteornomy 4:40: You will prolong your days upon the earth, which the Lord gives you.

Deuternomy 6:3: It will be well with you and you will increase mightily.

"And he will love thee, and bless thee, and multiply thee: he will also bless the fruit of thy womb, and the fruit of thy land, thy corn, and thy wine, and thine oil, the increase of thy kine, and the flocks of thy sheep, in the land which he sware unto thy fathers to give thee. Thou shalt be blessed above all people: there shall not be male or female barren among you, or among you cattle. And the Lord wil take away from thee all sickness, and will put none of the evil diseases of Egypt , which thou knowest, upon thee; but will lay them upon all them that hate thee." (Deuteronomy 7:13-15)

"Every place whereon the soles of your feet shall tread shall be yours: from the wilderness and Lebanon, from the river, the river Euphrates, even unto the uttermost sea shall your coast be: There shall no man be able to stand before you: for the Lord your God shall lay the

fear of you and the dread of you upon all the land that ye shall tread upon, as he hath said unto you."

(Deuteronomy 11:24-25)

Moses Prophesied Of Jesus

"The Lord thy God will raise up unto thee a Prophet from the midst of thee, of thy brethen, like unto me; unto him ye shall hearken; According to all that thou desirest of the Lord thy God in Horeb in the day of the assembly, saying, Let me not hear again the voice of the Lord my God, neither let me see this great fire any more. that I die not. And the Lord said unto me, they have well spoken that which they have spoken. I will raise them up a Prophet from among their brethen, like unto thee, and will put my words in his mouth; and he shall speak unto them all that I shall command him. And it shall come to pass, that whosoever will not hearken unto my words, which he shall speak in my name, I will require it of him."   *(Deuteronomy 18:15-19)*

After Moses presented the blessings of Deuteronomy 28, he listed the curses that would come upon the people of disobedience. It was a matter of choice between doing good and having a long life upon the earth, or doing evil and suffering under the curse of sickness, poverty, and death.

Prophetic

"And the Lord thy God will bring thee into the land which thy fathers possessed, and thou shalt possess it; and he will do thee good, and multiply thee above thy fathers. And the Lord thy God will circumcise thine heart of thy seed, to love the Lord Thy God with all thine

heart, and with all thy soul, that thou mayest live. And the Lord thy God will put all these curses upon thine enemies, and on them that hate thee which persecuted thee. And thou shalt return and obey the voice of the Lord thy God, and do all his commandments which I command thee this day. And the Lord thy God will make thee plenteous in every work of thine hand, in the fruit of thy body and in the fruit of thy cattle, and in the fruit of thy land, for good: for the LORD will again rejoice over thee for good, as he rejoiced over thy fathers. If thou shalt hearken unto the voice of the LORD thy God, to keep his commandments and his statutes which are written in this book of the law, and if thou turn unto the Lord thy God with all thine heart, and with all thy soul. For this commandment which I command thee this day, it is not hidden from thee, neither is it far off. It is not in heaven, that thou shouldest say, Who shall go up for us to heaven, and bring it unto us, that we may hear it, and do it? But the word is very nigh unto thee, in thy mouth, and in thy heart, that thou mayest do it. See, I have set before thee this day life and good, and death, and evil." *(Deuternomy 30:5-15)*

Moses Views the Promised Land from Mount Nebo

Chapter 16

THE DEATH OF MOSES

The Appointment of Joshua

Throughout the many chapters of the last four books of Moses, we hear the words, *"And Moses went and spake these words unto all Israel." And he said unto them, I am an hundred and twenty years old this day; I can no more go out and come in: also the Lord hath said unto me, Thou shalt not go over this Jordan."*

(Deuteronomy 31:2)

After all their years of wanderings together, Moses knew the hearts of God's people. He longed to go home to be with the Lord, but he feared for their souls. They were so bent on turning away from His commandments. Until now, Moses had been giving the people counsel and exhortation, but now he called them together to give them a word of encouragement, especially with reference to the wars of Canaan. Moses reminded them that God would be with them in all they were called upon to do.

"The Lord thy God, He will go over before thee, and He will destroy these nations from before thee, and thou shalt possess them: and Joshua, he shall go over before thee, as the Lord hath said. And the Lord shall do unto them as he did to Sihon and to Og, kings of the Amorites, and unto the land of them, whom he destroyed. And the Lord shall give them up before your face, that ye may do unto them according unto all the commandments which I have commanded you. Be strong and of a good courage, fear not, nor be afraid of them: for the Lord thy God, He it is that doth go with thee; He will not fail thee, nor forsake thee." *(Deuteronomy 31:3-6)*

We could not read these tender words of Moses without being struck with their peculiarly solemn tone. Moses felt the needs of his people; he foresaw their dangers as .they moved forward. From the depth of his loving heart, he made this last effort to prepare his brethren for what was before them.

Counsel to Joshua

"And Moses called unto Joshua, and said unto him in the sight of all Israel, Be strong and of a good courage: for thou must go with this people unto the land which the Lord hath sworn unto their fathers to give them and thou shalt cause them to inherit it. And the Lord, he it is that doth go before thee; he will be with thee, he will not fail thee, neither forsake thee: fear not, neither be dismayed." *(Deuteronomy 31:7-8)*

374

Counsel to the Priests

"And Moses wrote this law, and delivered it unto the priests the sons of Levi, which bare the ark of the covenant of the Lord, and unto all the elders of Israel. And Moses commanded them, saying, At the end of every seven years, in the solemnity of the year of release, in the feast of tabernacles, When all Israel is come to appear before the Lord thy God in the place which he shall choose, thou shalt read this law before all Israel in their hearing. Gather the people together, men, and women, and children, and thy stranger that is within thy gates, that they may hear, and that they may learn, and fear the Lord your God, and observe to do all the words of this law: And that their children which have not known anything, may hear, and learn to fear the Lord your God, as long as ye live in the land whither ye go over Jordan to possess it." (Deuteronomy 31:9-13)

Having written the law, Moses committed it to the care and custody of the priests and elders. He delivered one authentic copy to the priests, to be laid up by the ark, *"Take this book of the law, and put it in the side of the ark of the covenant of the Lord your God, that it may be there for a witness against thee"* (Detueronomy 31:26). It is supposed that he gave another copy to the elders of each tribe, to be transcribed by all of that tribe that were so disposed. He appointed the reading of the law before the ears of all the people every seventh year. This speaks to us of the importance of public assembly and the teaching of children who have never heard the Word.

The Lord Appeared to Moses

"And the Lord appeared in the tabernacle in a pillar of a cloud: and the pillar of the cloud stood over the door of the tabernacle. And the Lord said unto Moses,

Behold, thou shalt sleep with thy fathers; and this people will rise up, and go a whoring after the gods of the strangers of the land, whither they go to be among them, and will forsake me, and break my covenant which I have made with them. Then my anger shall be kindled against them in that day, and I will forsake them, and I will hide my face from them, and they shall be devoured, and many evils and troubles shall befall them; so that they will say in that day, Are not these evils come upon us, because our God is not among us? And I will surely hide my face in that day for all the evils which they shall have wrought, in that they are turned unto other gods. Now therefore write ye this song for you, and teach it the children of Israel: put it in their mouths, that this song may be a witness for me against the children of Israel. For when I shall have brought them into the land which I sware unto their fathers, that floweth with milk and honey; and they shall have eaten and filled themselves, and waxen fat; then will they turn unto other gods, and serve them, and provoke me, and break my covenant. And it shall come to pass when many evils and troubles are befallen them, that this song shall testify against them as a witness; for it shall not be forgotten out of the mouths of their seed: for I know their imagination which they go about, even now, before I have brought them into the land which I sware." (Deuteronomy 31:15-21)

The Lord God appeared to Moses, his faithful servant, and told him it was time for him to sleep with Abraham, Isaac, and Jacob. *"Their sorrows shall be multiplied that hasten after another god: their drink offerings of blood will I not offer, nor take up their names into my lips"*

(Psalm 16:4). Israel has ever proven the truth of these solemn words. She is a nation whose existence has been written in her own blood, and they have yet a tribulation through which they must pass, all of which proves to us that we encounter multiplied sorrows when we turn against the Lord. As one writer has said, may we learn well the lessons written upon the pages of this law. The Lord appeared in the tabernacle in the cloud, and talked with Moses in the door. He let Moses know that the people he had carried out of Egyptian bondage, through the wilderness, and to the border of the land of milk and honey, would go a-whoring upon his death; that they will break the covenant, and turn against the One true God for the gods of the Canaanites. The Lord told Moses to compose a song, divinely inspired, and sing it in the ears of the children of Israel as a testimony to them that He had been faithful to them. Again, Joshua is charged that he should be strong and of good courage, for he was the one whom God had selected to take the children of Israel across Jordan into the Promised Land. Moses knew that Joshua would need to put his total trust in God, and never rely upon his own strength. We are encouraged with the same word in Ephesians 6:10: *"Finally, my brethren, be strong in the Lord, and in the power of his might."* We can never overcome in our own strength; but, in the power of His might, we have the victory over every circumstance in life.

The Song of Moses

This song takes in the entire range of the history of the children of Israel, and God's faithful dealings with His people. Blessed be to God, this song begins and ends with Him.

Doctrine-Free and Abundant

"Give ear, O ye heavens, and I will speak; and hear, O earth, the words of my mouth. My doctrine shall drop as the rain, my speech shall distil as the dew, as the small rain upon the tender herb, and as the showers upon the grass."   *(Deuteronomy 32:1-2)*

God is the Rock

"Because I will publish the name of the Lord; ascribe ye greatness unto our God. He is the ROCK, his work is perfect: for all his ways are judgment: a God of truth and without iniquity, just and right is he."

(Deuteronomy 31:3-4)

No matter what may happen, the Lord God remains solid and steadfast as our ROCK. Our strength, our rest, and our solid foundation is in the Name of the Lord. Because the Lord is Holy, He was constrained to take down the rod of discipline and use it severely upon His own children, but He never dealt in justice without first offering mercy and grace.

The Lord's Portion is His People

"They have corrupted themselves, their spot is not the spot of his children: they are a perverse and crooked generation. Do ye thus requite the Lord, O foolish people and unwise? is not he thy father that hath bought thee? hath he not made thee, and established thee? Remember the days of old, consider the years of many generations: ask thy father, and he will shew thee; thy elders, and they will tell thee. When the Most High divided to the nations their inheritance, when he separated the sons of Adam, he set the bounds of the people according to the number of the children of Israel. For the Lord's portion is his people; Jacob is the lot of his inheritance."   *(Deuteronomy 32:5-9)*

He Led and Instructed Them

"He found him in a desert land, and in the waste howling wilderness; he led him about, he instructed him, he kept him as the apple of his eye. As an eagle stirreth up her nest, fluttereth over her young, spreadeth abroad her wings, taketh them, beareth them on her wings: So the Lord alone did lead him, and there was no strange god with him. He made him ride on the high places of the earth, that he might eat the increase of the fields; and he made him to suck honey out of the rock, and oil out of the flinty rock; Butter of kine, and milk of sheep, with fat of lambs, and rams of the breed of Bashan, and goats, with the fat of kidneys of wheat; and thou didst drink the pure blood of the grape."

(Deuteronomy 32:10-14)

At this point we reach another note on the scale of the Song of Moses. At verse 15, we change from God and His acts, purposes, and counsels, and view Israel's lack of appreciation for God and all He has done for them.

"But Jeshurun waxed fat, and kicked: thou art waxen fat, thou art grown thick, thou art covered with fatness; then he forsook God which made him, and lightly esteemed the Rock of his salvation. They provoked him to jealousy with strange gods, with abominations provoked they him to anger. They sacrificed unto devils, not to God; to gods whom they knew not, to new gods that came newly up, whom your fathers feared not. Of the Rock that begat thee thou art unmindful, and hast forgotten God that formed thee. And when the Lord saw it, he abhorred them, because of the provoking of his sons, and of his daughters. And he said, I will hide my face from them, I will see what their

end shall be: for they are a very froward generation, children in whom is no faith.''

"They have moved me to jealousy with that which is not God; they have provoked me to anger with their vanities: and I will move them to jealousy with those which are not a people; I will provoke them to anger with a foolish nation. For a fire is kindled in mine anger, and shall burn unto the lowest hell, and shall consume the earth with her increase, and set on fire the foundations of the mountains. I will heap mischiefs upon them; I will spend mine arrows upon them. They shall be burnt with hunger, and devoured with burning heat, and with bitter destruction: I will also send the teeth of beasts upon them, with the poison of serpents of the dust. The sword without, and terror within, shall destroy both the young man and the virgin, the suckling also with the man of gray hairs. I said, I would scatter them into corners, I would make the remembrance of them to cease from among men: Were it not that I feared the wrath of the enemy, lest their adversaries should behave themselves strangely, and lest they should say, Our hand is high, and the Lord hath not done all this.''

"For they are a nation void of counsel, neither is there any understanding in them. O that they were wise, that they understood this, that they would consider their latter end! How should one chase a thousand, and two put ten thousand to flight, except their Rock had sold them, and the Lord had shut them up? For their rock is not as our Rock, even our enemies themselves being judges. For their vine is of the vine of Sodom, and of the fields of Gomorrah: their grapes are grapes of *gall, their clusters are bitter: Their wine is the poison of dragons, and the cruel venom of asps. Is not this laid up in store with me, and sealed up among my treasures?"*

"To me belongeth vengeance, and recompence; their foot shall slide in due time: for the day of their calamity is at hand, and the things that shall come upon them make haste. For the Lord shall judge his people, and repent himself for his servants, when he seeth that their power is gone, and there is none shut up, or left. And he shall say, Where are their gods, their rock in whom they trusted, Which did eat the fat of their sacrifices, and drank the wine of their drink offerings? let them rise up and help you, and be your protection. See now that I, even I, am he, and there is no god with me: I kill, and I make alive; I wound, and I heal: neither is there any that can deliver out of my hand. For I lift up my hand to heaven, and say, I live for ever. If I whet my glittering sword, and mine hand take hold on judgment; I will render vengeance to mine enemies, and will reward them that hate me." "I will make mine arrows drunk with blood, and my sword shall devour flesh; and that with the blood of the slain and of the captives, from the beginning of revengers upon the enemy. Rejoice, O yenations, with his people: for he will avenge the blood of his servants, and will render vengeance to his adversaries, and will be merciful unto his land, and to his people. And Moses came and spake all the words of this song in the ears of the people, he and Hoshea the son of Nun." (Deuteronomy 32:15-44)

After Moses and Joshua had recited all these words in the ears of the congregation, Moses told them the impor-

381

tance of meditating upon the laws he had laid before them as a nation. Once again he encouraged them to teach these statutes to their chidlren, and their children's children. It was as if Moses felt he had to tell them just one more time that the way to a long and prosperous life was the way of the Lord. The Lord spoke to Moses on that same day and told him he was to get up to Mount Nebo and die there in the land of Moab near Jericho because he had disobeyed God in the midst of his anger at the Rock (Meribah-Kedesh, in the wilderness of Zen). Moses' life and ministry had come to an end, and he was to be buried by God. He had one more message to bless the tribes of Israel.

All Israel is Blessed

"And this is the blessing, wherewith Moses the man of God blessed the children of Israel before his death. And he said, the Lord came from Sinai, and rose up from Seir unto them; he shined forth from Mount Paran, and he came with ten thousands of saints: from his right hand went a fiery law for them. Yea, he loved the people; all his saints are in thy hand: and they sat down at thy feet; every one shall receive of thy words. Moses commanded us a law, even the inheritance of the congregation of Jacob. And he was king in Jeshurun, when the heads of the people and the tribes of Israel were gathered together." (Deuteronomy 33:1-5)

Reuben

"Let Reuben live, and not die; and let not his men be few." (Deuteronomy 33:6)

Judah

"And this is the blessing of Judah: and he said, Hear, Lord, the voice of Judah, and bring him unto his people: let his hands be sufficient for him; and be thou a help to him from his enemies."

(Deuteronomy 33:7)

Levi

"And of Levi he said, Let thy Thummin and thy Urim be with thy holy one, whom thou didst prove at Massah, and with whom thou didst strive at the waters of Meribah; Who said unto his father and to his mother, I have not seen him; neither did he acknowledge his brethren, nor knew his own children: for they have observed thy word, and kept they covenant. They shall teach Jacob thy judgments, and Israel thy law: they shall put incense before thee, and whole burnt sacrifice upon thine altar. Bless, Lord, his substance, and accept the work of his hands: smite through the loins of them that rise against him, and of them that hate him, that they rise not again."   *(Deuteronomy 33:8-11)*

It was at Massah and at Meribah that the Lord tried Levi, and he proved worthy; he is to be blessed for he obeyed the instructions of the Lord. It was there he destroyed many sinners, even family members for the Name of the Lord. The Levites shall teach God's laws to all Israel, and work before Him at the incense altar, and the altar of burnt offerings. Moses pleads with the Lord to prosper them, and give them a continued blessing.

Benjamin

"And of Benjamin he said, The beloved of the Lord shall dwell in safety by him; and the Lord shall cover him all the day long, and he shall dwell between his shoulders."   *(Deuteronomy 33:12)*

Benjamin is beloved of God, and dwells in safety with Him. God surrounds him with His tender love and care all the day long, and no harm will befall him.

Joseph

"And of Joseph he said, Blessed of the Lord be his land, for the precious things of heaven, for the dew, and for the deep that coucheth beneath, And for the precious fruits brought forth by the sun, and for the precious things put forth by the moon; And for the chief things of the ancient mountains, and for the precious things of the lasting hills, And for the precious things of the earth and fulness thereof, and for the good will of him that dwelt in the bush: let the blessing come upon the head of Joseph, and upon the top of the head of him that was separated from his brethren. His glory is like the firstling of his bullock, and his horns are like the horns of unicorns: with them he shall push the people together to the ends of the earth: and they are the ten thousands of Ephraim, and they are the thousands of Manasseh."

(Deuteronomy 33:13-17)

Zebulun and Issachar

"And of Zebulun he said, Rejoice, Zebulun, in thy going out; and Issachar, in thy tents. They shall call the people unto the mountain; there they shall offer sacrifices of righteousness: for they shall suck of the abundance of the seas, and of treasures hid in the sand.

(Deuteronomy 33:18-19)

Moses called Zebulun to rejoice, as outdoorsmen; and Issachar as lovers of the tents. They will summon the people to celebrate their sacrifices with them, and they will taste the riches of the sea and the land.

Gad

"And of Gad he said, blessed be he that enlargeth Gad: he dwelleth as a lion, and teareth the arm with the crown of the head. And he provided the first part for himself, because there, in a portion of the lawgiver, was seated; and he came with the heads of the people, he executed the justice of the Lord, and his judgments with Israel."   *(Deuteronomy 33:20-21)*

There rested a blessing upon all who helped Gad. He crouches like a lion with a savage arm; Gad chose the best of the land for himself, because it was reserved for a leader. He led the people because he carried out God's laws for the people.

Dan

"And of Dan he said, Dan is a lion's whelp: he shall leap from Bashan."   *(Deuteronomy 33:22)*

Naphtali

"And of Naphtali he said, O Naphtali, satisfied with favour, and full with the blessing of the Lord: possess thou the west and the south."

(Deuteronomy 33:23)

Asher

"And of Asher he said, Let Asher be blessed with children; let him be acceptable to his brethren, and let him dip his foot in oil."   *(Deuteronomy 33:24)*

Blessings to All Israel

"Thy shoes shall be iron and brass; and as thy days, so shall thy strength be. There is none like unto the God of Jeshurun, who rideth upon the heaven in thy help, and in his excellency on the sky. The eternal God is thy

refuge, and underneath are the everlasting arms: and he shall thrust out the enemy from before thee; and shall say, Destroy them. Israel then shall dwell in safety alone: the fountain of Jacob shall be upon a land of corn and wine; also his heavens shall drop down dew. Happy art thou, O Israel: who is like unto thee, O people saved by the Lord, the shield of thy help, and who is the sword of thy excellency! and thine enemies shall be found liars unto thee; and thou shalt tread upon their high places." (Deuteronomy 33:25-29)

Death of Moses

"And Moses went up from the plains of Moab unto the mountain of Nebo, to the top of Pisgah, that is over against Jericho. And the Lord shewed him all the land of Gilead, unto Dan, and all Naphtali, and the land of Ephraim, and Manasseh, and all the land of Judah, unto the utmost sea, And the south, and the plain of the valley of Jericho, the city of palm trees, unto Zoar. And the Lord said unto him, This is the land which I sware unto Abraham, unto Isaac, and unto Jacob, saying, I will give it unto thy seed: I have caused thee to see it with thine eyes, but thou shalt not go over thither. So Moses the servant of the Lord died there in the land of Moab, according to the word of the Lord. And he buried him in a valley in the land of Moab, over against Bethpeor: but no man knoweth of his sepulchre unto this day. And Moses was an hundred and twenty years old when he died: his eye was not dim, nor his natural force abated. And the children of Israel wept for Moses in the plains of Moab thirty days: so the days of weeping and mourning for Moses were ended." (Deuteronomy 34:1-8)

Joshua Ordained by Moses

"And Joshua the son of Nun was full of the spirit of wisdom; for Moses had laid his hands upon him: and the children of Israel hearkened unto him, and did as the Lord commanded Moses. And there arose not a prophet since in Israel like unto Moses, whom the Lord knew face to face, In all the signs and the wonders, which the Lord sent him to do in the land of Egypt to Pharaoh, and to all his servants, and to all his land, And in all that mighty hand, and in all the great terror which Moses shewed in the sight of all Israel."

(Deuteronomy 34:9-12)

Moses climbed from the plains of Moab to Pisgah Peak in Mount Nebo, across from Jericho, and the Lord pointed out the Promised land to him as they looked out across Gilead as far as Dan. There he saw the land of Naphtali, and Ephraim, and Manasseh; there he viewed Judah, extending to the Great Sea; there alone with God, he gazed at the Negev, and the Jordan Valley and Jericho, the city of the palm trees; and Zoar. *"This is the land that I promised to Abraham, Isaac, and Jacob. I promised that I would give it to their descendants. Moses, you may look over into the land, but you will not enter it"* (Deuteronomy 34:4)

So Moses died there in the mount at 120 years of age, and never before or afterward, was there a prophet like him with whom the Lord talked *"face to face."*

SUMMARY

Law And Grace

The only law to which we as Christians are responsible is the law of an Indwelling Jesus Christ. Christianity is centered in a Person, and not works of the law. It is not what we do for God, but what God has done for us through our Mediator, the Lord Jesus Christ. In Galatians 2:19-20, we read, *"Wherefore then serveth the law? It was added because of transgressions, till the seed should come to whom the promise was made. I am crucified with Christ: nevertheless I live; yet not I, but Christ liveth in me: and the life which I now live in the flesh I live by the faith of the Son of God, who loved me, and gave himself for me."* We are justified by the finished work of Calvary; no man is justified by the law.

We are not calling the law a curse. The Ten Commandments outlined the highest possible moral standards regulating human conduct. There is no higher rule of righteousnes than the law. Yet, we might ask the question, "Where does the curse lie that is spoken of in Galatians?" The answer is quite simple: the law insists upon total obedience by men. There can be no deviation from its requirements. Any failure brings the condemnation of the law. In James 2:10, we are told, *"For whosoever shall keep the whole law, and yet offend in one point, he is guilty of all."* In breaking one point of the law, we are guilty of breaking the whole law. Thus, it is man's inability to keep the law that brings the curse of the law upon him. The law shows man to be a sinner. The nature and intent of the law was not the way of salvation provided by God. It never was from the time of the first parents until now. It cannot save a man. It powerfully shows man he is a sinner and needs a Saviour. There had been no written law up to the time Moses was called up into the Mount to receive it from the finger of God. The law brought death instead of life. The Lord Jesus taught that the outward observance is not enough because the law dealt with the very intent of the heart. Jesus said He had not come to destroy the law but to fulfill it. He elevated it when He said, *"Ye have heard that it was said by them of old time, Thou shalt not commit adultery: But I say unto you, That whosoever looketh on a woman to lust after her hath committed adultery with her already in his heart"* (Mathew 5:17-18). On the subject of murder, He said that any man who is angry with his brother without a cause is in danger of judgment. Thus, we learn that the law strikes much deeper than outward acts. Our hope is found in Galatians 3:13: *"Christ hath redeemed us from the curse of the law, being made a curse for us: for it is written, Cursed is every one that hangeth on a tree."*

In Romans 8:1-4, we read *"There is therefore now no condemantion to them which are in Christ Jesus, who walk not after the flesh, but after the Spirit. For the law of the Spirit of life in Christ Jesus hath made me free from the law of sin and death. For what the law could not do, in that it was weak through the flesh, God sending his own Son in the likeness of sinful flesh, and for sin, condemned sin in the flesh: That the righteousness of the law might be fulfilled in us, who walk not after the flesh, but after the Spirit. "* Jesus was delivered for our offenses. It was our sins that nailed Him to the Cross. The law was given through Moses about 1500 years before Christ and at least 2500 years after Adam. The law placed alongside grace does not mean grace was removed. Grace was put there so man could flee to it when the law had done its work. The ones who live by faith are the true sons of Abraham.

What Then Is The Purpose Of The Law?

It was added later on (after the promise) to disclose and expose to men their guilt and to make men more aware of their need for a mediator between God and Man. Israel utterly failed in their keeping of the law, but their failure did not set aside the promise God gave to Abraham. Israel passed through centuries of chastening and discipline because of their failure, but God has not forgotten nor cast off His people. God cannot fail; He will prove faithful to us in the midst of our unbelief and faithlessness to Him.

The law had a beginning. It was added to something already in existence. It began with Moses as he stood between God and the sinful people. It must be remembered that the law was not given to make men better, nor to save them. Man was in need of a written document, moral code, to show up his sinful nature. The law was given until the Seed came, and the Seed had an appointed time to appear. In Galatians 4:4-5, we read, *"But when the fullness of the time was come, God sent forth his Son, made of a woman, made under the law, To redeem them that were under the law, that we might receive the adoption of sons."*

Two Mountains

The law revealed sin, but since Jesus Christ left, we find God has another method of convicting men of sin. The Lord said in John 16:7, *"Nevertheless I tell you the truth; it is expedient for you that I go away: for if I go not away, the Comforter will not come unto you; but if I depart, I will send him unto you. And when he is come, he will reprove the world of sin, and of righteousness, and of judgment."* The law came by Moses, but grace and truth came by Jesus Christ. The law was given on Mount Sinai, but God's grace was manifested on Mount Calvary. Jesus bore the sin of the entire world throughout all its generations. Mount Sinai belched out the fires of condemnation, while Mount Calvary soothed the desperate heart, and plead mercy for all. The law was dispensational; it served its purpose. Not only did the children of Israel receive a law which they could not keep, but before Moses descended the mountain, God had given them a way of escape through the sacrifices which pointed to the Lord Jesus, who would come in time and be the final sacrifice. They were immediately offered a way of escape. As our narrative continues, we find they broke the law before it was handed down to them.

The law was given to the nation Israel, and not to the whole world. As we have noted, the law was given to dem-

onstrate man's inability to make himself acceptable to
God by his self-efforts.

```
   MAN:
   I Thessalonians 5:23
   "And the very God of peace sanctify you
   wholly;  and I pray God your whole spirit
   and soul and body be preserved blameless
   unto the coming of our Lord Jesus Christ."

   TABERNACLE:  TRIUNE MEANS THREE IN ONE:  THIS  TABERNACLE
   WAS THREE IN ONE; this depcits the nature of God; the nature
   of heaven;  of man;  the church, and many other things.
```

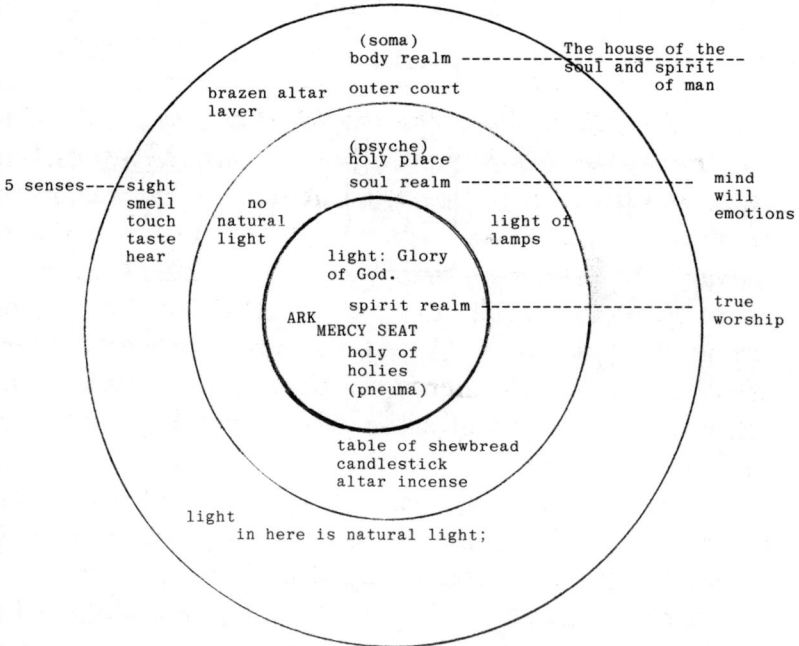

```
SPIRIT= awareness of God;new birth

soul:  mind will, emotions; awareness of self
body:  awareness of the  world;  five senses:
```

393

Jesus As The Fulfillment Of The Tabernacle In The Books Of John

Three aspects of Jesus in the 3 entrances:
"(1) the way (2) the truth (3) the life."
(John 14:6)

Three aspects of Jesus in the 3 entrances;
(1) the way (2) the truth (3) the life; (John 14:6)
JESUS AS THE FULFILLMENT OF THE TABERNACLE IN THE BOOKS OF JOHN;

GATE   AND   VEIL
DOOR

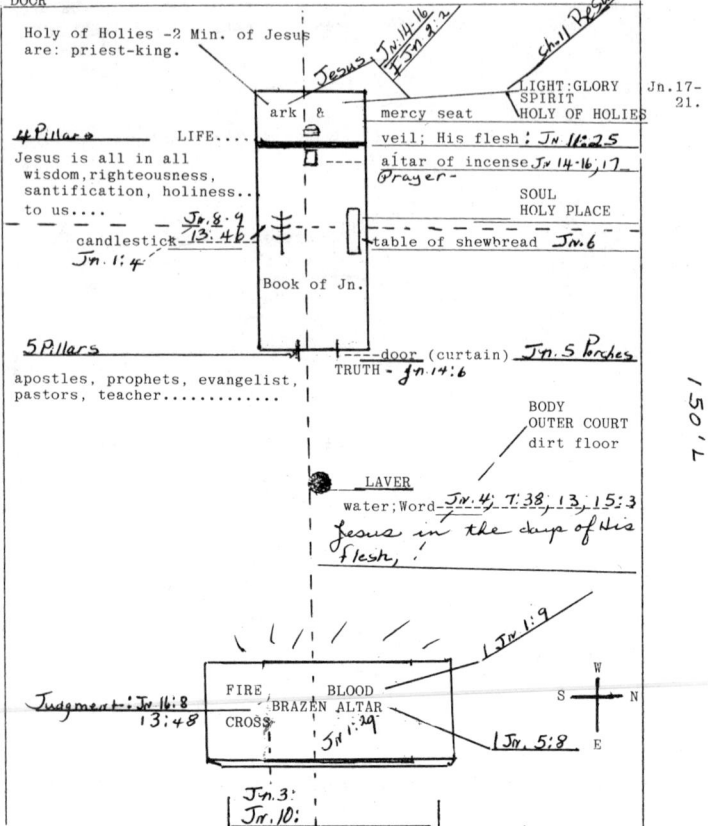

Holy of Holies -2 Min. of Jesus
are: priest-king.

Jesus Jn 14-16; 4 Jn 3.2

Ch.11 Resurrection

ark &

mercy seat

LIGHT:GLORY   Jn.17-
SPIRIT   21.
HOLY OF HOLIES

4 Pillars   LIFE....

veil; His flesh: *Jn 11:25*

Jesus is all in all
wisdom, righteousness,
santification, holiness..
to us....

aïtar of incense *Jn 14-16; 17*
Prayer-

SOUL
HOLY PLACE

Jn.8:9

candlestick *13:4b*
Jn. 1:4

table of shewbread *Jn.6*

Book of Jn.

5 Pillars

----door (curtain) *Jn. 5 Porches*
TRUTH - *Jn 14:6*

apostles, prophets, evangelist,
pastors, teacher............

BODY
OUTER COURT
dirt floor

150'L

LAVER
water; Word *Jn. 4; 7:38, 13; 15:3*
Jesus in the days of His
flesh,!

1 Jn 1:9

FIRE   BLOOD
Judgment: Jn 16:8   BRAZEN ALTAR
13:48   CROSS
Jn 1:29

W
S ⊢ N
E

1 Jn. 5:8

Jn.3:
Jn.10:

WAY *Jn.14:6-9,* 37   *Solemn Occasion*
Jn. 19:23

7-1/2   linen curtained
fence around it;
White speaks of His
righteousness.

East Gate
4 Pillars - 4 Gospels

Grace: Jn. 1-2 Incarnation
1 Jn. 1: 1-3

75' w

Jesus As The Fulfillment Of The Tabernacle In The Book Of Revelation

"Behold, the tabernacle of God is with men."

(Revelation 21:3)

pillar of cloud :1:7; 14:14.

Colors of tabernacle(rainbow)4:3
Gold....21:18,21;
Breastplate stones: 4:3;21:11,18-20;

Crowns of gold:4:4;14:14;19:12

ark of covenant, mercy seat
(throne)3:21;4:2,3; 11:19;

Laver: sea of glass-floor
4:6;15:2;

Cherubim:4:6-7;

Lampstand: 1:12; 2:1; 4:5

table-fellowship 3:20

shewbread:hidden manna:2:17

Lamb:(27 times) 5:6;7:17
(altar now a throne).

Tabernacle of testimony....
15:5;

Golden altar(4-horns)
5:8; 6:9;8:3,4; 9:13;

Priesthood:(redeemed)
4:9,10; 5:10,11;14:1-5;

Tribes of Israel: 7:4-8;
21:12;

Trumpets: 8:2

Mitre and crown..14:1;22:4;

Song of Moses: 15:3

copper-brass:1:15

brazer Altar

pillars: 3:12
Glory of God:4:5;11:19;15:8; — 21:23

golden or linen girdle:1:13;15:6

Stones with names (thummin)
2:17; 3:12c

Linen garments: 3:4-5; 6:11;
7:9,13; 15:6;19:8,14;

Notes

Notes

Notes

Notes

Notes

Notes

Notes